Changing Our Lives

Lesbian Passions, Politics, Priorities

Veronica Groocock

CASSELL

Cassell
Wellington House, 125 Strand, London WC2R 0BB

215 Park Avenue South
New York, NY 10003

First published 1995

British Library Cataloguing-in-Publication Data
A catalogue record for this book is available from the British Library.

ISBN 0–304–32899–5 (hardback)
    0-304-32901-0 (paperback)

Typeset by York House Typographic Ltd
Printed and bound in Great Britain by Biddles Ltd, Guildford and King's Lynn

*c*ontents

introduction

Lesbians have always been a diverse bunch, and as we move ever nearer the millennium this diversity seems to be increasing. Since the 1950s and 1960s representations of *lesbian* have expanded to encompass a multitude of images: SM dykes, lipstick lesbians, baby dykes and even lesbians who have sex with men. The latter group is regarded by some as a heretical notion, as almost a contradiction in terms, while adherents of lesbian chic or SM risk becoming as stereotyped as the stone butch or diesel dyke once was. Irrespective of such differences, eye contact between two passing female strangers can still often elicit a powerful frisson of recognition. Knowing looks between kindred spirits.

This book highlights changing lifestyles in a rapidly changing world. It is about looking back to a shared past and moving on to an uncertain but potentially exciting future. I interviewed more than forty women, each of whom talked openly with me about their experience of change, about their own individual rites of passage. We discussed ways of coming out, relationships (long-term and fleeting, passing fancies and 'significant others') and the joys and angst of 'pretended' family life. Most of my interviewees identified primarily as lesbian. Two are currently bisexual. Some, like Wanda Goldwag and Ann Wishart, had never had, or indeed desired, a heterosexual experience. Others, for reasons of cultural conformity at the time, had married (but never enjoyed sex with men) and continued to identify strongly with women.

I have attempted to record key changes or turning-points in their lives since (and, in some cases, before) the lesbian-feminist movement of the 1970s. 'Disaffected Dykes' charts the escape and subsequent recovery of Jill Posener and other fugitives from some of the more negative aspects of lesbian feminism. Part II contains first-hand accounts of the differing personal and political 'directions' of six women, among them activists such as Jackie Forster and Robin Gorna. An allied aim has been to place the idea of personal change and growth within the context of some of the main political, social and economic upheavals associated with these years, both in the UK and overseas: AIDS and Clause 28, to name the two most potentially catastrophic.

Since I began working on this project back in July 1993, it has grown into something much bigger and more complex than I had anticipated. I had originally targeted women aged forty-plus, on the basis that they had probably observed and experienced more changes than the younger women. And, indeed, women from this age range did comprise the majority of respondents to my advertisements in the gay press (*Pink Paper*, *Gay Times*), and the *Kenric* newsletter and *Everywoman* magazine. However, I found that I was also attracting a sizeable number of replies from women in their twenties and early thirties. So, I decided that it would be both valid and valuable to include and reflect their experiences, in order to convey a fuller, more complete picture of what it is like to be a young lesbian growing up in the 1990s.

About a third of my interviewees replied to advertisements. Of these, a few declined to respond to a follow-up letter, presumably having had second thoughts. The remainder came my way through personal recommendation. The majority of interviews were conducted face to face; for reasons of time and logistics, others were carried out on the telephone or, after an initial questionnaire, by letter and on tape. Like all writers, I had to be selective and did not use every interview, partly due to considerations of space, partly because of a gut feeling that a particular 'story' did not quite 'fit' or fulfil the tenor of the project. This still left me with a wide and representative spectrum in terms of age, class, ethnicity, work, and so on.

Nearly a third of the respondents were mothers, two of whom had conceived by donor insemination. More than half of all the women were in long-term relationships, including the two 'Irenes' who had been together for thirty-five years, surely something of an all-time record? (See Chapter 3.) Some lived separately from their partners, and approximately 20 per cent lived alone and had no regular partner. Five lived overseas: three in the USA, one in Australia and one in Spain. Of the UK contingent, seventeen were London-based, six lived in the North and Midlands, and the rest were scattered as far afield as Cornwall and Shropshire.

Areas of employment included teaching, academia, the caring professions, arts, the Church, housing, the police and prisons. In some cases, work and politics overlapped: **Robin Gorna**'s fervent belief in, and commitment to, the mixed movement correlates with her wealth of work experience in the AIDS field. **Brenda Ellis**'s chequered career has moved from journalism in the Fleet Street era ('parties every night, crazy people, drunken binges at lunch-time, terribly 1970s') through part-time office work, youth work, teaching adults, transactional analysis, photography, work in a créche, to her current job with the Greater London Federation of Disabled People where many colleagues, like her, have disabilities.

Others include volunteers. The Lesbian Archive owes its continued survival to women like **Jackie Forster**, who put in several sessions a week, gratis, at the London Women's Centre, where the archive was based until its move to Glasgow in July 1995. **Wilmette Brown** is a dedicated but unpaid worker for Wages Due Lesbians, which she founded, and **Sharley McLean**, a former volunteer with the Terrence Higgins Trust, has been a staunch member of Hyde Park Gays and Sapphics since the early 1980s.

Scottish-born **Ann Wishart** has managed to combine her job as an educational manager with an MA in women's studies ('for as long as it takes'). She is also a co-founder and area representative for Border Women, a lesbian community serving the Borders and Wales. Ann moved to Shropshire from Kent in 1973. She lived with her (then) partner in a house in the country and decided that she wanted other women to enjoy the benefits of rural life. As a result, many women would come and visit at weekends. They forged links with the Samaritans and advertised in *Sappho* magazine, initially calling themselves 'Sisterhood'. As Ann explains: 'We don't have any leadership. It is hardly even a collective. It is more anarchic . . . I write the newsletter and that is the main vehicle for networking.' There are around 400 members, aged from twenty-five upwards, and the catchment area stretches from the Welsh coast through Herefordshire and Worcestershire to the edge of Shropshire. As with the establishment of Border Women, Ann saw her contribution to my book as a way of supporting and keeping in touch with the changing lesbian political scene from the standpoint of a rural community.

Another teacher, **Hilde Morris**, had equally specific reasons for agreeing to be interviewed:

> I feel very strongly that I would like to give help and encouragement to other women like me who have for various reasons chosen one life and then felt the need, after many years, to change – particularly women who have had children. I would like to give them hope that they won't lose everything and that it is possible to get over this enormous disruption.

One of the principal changes affecting lesbians has been in the area of identity. The popularization of 'queer' in the 1990s represented a response to the more authoritarian elements of lesbian feminism. Queer, we are told, is about fucking with gender – a *laisser faire*, 'anything goes' concept whose appeal to younger lesbians is perhaps understandable. We all need something to rebel against, after all. Lillian Faderman considers it from a historical perspective:

> What I see is young people telling off the mothers and fathers, and it happens in every generation – lesbian feminists were doing it to the butches and femmes of the 1950s, and I imagine that's what the butches and femmes of the 1960s were doing to the 'romantic friends' of other eras. What it shows me is that we're alive and well, and young women . . . aren't complacent and they want to do it their own way. . . .
>
> It also suggests the impatience of youth, which I think is terrific.[1]

For her, the queer notion, at its best, is 'an umbrella term that refuses the distinctions of lesbian feminism and lesbian separatism, that insists on the inclusion of people of colour'.[2]

We have moved beyond the didactic notion that 'feminism is the theory and lesbianism is the practice', to a kind of multi-sexual free-for-all. Bisexuality, once again, is considered acceptable, even chic, in some circles while remaining a source of dissent elsewhere, as Robin Gorna has found (see Part II). Just about every event, festival, group or organization is advertised as open to lesbians, gays and *bisexuals*. In March 1995 a notice publicizing 'Sex Talk' at the University of Sussex, read: 'All welcome: M/F, transgenders, straight, bi, gay and explorers.' *Plus ça change* . . .

British publisher of erotic fiction, Black Lace, has conducted surveys to find out just what turns women on. Top of the list is the submission fantasy; number two is having sex with another woman.[3] Meanwhile, the genetics-versus-environment debate looks set to continue indefinitely. One 1994 study, co-authored by Harvard University's David Wypij, revealed what Kinsey et al. had discovered earlier this century: namely, that sexual orientation encompasses a *range* or spectrum. Wypij found that nearly one in five Americans had been attracted to someone of the same sex since the age of fifteen.[4]

In Britain in the 1990s public opinion on homosexuality and AIDS is improving, albeit slowly. In the British Social Attitudes Survey of 1994, 64 per cent of 3500 people questioned believed homosexuality to be 'wrong' (compared with 74 per cent in 1987).[5] This is no cause for complacency, let alone celebration. Stonewall claims that of 2000 lesbians, gay men and bisexuals surveyed in the workplace in 1993, 48 per cent had been harassed and 8 per cent sacked because of their sexuality, while 68 per cent were not fully out at work.[6]

Despite such discrimination, one thing seems certain: the closet door is well and truly open, and any attempt to lock it against the 'real' world outside would be akin to shutting the stable door after the 'mare' had bolted. In their reference to the Christopher Street riots of 28 June 1969, Del Martin and Phyllis Lyon declared: 'Once the bottle containing the genie is open, it is not easy to get the genie back into the bottle.'[7] Many of the women in this book are free like the genie. Others, wary of being outed, even in 1995, find this problematic and have chosen to remain anonymous. They would probably welcome the genie's magical powers to banish fear and homophobia from our society, transforming it into one where to live as a lesbian is seen as a source of genuine acceptance and pride rather than simply the latest fashionable media bandwagon.

Most of the interviews for this book were completed during 1994, and women were describing their ongoing 'life' situations at that time. I have tried wherever possible to update these, but have been unable to contact everybody concerned. In some cases, therefore, certain aspects of individual 'stories' may well have changed in the interim (this, after all, is the theme of the book!) – aspects concerning relationships, work or social life. One example is the demise of *Sappho Rising* (see page 160), the 1990s successor to the original *Sappho* of the 1970s. For this and any other discrepancies that may have arisen due to the time lapse since the interviews, I hope that readers (including interviewees) will make allowance.

*a*cknowledgements

There are many people to whom I owe a great deal for helping me to initiate and complete this book.

At Cassell: I would like to thank Sandra Margolies for her thorough, yet sensitive, editing of the final drafts, and for her patience in dealing with some last-minute additions and alterations; Roz Hopkins for her interest and co-operation throughout; and Liz Gibbs for her consistent encouragement and support, and for believing in this book enough to commission it in the first place.

Thanks also to Chris Padmore, for her help in the laborious task of typing up most of the interview transcripts.

For permission to use the photographs of Jackie Forster and Linda Bellos in Part II, thanks to Brenda Prince and Sharon Wallace, respectively.

Special thanks to all the women who, having responded to my initial letters and advertisements, agreed to be interviewed. I really appreciate the time and hospitality they gave, willingly and sometimes at short notice, often referring me to other possible interviewees and so helping to make this a truly wide-ranging book that reflects a diversity of attitudes and lifestyles. I am sorry that pressure on space has led, inevitably, to heavy cuts in some cases.

I

Coming Out

1 *initiation*

To 'come out' is to 'be revealed, declare oneself . . . *emerge from clouds*' (OED, my italics). When applied to lesbians and gays, this latter definition seems oddly apposite, and yet misleading – as if the clouds in question represented some fragile, wispy obstacle which have only to be brushed aside to create a space for the 'new' persona. Rather than a sense of change and transformation, it suggests a gentle easing away of flimsy barriers. For many lesbians and gays the reality is often very different and can be far more dramatic, even overwhelming. In any sexist, homophobic society such as Britain's, the numbers of *out* lesbians represent the tip of a massive iceberg beneath which lies, at any one time, a vast 'closet' of women whose sexuality remains hidden to family, colleagues, neighbours and friends.

Since the feminist and Gay Liberation movements of the late 1960s and 1970s, this closet has diminished in size as, like Nora in Ibsen's *The Doll's House*, many of its occupants have, individually and collectively, chosen to escape its confines, slamming the door behind them. More and more women have become disenchanted with leading double lives, with the pretence and duplicity involved in 'passing for straight'. In deciding to be open about their sexuality, they have come to realize the significance of the maxim: 'To thine own self be true'.

Far from being a one-off event, however, coming out is a continuous *process*, indeed a lifelong experience or 'journey'. Precisely when it occurs and what it entails is open to question. At what point can we claim to have adopted a lesbian identity? Is it the very earliest glimmer of sexual or emotional attraction to another woman? The first expression of physical affection? Living (and perhaps working) openly in a lesbian and gay community? What degree of 'outness' is needed before the word 'lesbian' can be owned? Is it only in cases of complete honesty with *everyone* –

family, friends, acquaintances, colleagues – that coming out can be considered genuinely to have taken place?

Certainly, every person to whom one comes out in effect embodies a separate stage in the process. Many interviewees spoke of the experience of being out to *themselves* – the idea being that loving and accepting oneself and one's sexuality is a prerequisite to love and acceptance by others. For Heather Cowan (thirty-one, postgraduate student/mother, Plymouth) by far the greatest stumbling-block was acknowledging to *herself* the fact that she had fallen in love with another woman:

> The final piece fell into place while I was writing an essay for a feminist module at university. I had to place myself in the context of a very anti-feminist diatribe, and the whole denial/running-away process became very clear to me.

Ann Wishart (forty-seven, educational manager, Shropshire) claims to have been out to herself for as long as she can remember, and since 1983 Gill Storey has been out in all areas of her life, including 'completing' the process of coming out to herself:

> Whereas I feel completely at one with myself as a lesbian, I think that we all have internalized homophobia, and every now and again I will realize that perhaps I have kept some knowledge to myself, whereas had I been heterosexual I wouldn't have done. In a work environment, for instance, if a parent said to me: 'I bet your fellow thinks *that*', I am conscious that I have to make a *choice*. .... I work with disadvantaged families and it would be fairly inappropriate suddenly to raise an issue about *me*.

Out to parents

Despite a climate of increasing public awareness of lesbian and gay issues in the 1990s, coming out to parents continues to be a source of immense personal trauma. Homophobia in families in the UK and the USA is alive and overt. In a volatile edition of *Ricki Lake* (an American 'audience' show similar to *Oprah*) that focused on homophobic siblings, the degree of sheer naked malice shown seemed the best possible advertisement for being an only child. One young gay man's sister, heavily heterosexual and premaritally pregnant, was particularly vicious. Also appearing on the programme was Andrea Sheldon, who purported to represent WACO, an anti-gay organization, and used the opportunity to air the group's obnoxious views.[1]

The programme also revealed some alarming statistics, courtesy of the Hetrick-Martin Institute: of the 40 per cent of young lesbians and gays *out* to family and friends, 50 per cent are subsequently rejected. The average age when boys first acknowledge their sexuality ranged from sixteen to nineteen; girls tended to be younger: fourteen to sixteen.[2]

For most lesbians and gays, telling parents has always represented the ultimate test of courage and stamina. In some cases, the degree of disapproval and hostility encountered can lead to ostracism. Wanda Goldwag (forty, managing director, travel agency, London) was sixteen when her parents discovered she was lesbian:

> My mother rummaged through my pockets and found a love note from a friend, which was very explicit. In retrospect, I am very pleased that happened, because by that time my parents and my brother were the only three people in [my] world who didn't know. I was fourteen when I first had an affair with a woman and I started coming out to school friends.
>
> My relationship with my parents has never recovered. They took it appallingly. I'd told my headmistress, teachers, I was completely out, but I knew my parents would be abysmal – and I was right.

Her father's response proved to be worse than her mother's: 'In the last ten years I've seen him once, for about three hours, and I've seen her twice – for a day and the same three hours.' A case of 'Never darken my door again'?

> It wasn't quite that bad. They continued to let me live in the house, but only just, and they funded the first two years of my university course. Then in the third year they cut off funds completely, so I survived off a lover. A lover kept me – that's what got me through it.
>
> I read economics and history at LSE. I was there for four years: three years for my degree, and I was elected president of the Students' Union for my fourth year. I ran the LSE's Gay Cultural Organization, which took over from GLF [Gay Liberation Front] when GLF moved out of LSE, and I ran the University of London Gaysoc ... and most of the major central London Students' Union Gaysocs.
>
> When I got the year as a sabbatical president, the fact that my parents, who had completely believed this was going to be a *phase*, now realized there was no possibility it could be, finally finished them off.

It sounds naive, but I came out at a time when I was so young I didn't realize that people objected. Close to my sixteenth birthday I had sex with my sixteenth woman, and I had learned a lot of things in those two years. I learned to lie about my age . . . I was very often taken for a young boy, and so I could lie effectively about my age.

One of my lovers committed suicide because she could not cope with being a lesbian. I was about fifteen at the time, and I just could not believe she had done something so stupid. She was much older, in her thirties. What happened to me was that I came out without any qualms about it: I was having sex with a woman. I adored it. I told everybody. . . . My parents wanted me to go to a psychiatrist, they thought I was sick, but I knew I was fine.

I don't generalize, but I think what sometimes happens to people who come out very young is that they have that total self-confidence of the young – 'Nothing bad can happen to me' – and that affected the way I think about myself.

Like Wanda, Hilde Morris (forty-seven, teacher, Guildford) came out to friends before family:

A few well-chosen close friends: first, my oldest friend, Anne, whom I met in the maternity home when I was expecting my daughter, and subsequently, to one or two other friends. When I finally left my husband and my home, I then came out in a short space of time to quite a few people, including colleagues.

[Coming out] wasn't something that I planned to do at a certain time in a certain place. It had to be appropriate in the conversation, not forced, and it still does. It was a way – when I knew that I would be leaving my husband – of preparing my friends and also of establishing some sort of base: knowing they were still with me even if I was going to walk away from the life that I had known. I just said to them: 'You do know that I'm gay, don't you?' . . .

One friend was shocked, but everyone else said: 'Well, I suppose I might have guessed it because you're such a strong feminist', or just: 'Well, yeah, I thought you were'. Some said: 'Well, so . . . ?' And some said: 'That's OK' and gave me a hug.

My family was different. My father was horrified. My mother hit the roof, she went completely ape. She wrote me out of her will, refused to see me or speak to me for a year and was very bitter and vitriolic. I expected this from her because I always thought she had some peculiar hang-ups. She always said that she didn't like women, that women were only out to steal your man, etc.,

etc. She had no women friends. Maybe she 'protested too much' – I don't know ...

During the first half of the twentieth century, homosexuality was commonly perceived as a sickness, and aversion therapy often recommended as a mode of 'treatment'. The sexual revolution of the 1960s had barely begun when Del Dyer (forty-eight, careworker, London) came out to her parents. She was seventeen and their immediate response was to drag her off to the doctor:

> I was quite lucky: that was the first 'break' I ever had as regards coming out, because the doctor, a woman, was gay. In a way my parents completely changed then, and that annoyed me – because, you know, I'm their daughter and I'm telling them I'm gay and they can accept or reject that. But because a *doctor*, a *professional*, was saying: 'There is nothing wrong with being gay, it is not a disease, I can't give you a prescription for it', suddenly it was *acceptable*.
>
> At the time my mum was more concerned about the *type* of people I was mixing with, rather than the fact they were gay. She was concerned about this 'den of iniquity' I went to in Soho, the Huntsman in Berwick Street, with gay people, bisexuals, prostitutes and drug addicts and drop-outs – a collection of people who didn't fit in. But because there was a small gathering of gay people and there weren't many places at the time to go to, I used to go there. She said: 'I don't think much of this crowd; aren't there any gay people who are successful, or who live ordinary lives?'
>
> The doctor asked me if I wanted to go to this group in Hampstead. I felt out of my depth. I was only seventeen and most of the women there were in their thirties or early forties. As a *young* woman coming out, I felt totally alienated.

At first the whole family completely rejected her, but within a year their attitude changed for the better: 'I think they'd been waiting for *me* to change, but I didn't.'

SOCIAL PRESSURES

Young women are still subject to all kinds of subtle (or more overt) pressures from parents, relatives – and peers: it is still important to be seen to be dating boyfriends, and marriage remains one of the most significant yardsticks of social success. Bridget (thirty-five, single mother/

health campaigner, Sheffield), had always envisaged getting married one day ['Bridget' is not her real name]:

> It was just the assumption that that was the way things were. In our family, there was often a lot of talk about 'Have you got a boyfriend?' . . . I told my mum and she told my father. . . . When I told her, my mum seemed OK, but she wrote me a letter where all her true feelings came pouring out. It hurt me a lot. I wished she had said it to me face to face. She said how it was against the Church, and I felt she used that as an excuse, rather than coming to terms with her own feelings.
>
> Since then I haven't mentioned lesbianism as such to her, but I was living with my girlfriend [T.] at the time and I made sure I talked about T. as much as I would have done if she'd been a bloke, so it was clear to them that she was part of my life. They visited us and they were all right to her, but I knew that my mum found it very difficult.

For Beth Lambdon (forty, police officer, Exeter) coming out was more like being 'pushed' out, with consequences not so far removed from the young Jeanette's experience in *Oranges Are Not the Only Fruit*:

> I and another girl at school had been caught kissing in the toilets and it got around the school in ten seconds flat. My mother went berserk and threatened to tell my dad, which would have been painful to say the least – he had a heavy hand. I would have got a whipping.
>
> First, she demanded to know if it was true. When I said yes, she threw up her hands in horror and had a mild bout of hysterics. . . . She demanded to know where she had gone wrong.
>
> I wasn't able to reason with her. I was sullen and defiant, so she dragged me off to the priest to see if he could talk sense into me. I was brought up a Catholic. I could say my Hail Marys before I could read or write. . . . The priest gave me a lecture about mortal sin. Being quite young, I wasn't able to argue back. The most I could say was that it didn't *feel* wrong. It always felt right to me, because I had been attracted to girls for as long as I can remember. . . . But I was definitely 'going to hell' and he didn't want me back in his church until I had confessed my sin. All I could do was to put my head up high and say all my friends were going to hell anyway, so I would at least know people.
>
> It did upset me, very much so. I was very depressed, and thought I was somehow evil or sick. I didn't want to be different. I had absorbed all the negative things people threw at me. I was being defiant, but in no way was I proud. I was very much a dyke: even at fifteen I was being mistaken for a boy

all the time. I wouldn't wear dresses on pain of death, apart from school uniform. I had no interest in boys at all. . . . Boys were for climbing trees and playing conkers with.

JUST A PHASE

The previous testimonies represent extreme examples of what can happen when dykes decide to be upfront with their parents. Not all coming-out stories, however, are quite so agonizing. Many mothers resort to a kind of 'wishful thinking' mode, a ploy which is generally well-meaning rather than deliberately reactionary. Gill Storey was sixteen when she told her mother:

> It just seemed perfectly natural and normal to tell her I was in love with another girl. She was very supportive from day one, in terms of saying: 'Don't worry, darling, you will grow out of it'. She has admitted since that she stopped saying 'It's a phase' when I was about twenty, and that she stopped *hoping* by the time I was about twenty-three.

It was her therapist in New York who told activist Joyce Hunter (fifty-six, social worker HIV Center for Clinical and Behavioral Studies, New York) that her overpowering feelings of attraction towards women would 'go away'. Joyce was in her teens at the time and had fallen in love with her best friend:

> I made the mistake of telling her. I lost the friendship. Then I really was back in the closet . . . I went into therapy, and the therapist, a woman, said. 'You will get married. You are in an arrested state of development'. I quit high school. A lot of traumatic stuff was going on, it was a real mess and I wound up trying to hurt myself.
>
> I grew up in an orphanage. I was there from five until about fourteen, when my parents came to get me. My mother came to visit me on and off during those years, but I never saw my father. He was black, she was an orthodox Jew . . . I've always known I was gay since I was ten years old, but I never spoke to anybody about it. . . . We'd go to movies and I would be only wanting to stare at the women. . . . In the home, there was a lot of sexual experience, kids fooling around with each other, and I got involved with that. I was more interested in the girls than the guys. I found the guys boring and rough. I thought off and on about being different, but never told anybody.

Ann Wishart has two sisters, both married with children. She came out to her mother twice, first at twenty-one:

> I asked her to tell my father, and then came out to my younger sister. I think my parents just kind of accepted it. The first time I took a lover home, they accepted it because she was also a teacher, the same age, and we clearly got on very well. Interestingly enough, my father never referred to it and my mother appeared to forget about it ... I was a bit in the closet after that because of a particular long-term relationship.

Ann came out to her mother a second time (aged forty-one) when the relationship ended. 'I wanted her to know what a major change it had been in my life, so I told her again. She said she had always thought of us as just *pals* and that my lesbianism was "how you were when you were younger".'

Diane Langford (fifty-two, novelist, London) was brought up in Christchurch, New Zealand, where her parents still live. She has two younger brothers, one of whom is gay. He came with her to live in London in 1963, and, like most Australians and New Zealanders, they gravitated to the Earls Court area. Coming out to her parents was not a traumatic experience, Diane recalls, as the issue had already arisen with her brother.

> From a very early age he was accused of being a 'poofter' or a 'candy' ... but he is very closeted. He lives with a bloke, they've been living together for about twenty-five years ... and my mother has said: 'I've given birth to two deviants. Where did I go wrong?'

Diane did not *formally* tell her parents, but simply allowed them to draw their own conclusions if they happened to see a woman coming out of her bedroom.

> It was *that* kind of coming out, rather than sitting down and having a sensible heart-to-heart. They come over here quite often, and my father has never ever referred to it. Only once, when we were sitting watching the telly one evening, and an old Rita Hayworth film came on and all of a sudden he said. 'She was a lesbian.' There was a stunned silence, then my mother said. 'How do you know?' He said. 'I just *know* ... '.

For some years Harriett Gilbert (forty-six, broadcaster, teacher, writer) was out to everybody except her parents. She is the oldest of seven.

To my siblings I was out, which was a long process, there being so many of them. The younger they were, the more they just sort of said: 'So what?' or 'Yes, of course, I know', or whatever. To my parents, I only ever indirectly came out. I wrote a novel, published when I was about thirty, called *The Riding Mistress*, which had a lesbian heroine. I don't think I ever actually said to them: 'I am lesbian.' I find it difficult to talk to my parents anyway about anything remotely personal, but I was constantly aware that I ought to be out to them and wasn't.

The book became a kind of vehicle for a more public coming-out when she gave a talk to promote it at London's ICA.

A lot of the audience had come along because they were lesbian and wanted to talk about being lesbian almost more than about the book, and therefore it seemed necessary for me to try and define where I was standing sexually. I didn't feel I could hide behind the thing and say. 'This is a novel; my sexuality as the writer is nothing to do with it.' I think some sections of the book are in the first person anyway ...

I wrote the book partly as a communication to my parents – my mother in particular. It wasn't so much not wanting her to know, it was not being able to cope with the moment of telling her, with the mixture of fury and pain. I know it's a terrible cowardice ... I think she'd long suspected. She did feel that it put her in a difficult position, but I think more than that, she was worried that I was unhappy. Also, there was a level at which she could find it difficult to reconcile, because I'm her daughter and she actually finds the whole thing quite repulsive, but she would have such a conflict because I think she does love me.

The loudest whisper?

This conscious decision not to 'spell out' one's sexuality to avoid upsetting the status quo can be a necessary, albeit regrettable, compromise in certain situations. Lesbian couples in long-term relationships where each woman becomes a friend of her partner's family are both more accepted and, by virtue of their greater mutual ease and familiarity, potentially more vulnerable. Karen and Pat (not their real names) have lived together for more than twenty years. Both are in their late forties and they share a house in Cambridge. Karen describes how one of her friends almost invariably introduces herself to others as a lesbian.

It's just not something I would do. Nobody normally goes around saying: 'I'm heterosexual'. I just allow other people to see and accept what I am and the sort of relationship I'm in ... so I don't think I've gone through a *process* of coming out as such, although I have become less sheltered over the years. I don't hide things now – neither do I wear badges.

I suppose I've adopted the same attitude with my parents. I introduced them to Pat when I first knew her and we went to stay with them, and I always insisted that we slept together. For many years we slept in a double bed, but had two single quilts on it: that was the way we presented it. So I feel they must have known and yet, when I was having problems with my younger daughter about six years ago, I did actually say to my parents at one stage: 'One of the problems J. has is in accepting our relationship'. My father said: 'What relationship?', and my mother immediately changed the subject.

I feel they know on one level but they don't accept it, intellectually or emotionally. . . . It's not something we can talk about. My mother, if she meets someone, introduces Pat as her other daughter, and I think this is her way of coping with it. She can accept her as another daughter, she can't accept her as my partner. It's avoidance tactics ...

Initially, we were very secretive. You can be secretive without telling lies and I don't think we ever told lies about it, but we certainly didn't expose it to the outside world. We have over the last ten years become much more confident. I don't think I care any more about what people think.

In practice, the act of coming out can prove to be something of an anticlimax, as recipients of the information may claim to have known or suspected all along. When Becky (twenty-three, police officer, London) came out to her family, her twin sister remarked: 'I was wondering when you were going to realize.' As Becky acknowledges: 'She spotted it months before I did.'

Mention coming out to Maggie Ford (fifty-three, ex-prison governor, now English teacher, Spain) and she will reply with a laugh that she has never had the luxury of being *in*. Work colleagues had privately outed her before she herself had even become aware of her lesbian feelings, let alone acted on them:

I changed from a completely heterosexual lifestyle to a lesbian lifestyle when I was in my mid-thirties. I was working in the prison service and almost everybody, including the staff of the establishment where I was working, had decided I was a lesbian a long time before I did, and so it was all very public and not at all what I really wished for. I would have liked some privacy to sort out this change for myself, but I wasn't allowed it. They were quite convinced that I was lesbian and I was treated as such.

They just assumed that any relationship with a female friend was a lesbian one. . . . Any time when I became only *slightly* friendly with another member of staff this was immediately blown up into a lesbian affair. What's more, the governor was convinced that it was and since he was rabidly anti-homosexual, that made a lot of problems for me in my professional life. And the fact that it coincided with *me* deciding that I was lesbian, made life even more difficult.

Maggie knew a number of prison officers and governors who were lesbian, and had helped some of them through traumatic changes of partners or, in one case, to make the change that she would later make herself:

An officer at my first establishment had left the prison service and I met her at a party in Durham, and she said: 'I thought I'd meet you at one of these dos one day. I said to the deputy governor when you walked through the gate: "That little girl is one of us; the trouble is she doesn't know it yet."' She was right, but it took me several years!

One early woman lover, a writer from Scotland, asked her how it felt when she made the 'change'. 'She expected tales of internal trauma and there just weren't any! I said it felt like putting on a very old, very comfortable sweater. The drama was everybody else's. Inside me I knew where I was.'

One of Britain's few out lesbian celebrities is actress Pam St Clement who, when offered the part of Pat Butcher in BBC TV's *EastEnders* in 1986, decided that although she would not make 'a song and dance about it', she would not attempt to hide it either: 'Certain people at work knew, it was never a secret. Although I got "outed" by the tabloid press, in fact I had never been "in".'[3] A long-time member of Stonewall, she describes how she has felt 'incredibly sustained' by the gay movement:

I suppose now I am something of an icon, both in my TV character and because I am still one of the very few out lesbians in this country. It's silly to talk about this as a burden, but I do feel a bit alone, I don't believe in outing, but I wish other lesbians would join me.[4]

Far from damaging Pam's popularity, her openness seems to have enhanced it and gained her new respect. Nearly two decades earlier, MP Maureen Colquhoun was less fortunate when her local Labour constituency of Northampton North voted to deselect her after her lesbianism became public knowledge. A massive campaign was mounted on her behalf. The *Daily Mirror* published a rather pious front-page editorial ('The case of the gay MP'), containing words such as 'normal' and 'confess', and regretting the fact that Colquhoun had concealed her lesbianism from those at her selection conference:

> Homosexual MPs should be candid about their private life, even if it affects their political life.
>
> Voters have a right to know the influences and pressures which shape the actions and the judgments of their representatives.
>
> The day may come – we hope it does – when a man's or a woman's sexual preferences within the law will be of as little concern to others as the colour of a tie or skirt.
>
> But it hasn't come yet.[5]

In the 1990s we are still waiting. Chris Smith is one of the few out gay men in the House of Commons, and there are no out lesbian MPs. Coming out in public life still appears to be as fraught with pitfalls as it ever was. Remember Jane Brown, the Hackney head teacher hounded by the press for declining to take her pupils to see *Romeo and Juliet* on the grounds of its heterosexism? This widely publicized story prompted a former head teacher (now a therapist), Deirdre Haslam, to respond. Throughout her teaching career she remained in the closet and knew of no colleague who admitted to being gay: 'All around me I see people who cannot, for whatever reason, openly acknowledge that they are lesbian or gay, even though we have laws to protect us from discrimination. What angers me is the waste.'[6]

As Jackie Forster recalls:

> When we were at [Sappho] meetings the last thing that any of us would dream of saying was 'What do you do?' because of revealing what the job was – it would be highly sensitive. We were much more likely to say 'What sign are you?' or 'What do you drink?' And certainly on my first getting-together on the lesbian scene there was no overt racism. Black women were welcome, prostitutes, working-class women, middle-class women ... It was a very democratic kind of mixing, probably because we were all outside the

mainstream, and I haven't met it anywhere else. But now I notice that there are many more black women – and men – who are out.

As a police officer who is *out* at work, Beth Lambdon can 'relax' and take her partner to police events.

I can go to the local gay bar and don't have to worry about being seen if the police van turns up to break up a fight or I'm leaving the bar at closing time . . . The gay bar is in roughly the same area as straight bars and there is often trouble on a Saturday night, the police are just waiting and the vans cruise around in a circle. Sooner or later a van will turn up, you might see the same lads and wave.

There are a couple of guys who don't really like me and make comments behind my back, and another two who still insist on treating me as one of the lads. They have lousy taste, they see a couple of women from the van and I am supposed to say, 'Cor! Look at the tits on that!'

None of the women are any problem at all. Because I am out I have had several officers approach me and say, 'I am gay but would you mind not telling anyone?' One of the women looks so 'obvious', but even she doesn't want to come out and I am not about to *out* her.

Heather Cowan recalls homophobia in the WRAF at Brize Norton:

Lesbianism was the horror of the WRAF block. Women would run around half-naked in the block and feel OK with that, because it was implicitly understood that 'we are all heterosexual and no one had better threaten the status quo'. Women who weren't feminine enough were considered suspect and jokes would be made behind their backs – about not finding oneself alone with them. Rooms were single, or had three or more beds. Two WRAFs could not share a room, we all knew that was in case of lesbianism! There was no privacy: shared bathrooms, communal toilets, but emotional closeness was discouraged. I can't ever remember hugging any of my friends during my time in the WRAF. It's odd – because I'm a very 'touchy-feely' person.

POLITICAL ACTIVISM

During the 1970s and 1980s many women came out through their political activism. For Nettie Pollard (forty-four, worker at the National Council for Civil Liberties, aka Liberty, London) coming out was an outward gesture of sisterhood rather than an action generated by an inner personal need:

> I came out in 1971, through GLF, because my best friend turned out to be gay
> ... I wasn't actually a lesbian at the time, I was entirely hetero-identified. What
> I was doing was to wear a gay badge around the place. It's beyond just giving
> support, it's to do with showing solidarity.... At the time I identified with Gay
> Liberation and Women's liberation. It's all within the context of liberation for
> everyone, which is very much how I still think of this.

Being open with her parents presented few problems, because they themselves had quite unconventional views:

> My mother's family moved to Canada in the 1800s – they came from Scotland.
> My father's family virtually lost touch with him. They didn't approve of him
> because he was a communist and a trade unionist, and they were all in
> insurance and banking. My mother came from a fairly privileged background.
> She was one of the first people to do philosophy, politics and economics at
> Oxford. She also became a socialist and was involved in women's issues at a
> very early age, so she didn't fit into the conventional lifestyle ...
>
> I wasn't successful at being heterosexual. I found that my relationships with
> men, particularly back in the early 1960s, made me feel uncomfortable ... and
> I didn't feel I could pretend and act a part. It wasn't that I didn't fancy men –
> I did, I wanted to have sex with them – but I didn't want any of those things
> that go with it, like the courting and dating and engagements. I really wasn't
> into that, I wanted something real and intimate.
>
> My mother was a bit concerned about me making myself more 'different'
> than I already was. I was already not particularly conventional politically, and
> I was a vegetarian and not religious ... and she was worried that this was yet
> another thing and that it would make me even more of an outsider. But I said
> no, this is something I feel very confident about and happy with. I think I did
> convince her, and by the time she died she was quite comfortable with it, and
> was very close to my partner.
>
> My father thought lesbianism was really good fun. He rather liked it.

Wilmette Brown (forty-eight, co-founder of Black Women for Wages for Housework, London) came out on two separate occasions: first socially (in 1966), in lesbian and gay bars in San Francisco, and politically ten years later, at a Wages Due Lesbians conference in Toronto. It was in the early days of the Wages for Housework campaign, from which Wages Due Lesbians had evolved the previous year:

That was our first conference and the first time I spoke publicly as a lesbian woman, so that was a much more public coming out, declaring myself and saying what my life was about. Whereas in 1966 there was a very limited number of people I was able to tell. During that time, too, I lived in Africa for four years, and I certainly couldn't come out there because the level of power of women was even lower in Africa than the USA; so to mention being lesbian then was out of the question.

I didn't come out to my family until the 1970s. I was away at university and then in Africa, so there wasn't even the time to sit down and discuss that area of my life with them in such a way that they could really deal with it. It wasn't something I felt I could just drop casually into the conversation. When I came back from Africa in 1974 I told my mother (my father was dead). Her question was: 'What about children?' and I said: 'That will take care of itself. If I decide I want to have children I will organize that in some way.' Other than that, my mother has always been very supportive of me.

Elaine Willis (forty-three, director of an educational charity and Vice-chair of Stonewall Coventry) has worked in the voluntary sector since 1984. Before that she had trained to be a minister at a Methodist and Anglican college in Birmingham, where she came out as a lesbian. Her lover was a Methodist and Elaine an Anglican.

We wanted to continue our relationship after college and we wanted postings near each other, which obviously caused huge ructions and tested the system somewhat ... so the next five years of our relationship became overshadowed by the traumatizing of that experience. In the course of that she decided she didn't want to be a Methodist minister after all because, for her, part of wanting that position was a substitute almost for relationships, so she gave up on that. Then I got a job, but the bishop wouldn't give me a licence because of my sexuality ... The principal of my college felt duty bound to put him in the picture, so that was that. You can't fight the whole system, all at once, particularly as the Church is not renowned for its pastoral skills in dealing with women at any level ... I didn't have a job or anywhere to live, and I was shaken by the hand by the principal of the college, who hoped I'd find my vocation one day. I've hardly been inside a church since.

Although Mary Jennings (forty-two, PhD student, Cambridge) moved to London in 1967 partly for economic reasons – job opportunities in her native Dublin were limited – her decision was motivated more by a wish to avoid coming out to her family:

London has a large Irish gay population and it enabled me to segment my life so that I could have a family life. When my mother came to visit, I took down my books and posters. I was living with somebody, but we had a very 'distant' relationship.

Mary did not come out to her mother until July 1991, and then mainly because circumstances forced her to do so. She had been asked to take part in a BBC TV programme about gay people in Ireland:

The whole of Ireland watches British TV, and I felt that even if I didn't tell my mother somebody in my family would see it (and of course they did). . . . I said: 'I'm going to be on television, as part of an evening of gay TV', and she said: 'Are you trying to tell me you're gay?' She almost said it for me! It was easy in the end. She'd met most of my friends when she came to London, and in the intervening years she'd had to deal with a lot of difficult issues to do with abortion, divorce (my sister married a divorced man), all of those kinds of things, so this was just one more.

We went to a wine bar in London and I talked to her. We were there the whole evening, and I told her two minutes before my brother-in-law was going to pick her up. She just threw her arms around me and gave me a big hug and asked if there was anybody special in my life. She's been really amazing.

For Linda Semple (thirty-eight, freelance editor, London), it was through the broader umbrella of the Women's Movement that she first discovered Sappho, the campaign of support for MP Maureen Colquhoun and lesbian politics generally.

When I was at LSE I went along to a Sappho meeting with a friend of mine. I went to hear Maureen Colquhoun speak. Our college supported her when she was having trouble with the Labour Party, and I went to this meeting with some of my straight friends to hear her speak and started going along to meetings on a regular basis, and came out through that.

In 1979, at the age of twenty-two, she joined the Sappho collective, helping to run the magazine. She also lived next door to Sappho's (then) basement premises in Dorset Square, NW1.

It was fabulous, great fun, a good community of women across class, race, age. Interestingly, it was racially mixed in a way that a lot of lesbian groups weren't in those days. It was a broad church. It was also about the only place where older women coming out could go at that time. Sappho fought battles about advertising in newspapers, answered hundreds of letters, provided a penpal service and had a weekly disco. It did all of those things that were important for people who were finding it difficult to come out.

London was, even then, very gender-divided – loads of stuff for gay men but very few places where women were welcomed.

Linda has also worked with Lesbian and Gay Switchboard, OutRage! and Feminists Against Censorship. About two years after joining Sappho she came out to her parents.

My mother was very, very supportive and decided to set up her own phone line for parents of lesbians and gay men coming out, and she ran that for about eight years. She's disabled and doesn't have a lot of time or energy any more. Now there are a lot of very active groups in places like Manchester and Leeds, and I think she feels that *they* can do it.

Despite the higher public profile of lesbianism in the 1990s, the prevailing feeling within society is that lesbianism is still not 'normal' and is a less valid lifestyle than heterosexuality. This being the case, each coming-out experience is no less problematic to the individual concerned than in more repressive, pre-Gay Liberation times. Many parents adopt a stance of woolly liberalism, dissociating themselves from the idea that *it* could ever happen to *them*. The mainstream media has, during the latter part of the twentieth century, published articles on various aspects of lesbian lives, especially those with a 'coming out to parents' slant. And, whereas once these were relatively rare, the 1990s has seen a marked increase in coverage of lesbian issues, both in the written and spoken media (including several series of Channel 4's *Out*).

Linda Semple's mother was interviewed by the *Daily Mail* in a piece headlined 'The night I learned that my daughter's lover was a woman'.[7] There have been a number of similar features in both the national and provincial press. In October 1992 the Brighton *Evening Argus* featured twenty-seven-year-old Jo Davies, who was already out to her friends and planned to come out to her parents, who lived in Birmingham, on the first International Coming-Out Day (11 October 1992). 'I am scared of their reaction,' she admitted, 'but I do not feel I can have a proper relationship without telling them . . . I love them and I want them to know who I am.' The article, although sympathetic, was spoiled by the sub-heading: 'Gays' *confession* to friends' (my italics).[8]

In the next month the *Guardian* Women's Page highlighted mothers' feelings about their lesbian and gay children. All agreed that discovering that their child was lesbian or gay had changed them profoundly. There seems to be a parallel need in parents in this situation to 'come out' to the straight world and to each other, and to garner mutual support. Angie, forty-six, said that at first she worried that her daughter might be treated as a second-class citizen. ('I had this view that being gay is OK, but it wasn't something that you would choose or hope for. My overwhelming feeling was guilt.') But coming to terms with her daughter's sexuality turned out to be one of the best things that had happened in her life. 'I like to think I was a reasonably open-minded person before, but since I have known my gay daughter properly, I feel the world has opened up.'[9] Angie belongs to FFLAG: Families and Friends of Lesbians and Gays.

Mothers always tend to blame themselves for any perceived shortcomings in their children, as psychologist Jane Firbank explains:

> It is still a mark of how well you are doing in society that you get married, mortgaged and have kids. Which is why women will turn to their incredibly successful single children and ask, 'When are you going to settle down?'[10]

When it is married women who find themselves sexually and emotionally attracted to other women, a very different and more complex scenario emerges. An article in the *Guardian* entitled 'Hopelessly devoted – living with a love that dare not speak its name', represented a kind of anonymous coming-out, a *cri de coeur* from a married woman in love with her best friend.

> Marriage [she wrote] can be a convenient camouflage for any woman without the confidence to accept, or even to acknowledge, other aspects of her nature. Yet I have never been able to forget my other self. I cannot begin to guess whether I am truly bisexual, homosexual or heterosexual, but I have always known there is a part of me that is attracted to women.[11]

The article generated an influx of highly charged and empathetic correspondence from other women facing similar dilemmas, some of which were published in subsequent weeks. One woman, in particular, was involved in an affair that she described as

> one of the most romantic, rewarding and valuable experiences of my life. I continue to enjoy the sexual relationship with my husband and am saddened

only by the unavoidable duplicity. I am now convinced that we are all much more complex creatures than the common consensus would allow, that the labels of homosexuality and bisexuality are inadequate, and that the notion of love being exclusive to a single other person is misleading. I am deeply committed to both my husband and my lover and consider myself lucky to be loved by each.[12]

Most of us tend to idealize our mothers, imbuing them with all kinds of unrealistic expectations. While young heterosexuals may accept lesbianism in theory and at a distance, when it comes to their own mothers' sexual behaviour they often take a much more censorious view. Living openly as a lesbian mother has never been an easy option. In many ways it can be even more of a potential minefield than coming out as a lesbian *daughter*. About a third of my interviewees are mothers, most of whom have been married at least once. While most children have been supportive, a minority of women have experienced serious family friction (see Chapter 2).

Bisexuality

Many women made tentative inroads into lesbianism via bisexuality. Gillian Rodgerson (thirty-five, writer/broadcaster, former editor of *Capital Gay*, London) was at high school in Canada and came out in the mid-1970s, a time when bisexuality had become 'fashionable' in that country. Having first identified as bisexual, she came out a second time as lesbian, through the time-honoured 'crush' on her best friend:

> We wrote long romantic letters and exchanged paintings and poetry, but it didn't develop into anything physical. But I was really lucky, in that I was at an 'alternative' school. I suppose the closest thing in Britain would be Somerville. ... It was very progressive, the other students' attitudes were very open. There were people who identified as bisexual and one woman had had the courage to say she was a lesbian, so it was a very easy environment to come out in.
>
> I went on to have a few more fairly successful relationships with men, but then, when I was nineteen, had my first physical relationship with a woman. She was married at the time, so we didn't live together. She would come down to visit me at college at weekends. After that I moved to Toronto and was living in a house with three gay men. They set me up on a blind date and

this woman arrived and we moved in together. I came out to my parents after that. I suspect that they were initially less accepting than they are now, but they dealt with that themselves. They asked all the usual questions ...

Her father is a GP and her mother was in town planning but gave up work when Gillian was born. She describes them as 'Methodist, very liberal, conventional middle class'. She has two younger sisters: one lesbian, the other one heterosexual. The latter was the first person to whom she came out:

> She is five years younger than I am, so at that time she was in her mid-teens. She was fine, and she's always said that because she has two lesbian sisters she's thought about being a lesbian more than most straight women do, but she's decided she likes men. I think that's good because a lot of straight women feel quite comfortable asking lesbians: 'Why are you lesbian?' but don't ask themselves why they are heterosexual, but Jane *knows* that she is. When I was living in the house with three gay men, we had a party and I invited Jane. She always knows the socially correct thing to do – she brought another girl!

Gillian's lesbian sister delayed coming out to her until each of them was living with their respective girlfriends: 'She invited me to dinner and she drank much more than she usually does and it finally came spilling out.'

Only two interviewees currently identify as bisexual; a few others, like Bridget, continue to be open to relationships with men. Sophie Mills (thirty, college lecturer, North Carolina) identifies, very definitely, as lesbian, but still sleeps with men occasionally:

> I wouldn't rule it out. I'm not at all prescriptive about that kind of thing ... I was going out with a man before I came up to [Oxford] university and I chucked him for the woman I met when I started college. He was actually very good about it, really nice when it broke up about ten months later, nicer than he need have been, and let me cry on his shoulder.
>
> I've no problem with men *sexually*. It's *spiritually* that I just don't have a lot to say to them; whereas there's a certain type of woman that I instantly click with. I go out looking for women in a way that I wouldn't go out looking for men. I think it's easier. Maybe I'm lazy. I find it easier to relate to people who are more like me, and I think men and women have really quite little in common.

Some, like Harriett Gilbert, have reverted from a lesbian lifestyle to an entirely heterosexual one, a change which has necessitated a considerable readjustment, almost a second 'coming-out' (see Part II). Others, including Nettie Pollard, question the need for self-labelling altogether, regarding it as a retrograde idea:

> I just think of myself as a sexual person. I don't have a particularly strong lesbian identity now because times have changed ... I'm not a separatist, never have been. I think it all changed in the 1980s: [identity] became less and less important. The lesbian and gay movement became very 'establishment'. It stopped being radical and became a rights movement rather than a liberation movement.
>
> I think we adopt labels like 'lesbian' for political reasons. They don't really say a great deal about what we want. I think that lesbians, for example, like to identify as lesbians because they are identifying with the subculture where they've been rejected by the mainstream culture. There are so many different aspects to our sexuality – there's how we define ourselves, what we actually do sexually, what kind of materials we might like reading, and then there's fantasies that go on in our heads. I don't know where you draw these lines – about who we're attached to and what that means. I don't think these things are in fact very meaningful.

How and to what extent people come out depends on individual circumstances, personality type, inclinations. Parents may be more likely to accept a daughter's sexuality in the context of an existing relationship (as in the case of Pat and Karen; see Chapter 2). They are then faced with a *fait accompli* rather than some remote, abstract notion from which they are several steps removed.

Elaine Willis took her lover home to meet her parents so that they could tell them together:

> I was at theological college at the time, so I think my parents probably knew after quite a lot of other people ... I made a special trip home. I think it was OK, except my mother has said to me since that she spent quite a long time talking my father through things in order to get him to understand. I think they just accept that if you want to keep a relationship with your daughter, then you have to accept where she is coming from.
>
> It was all a bit dramatic – and terribly formal, which I never have been with my parents except, I suppose, with the big things. There never seemed to be

an easy, natural way to say the big things casually. It seemed easier to do and explain in terms of having a relationship with someone. My parents could understand the fact that you would make some choices because of having met someone. I doubt they could understand if you just decided, one day, that you were a certain sort of person.

A good test of family support is feeling able to confide in a parent when a relationship founders. Because lesbian and gay relationships are not legally sanctioned, the trauma of separation is exacerbated. The absence of any 'divorce' procedure for same-sex couples merely serves to devalue the relationship in the eyes of mainstream society. When lesbian couples split up, few have access to the same extended family network of support which heterosexual couples have traditionally taken for granted (see Chapter 3).

Sophie Mills finds her mother a willing confidante:

> If things go wrong – if I split up with somebody – I can go and cry on my mother's shoulder. She always says: 'Well, I never liked her anyway, she wasn't worthy of you' – which is really nice. On the other hand, there are things I wouldn't tell her. I wouldn't be absolutely explicit and say: 'I'm going out with so-and-so ... '.
>
> She's really sweet. If there's a book with a gay theme, she says: 'I've read this book and you'll really like it'. ... That's her sort of supportive *code*.

Sophie's coming-out began at school in her early teens. She never felt 'comfortable' with the term 'lesbian' because she tended to associate it with one particular teacher who was 'a strange piece of work and, you know, one didn't really want to be like that. ... But I'd read a lot of literature – Virginia Woolf, Vita Sackville-West, and so on – and that was where the role models came from.'

She recalls, too, one 'amazing' girl who, aged about twelve, declared that she was bisexual:

> Everybody was terrified of her and wouldn't sit next to her in prayers in case she made a pass at them, and I thought: 'God, that's really terrible.' By about fourteen I started thinking: 'Uh huh, does this perhaps relate to me rather more?' ... I had a very brief and disastrous affair with this girl, partly because I was much too clueless to cope with what was going on, and she was mature and sophisticated, which I certainly wasn't. I was unbelievably in love with her for about two years, much more so than she ever realized, and I couldn't really handle it.

A few people knew and weren't incredibly pleased, particularly my best friend ... I think she thought: 'God, what does this say about *me*?' But when I came up to Oxford, I thought: 'Right, this is the moment to be completely out' ... so I had literature around and posters on my wall. I also acquired a girlfriend during the first week of the first term. We were a notorious couple around college, and one or two people said nasty things. There was one girl who wouldn't stand next to me in the dinner queue, but on the whole I had a very positive response ... I enjoyed the notoriety – everyone knew who I was, for good or ill, which was quite exciting. But college dyke, and *only* that, was also a bit limiting. I don't wear badges or proclaim my outness any more, just because I prefer to be more understated.

Sophie is now thirty, the age at which prurient questioning about women's marital intentions generally ceases. This sometimes makes it simpler to pass as straight, to remain in the cosy, safe space of the closet. Many women's experience has shown, however, that the sheer sense of relief felt at the *telling* often outweighs any remaining doubts or qualms about the anticipated response. A life of pretence or concealment is merely 'a life half-lived'.[13]

For women from different cultural and ethnic origins, where families are often closer-knit and parents may have more traditional expectations of daughters, the risk of rejection may be greater still. Sri Lankan-born Savi Hensman (thirty-two, trainer/community worker, London) was fortunate in belonging to a 'progressive' family who accepted everybody's right to equality:

> I wasn't under the same kind of pressure that a lot of young women are under – to prove their femininity. Maybe that helped ... I didn't have to prove anything, or be dependent on a man in order to be a *person*. ... There is also a certain advantage in terms of my background, in that if I didn't go out with boys it might simply be assumed that because I was from an Asian family my parents might not approve.

By her mid- to late teens, having decided she wouldn't make a very good 'go' of heterosexuality, she had started to explore lesbianism. Although still afraid to go into a bookshop and openly buy a book on the subject, she had read *The Well of Loneliness* and watched TV programmes which, even in the early 1970s, had begun to move beyond depicting lesbians and gays in silhouette with first names only:

I read books around religious issues. Whether it was right and proper to act on my feelings rather than live a celibate life was an important question for me. By the time I was seventeen or eighteen I had a clearer picture of who I was and where I wanted to go. I began reading *Gay News*. . . . Living in Hackney I must have been surrounded by other lesbians and gay men, but in those days the lesbians and gays on my estate didn't walk around holding hands and wearing badges. When I went to university it was a bit of a shock to come to terms with what I had kept hidden – not always very successfully.

She first tentatively raised the issue of sexuality with her parents several years ago, and later, more overtly, when she was at university (she read chemical engineering at University College, London):

By that stage I was aware that my feelings were unlikely to change. I was unlikely to become strongly attracted to men. For me, being a lesbian wasn't initially a choice made because of politics ... I had decided there was a possibility of having a fulfilling relationship with another woman and that there was nothing wrong with that.

She told her parents just as they were preparing to go back to live in Sri Lanka:

I wanted to know whether they could accept that this wasn't 'a phase I was going through', that this was the way I was. So before they left I discussed the issue with them. My mother didn't say very much at the time, and my father was rather hesitant: I think he still hoped that I would change.

Looking back, I don't think there was ever any serious danger that they would have rejected me – they weren't those kinds of people. They were heterosexist, but not strongly homophobic. They didn't make hostile comments; I think they just had an idea that 'straight is best'.

At thirty-two, Savi is the youngest of three. Rather than coming out via a particular relationship, she took a more cerebral 'route':

I did a lot of thinking about who I was before I actually got involved with anybody, so it wasn't a case where I met somebody, fell in love and then came out. But I think it is important to acknowledge that a lot of women may have strong *emotional* relationships with other women but not, for whatever reason, a *physical* relationship.

Being black and lesbian have always been important components of her identity:

Growing up here in England, being black, you have to make certain choices: how much do you affirm your identity? Do you try to act like the white girls and hope that people will take you for one of them? Going through all that maybe made it easier for me to come out as lesbian. If others are being put down, for whatever reason, sometimes it's important to take up the issues, not just in an abstract way but also by saying who you are, even if that doesn't fit in with what society thinks you should be. Which was why, when I did come out properly, I did it in grand style. I'd been influenced by the lesbian and gay movement – by the early 1970s there were helplines, and so on – and at that time there was almost a strong moral imperative to come out ... an important *core* feeling that if you are able to come out, it does help other lesbians and gays, yourself and the world in general.

So I came out to family members, students – and my [Christian] congregation – fairly rapidly. I didn't have any really heavy reactions, though some of my congregation were incredulous. There's that assumption that lesbians are sophisticated people who come in from outside, and ordinary people who grow up in Stoke Newington just don't turn out that way. .... I started going along to the Islington and Haringey gay group, which I found very helpful.

When I was growing up, there were very few positive images of black lesbians or, indeed, black gay men. ... I'd read in a book that there were lesbians and gays in all sections of society, so I figured out that the 'one in twenty' must be there somewhere. I trusted in the fact that they must exist, and when I began going on the scene I tended to find myself mostly in the company of other black *straight* people, or of lesbians and gays, almost all white.

The first time I went on a demo, I noticed a black man with a pink triangle badge and thought: 'That's brave'. Then there were others and they had a banner: they were the Gay Black Group. [This later became the Lesbian and Gay Black Group and helped to set up the Black Lesbian and Gay Centre in South London.] So the black lesbian and gay movement in this country was beginning and was making a difference. And when I found myself, in 1985, working for the centre, I discovered just how many of us there were.

'MIDLIFE' LESBIANS

A change in sexual orientation may be especially traumatic for women who, for perhaps the greater part of their lives, have led a conventionally heterosexual existence, with all the trappings of marriage and nuclear family life. In 1984, the National Lesbian Health Care Survey, developed and distributed throughout the USA, found that of 'midlife' lesbians (aged forty to sixty), 34 per cent had been married at some point. The least out were those who had had their first sexual experience with another woman after forty (eight per cent). Degrees of outness were assessed in the context of four different groups: family members, gay friends, straight friends and co-workers. Only one in four were open with all or most family members (24 per cent). Sixty per cent were out to more than half the people in *all* their networks. Only 7 per cent were out to *everyone*, and an equal proportion were out to *none*.[14]

It was concluded that although coming out was considered a healthy step and also the key to finding a partner and a place in the gay community, many midlife lesbians paid a high price for their openness. A significant connection was identified between such disclosure and the long-term use of counselling: of the sample in question, 73 per cent had sought counselling at some time during their lives.[15]

Several interviewees in this book belong to this category of women over forty who have been married. For those who were around in the 1970s, the combined influence of the Women's and Gay Liberation movements acted as a kind of catalyst, helping to ease their transition into a lesbian lifestyle. Before this, many women had rejected the possibility that they might be lesbian, regarding the stereotypically butch imagery with which lesbianism was then associated as alien and repellent.

Born and brought up in Adelaide, South Australia, Brenda Ellis (forty-six, worker with the Greater London Federation of Disabled People, London) has been married twice. She was married with small children and living in London when, in 1970, she joined the GLF:

> I defined myself as bisexual. I had fallen madly in love with a man, but I had these other feelings for women. I was exploring my sexuality. I was very into Biba clothes and double sets of false eyelashes and being very glamorous. And I remember going to these meetings in some underground cave in Covent Garden and seeing all these real bull-dykes and being horrified, thinking: 'God, I can't look like *that*! I can't possibly be a lesbian.' So I more or less put it on hold until thirteen years later, during the process of my [second] husband dying.

I'd been in a women's consciousness-raising group for four years and S., one of the other women there, was also married. I was really surprised when I ended up having a relationship with S. because she seemed the least likely person that I thought would come out. She gave me a lot of emotional support during my husband's illness. I don't think I could have got through it without her. She was magnificent.

My women's group were like my family. They came round, they babysat my children. I used to drink a bottle of wine every afternoon because it was the only way I could get through the day. My husband was in a lot of pain ... It was a horrendous time and they kept me 'together'. They cooked meals, cleaned my house, took me places, took my children out. They were fantastic. That reinforced my feelings about feminism and sisterhood. I think a lot of younger people take feminism for granted, but if you've been on the receiving end of what feminism can do, you really do appreciate it. It gave me the confidence to come out as a lesbian.

Before moving to London she had lived a hippie lifestyle for a year in Laugharne. West Wales, with her first husband:

That's when I had my first proper stirrings of lesbianism – I had an affair with a Welsh opera singer. I met her mother, and then her mother introduced her to me and said it would be nice for H. to have other friends. At the time she was having problems about her own sexuality: she said she had been pursued at Sadler's Wells by all these butch opera singers and was finding it horrendous, and the next thing I knew the woman was leaping on me and seducing me. . . . It lasted about six months. We used to have to get rid of my husband, we sent him down the road to buy things to give us five minutes alone. We spent a lot of time sheltering in doorways when it was pouring with rain or snowing, holding hands and walking past Dylan's [Thomas] workshop overlooking the estuary and gazing into the estuary, and gazing into each other's eyes. It was wonderful.

I was besotted with this woman. Most of our friends were hippies, there were large hippie communes in the mountains. . . . Friends used to come down from London. It was hip then to be bisexual. . . .

I had always had incredibly intense relationships with women friends. My best friend at school and I slept in the same bed together between the ages of thirteen and fifteen and never thought anything about it, and used to spend every living, waking moment together. Then I got a boyfriend, who was my first husband. I used to even take my girlfriend when we went out on dates together, and eventually he said it's got to be one or the other, and poor

Aileen got left behind. I hadn't had any consciousness about lesbians, except perhaps when I was playing hockey. There were these older, independent women, who I thought were great role models. There was something about them, I couldn't put a word to it. They didn't spend their lives talking about boyfriends like all my other friends did, and they had good jobs, their own places to live and seemed really strong and powerful. I liked that and felt attracted to them, followed them around and they were my heroines. But it wasn't until afterwards that I realized they were dykes.

Sally Cline (fifty-six, writer/academic, Cambridge) realized very early on in her life that she was open to the idea of lesbian relationships, but grew up in the 1950s when there were no positive role models and lesbianism was perceived as 'wicked and sinful':

so I dutifully followed the typical and expected path for a nice Jewish girl – heterosexuality, marriage, motherhood, career. I had discreet lesbian relationships during my so-called heterosexual years. The decision to finally discuss with my second husband my affair with my younger lesbian lover broke up my marriage. He could not handle it. . . . I came out in stages over the years. The Women's Movement facilitated this process.

Like Brenda Ellis, although aware that she wished to adopt a lesbian identity, Sally defined herself initially as bisexual. This was because 'lesbian' was a taboo word and she was behaving 'in a bisexual manner'. However, with her increasing involvement in radical feminist politics, it wasn't long before she began to identify as a *political* lesbian.

In the 1990s the mainstream media has given dykes such a high profile that young women barely into their teens are not only acknowledging their sexuality but acting on it and outing themselves to the world. In one edition of Channel 4's lesbian and gay series *Out* (August 1994), one fifteen-year-old dyke seemed to get a real *buzz* out of each coming-out situation. She described how she would 'psyche herself up' for the occasion and feel 'quite excited' by it. Since the age of thirteen she had come out so many times that she was 'running out of people' to tell. She clearly relished the curiosity shown by her female peers, several of whom had followed her home from school when she was with her girlfriend, eager to know who did what and 'who plays the boy?'

What marked this out as impressive – and fundamentally *different* from previous decades – was the absolute certainty, and pride, with which this young woman proclaimed her sexuality. No tentative 'testing the water' tactics here. In the 1990s these in-yer-face strategies by stroppy dykes are directed at people of all sexual persuasions. Nonetheless, despite claiming to have been 'sure' of her lesbianism at thirteen, she had the insight to concede that in fifteen to twenty years' time her sexual preferences might have changed. This reflects the trend which began in the 1980s towards a broader perspective on gender and sexuality, a reaction against the more prescriptive 'identity politics' promulgated by lesbian feminism.

It can be argued that the very notion of 'coming out' presupposes sexual orientation as a fixed, static concept, the antithesis of a sexuality that is socially constructed and, consequently, fluid and flexible, bearing within it the seeds of change. The latter concept, by definition, is infinitely more threatening to heterosexuals – and, indeed, to those women who see themselves as unequivocally or predominantly lesbian.

In the lesbian-feminist culture of the 1970s and early 1980s, bisexuality was deemed politically incorrect or, in the terminology of those times, 'ideologically unsound'. Bisexuality in the 1990s, although largely free from the stigma and taboo which previously surrounded it, is still – and probably always will be – a source of passionate debate and dissent. Indeed, some women have found coming out as bisexual to be infinitely more contentious than coming out as lesbian. There is a sense in which they are made to feel they cannot 'win': they are judged and found guilty, particularly by lesbians. However, the 1980s and early 1990s have been informed by a far greater diversity of images and behaviour, by the fantasy element and gender-bending potential of queer politics.

Like many of her 'lesfem' contemporaries from the 1970s, Carol Uszkurat (forty-five, academic/musician, London) has shifted from an essentialist stance on sexuality to a broader, social constructionist view, incorporating the idea of sexual *preference*:

> I've been to these different 'places' in my life where I thought first of all I was following some sort of basic instinct – that that was what my attraction to women was, that I was 'finding myself' as a lesbian. I am ambivalent about that, which doesn't understate in any way the passion I feel with women, because that to me is a wonderful thing, but the explanation of it is something I haven't really decided upon.
>
> I think if I look at all the different points in my life I can reread my past differently ... I've had different opinions throughout my life as to what my lesbianism is. I now see it as my 'lesbianism', not 'being a lesbian' – and that's an important distinction. ... So I see myself as having done what people call

'coming out', although I don't any more see myself as someone who 'came out', because of the essentialist nature of that description – all the stuff about being an essentialist person repressed by heterosexuality – as distinct from choices that can be made.

In any debate on coming out, it is important to take into account the *economic* changes that have taken place in both British and American society since the affluent, 'never had it so good' 1960s. Both the Gay Liberation and lesbian feminist movements were premised on the economic prosperity and full employment of the late 1960s and early 1970s. In the 1990s climate of high unemployment and constant fear of job loss, many lesbian and gay people have different, more mundane preoccupations, and consequently, sexual politics figures low on their agendas. The exceptions to this are perhaps those who work in gay-friendly environments such as AIDS therapy, or some branches of academia (witness the growing influx of gender studies courses, alongside women's studies courses, into the mainstream curricula in universities).

Coming out in the 1990s may be seen by some, therefore, as something of a luxury, an indulgence, a festival or carnival to be looked forward to and celebrated once a year at Pride – with badges, banners, placards and *attitude*. But for the remaining 364 days many lesbians revert to a position of invisibility.

It is a tragic irony that in the 1990s, which has seen the burgeoning of Pride into a major political and cultural landmark, the British mainstream press chooses largely to ignore it. Perhaps the sheer *numbers* of lesbian and gay people marching and honouring this historic event is considered such a threat to the rest of society that the media feel compelled to focus only on the *negative* aspects of the lesbian and gay community, such as homophobic harassment or violence.

It has been said before many times, but bears repeating, that lesbianism is not simply about 'private sexuality'. What lesbians do in bed has important implications for, and repercussions on, the rest of their lives. It can result in multiple losses: of children, job, home, status. Lesbianism is about life beyond the closet door. Each coming-out experience is unique, a continuous process of growth and change.

2 pretend families

Research in the 1990s has shown that increasing numbers of lesbians in the UK are choosing to get pregnant by donor insemination. Others already have children from previous relationships, but are still sometimes denied custody by the courts on the grounds of their sexual orientation. Institutionalized homophobia militates against the lesbian household, disparagingly referred to by the British Conservative government as a 'pretended family relationship'. Underlying such blanket condemnation is the kind of blinkered thinking that regards almost any heterosexual ménage as, by definition, superior when it comes to the job of parenting. Lesbians are frequently seen, by society at large and the judiciary in particular, as 'bad women', and consequently unfit mothers, whose sexual proclivities debar them from any right to bring up the next generation.

As with gay men, such bigoted attitudes stem from the pernicious belief that any child in a lesbian household is in imminent danger of being abused or corrupted by the parent's lover. A widespread belief, this has influenced judges in custody cases even though, historically, the incidence of such acts has been proven to be far higher in the case of a *heterosexual male* step-parent.

Moreover, an equally erroneous theory prevails that the child of a lesbian mother 'risks' becoming homosexual. This, again, is based on irrational fears stemming from society's homophobia. Indeed, countless cases have shown that a parent's sexual orientation does not, of itself, detract from a stable environment. In the mid-1970s, American researchers studied the development of twenty children brought up by lesbian mothers. The results, published in the journal *Human Behaviour*, refuted claims made in custody battles 'that children who live with homosexual mothers will form a transsexual self-image, become gay themselves, or learn the social roles of the opposite sex'.[1] And in 1983 a British study by the Institute of Psychiatry found that being brought up in a lesbian household did not increase the likelihood that a child would become homosexual.[2]

However, when attitudes are so deeply ingrained, any attempt to change them elicits accusations of 'subversion'. Popular prejudice, in turn, is fed by the sensationalist treatment of lesbian mothers in the tabloid press. It is the type of coverage which, through the post-hippie 1970s to the repressive, Thatcherite Britain of the 1980s and beyond, has become increasingly vitriolic. Back in 1976, Eleanor Stephens, co-founder of Action for Lesbian Parents, wrote:

> To choose to live openly in a homosexual relationship is a direct challenge to the norm of the heterosexual family which the law upholds. This is doubly threatening where the woman is not only a lesbian but holds feminist views. Court cases of this nature combine the usual morbid obsession with the mothers' sexuality (questions such as 'Do they do it in front of the children?', which would never be asked of a heterosexual liaison, are commonplace) together with a strong element of political witchhunting.[3]

To live as a lesbian mother in the 1990s continues to be regarded as socially confrontational and provocative. Since the 1960s and 1970s, however, judges have begun to rely less on the testimony of 'expert' psychiatric opinion concerning the possible effects on a child of being brought up with two 'mothers' and no father. This is reflected in the greater incidence of tug-of-love cases in which custody is granted to the mother. Until November 1976 custody in cases involving lesbian mothers invariably went to the father, despite the fact that the children may have spent considerably longer periods of time with the mother. The turning-point came when three Appeal Court judges awarded custody of eleven-year-old twins to their lesbian mother. Although a historic decision, it was a limited victory, based partly on the father's inability to provide immediate housing for the twins.

Nonetheless, its significance should not be underestimated; indeed, in another important respect, the case represented a milestone: previously, courts would often instruct a mother not to associate with her lesbian friends in her children's presence because of the alleged fear of molestation or corruption. No such recommendation was made in this instance. Indeed, the judge ruled that he would leave it to the mother's 'good sense' not to conduct her personal life in a way that would impinge upon the children, a statement seen by Action for Lesbian Parents (ALP) as a significant breakthrough 'since it acknowledges that some areas of people's lives are beyond the law's jurisdiction and must be their own responsibility'.[4] One of several campaigning groups which emerged from Sappho in the 1970s, ALP regularly intervened in custody battles, campaigning against injustices in the courts and supporting lesbian mothers in their fight to keep their children. Eleanor Stephens, a founder member of ALP, cites one couple who, having tried to follow the court's injunction to sleep apart, found that this upset the children, who assumed they had quarrelled.

Although not herself a parent, Wanda Goldwag was very deeply committed to ALP:

> I was a complete gay rights activist at the time. For four years I never left the house without wearing a badge that said: 'Lesbians Ignite'. I was very heavily involved in ALP, because that was a period when women were always losing custody of their children. This self-help organization had been set up, but no one could be a contact point or be the treasurer or run the cheque book, because in a test case someone had been found to be a member and they had used that against her as a reason for her not keeping her children.

Linda Bellos's daughter and son live in Brighton and they all meet up as often as they (and she) choose to. But when her children were much younger and her marriage had ended (about 1980), she did not see them for some considerable time. She had come out, and her ex-husband was given custody:

> I came out completely. (My mother was great about it. My father wasn't over-pleased.) To some extent it wasn't entirely wise, in the sense that it jeopardized the custody of my children, but I never do things by half measures. We had fought a custody case and I withdrew because I thought it was extremely damaging for my children. It was devastating. . . . On the other hand, I remained their mother and I had to fight for access, which my husband for a long time denied me.

The lesbian mother has long been regarded as the pariah of 'respectable' society: *persona non grata*. In 1972 Del Martin and Phyllis Lyon (founders of the Daughters of Bilitis) responded eloquently to such perceptions:

> There is no provision in this hetero-sexist society for the Lesbian mother. But her existence cannot be denied – nor can her relationship to her children. In

the past she has been treated like a leper, a threat to her own children. . . . Husbands, by their sole claim to heterosexuality, have been awarded custody regardless of their suitability as parents. The onus is on the mother, and the label 'Lesbian' is enough to deny her her children.

As a result many women have been held captive in unsatisfactory marriages. Others, who have managed to obtain divorces and custody of their children, live under the constant threat of exposure, of being declared unfit mothers because they are Lesbians.[5]

When it comes to adoption or fostering, the same stigma applies. Following the November 1993 White Paper on Adoption, the then Health Secretary Virginia Bottomley reassured the bigots by restating the legal ban on homosexual *couples* becoming adoptive parents, while – technically – leaving the way clear for *individual* lesbians to adopt, whether or not they have a same-sex partner. Although still no easy option, the rules surrounding fostering have become more flexible. An *Independent* feature ('When two "mums" are better than one') included interviews with Kay (nineteen) and Jo, one of her lesbian foster parents. Jo and her partner Liz had fostered more than twenty children over five years:

> I was working in a children's home and Liz trained as a teacher and was working as a minister when we met. We only decided to live together in order to foster, because we didn't think we could do it alone. You don't just walk into fostering – you have a whole year of interviews, and they take lots of character references.[6]

Kay described how living in a home with two women had transformed her life:

> People have these totally wrong stereotypes of lesbians, and if I've learned anything, it's that all stereotypes are wrong. You only have to look at a family like mine to see that. Everyone thought we were perfect. My parents were the type who always turned up at parents' evenings. We seemed like a normal family, but we were sick; now I'm part of what may not seem a normal family, but it's a healthy one.
>
> I think two women can get their heads together much more than a man and a woman. Liz and Jo may yell and scream at each other, but they will always talk things through. . . .
>
> It annoys me when people say they don't think lesbians should be allowed to be foster parents. I think there are so many children in care like me who need two-women households.[7]

In cases of biological parenthood, the kinds of conflicts that can arise between children and lesbian co-parents are no different from those in newly formed *heterosexual* households. They tend to focus on feelings of jealousy and resentment towards the new partner who has (in the child's eyes) 'supplanted' the father in their mother's affections, altering irrevocably the dynamics of the family unit. However, these feelings may be accentuated by homophobic harassment, both physical and mental, from their school peers. Such attitudes and behaviour have been fuelled by the relentless diatribe of British Tory ministers against single mothers in general and lesbian mothers in particular.

There has been a corresponding spate of actions, often highly effective, across the UK, protesting at such scapegoating tactics. At the International Family Conference in Brighton Centre in July 1990, a group of angry women interrupted Princess Diana's speech, invading the platform and brandishing placards proclaiming: 'Lesbian mothers are not pretending.' Then there was the campaign in support of comedian and mother Sandi Toksvig (pp. 49–50).

Whereas the attitudes of most mothers towards their children are informed by the concept of unconditional love, this situation is not always applicable in reverse. Hilde Morris has two daughters, both in their twenties. Each reacted to her mother's lesbianism in very different ways. The elder of the two was accepting from the start, but the younger one found it more difficult: 'Rationally, it isn't a problem, but emotionally, she's still coming to terms with the shock – and this has been over four years now.'

It was in the late 1980s that Hilde embarked on her first 'full' lesbian affair. Like many women who had previously lived and identified as heterosexual, it had taken her several years to confront her feelings of erotic attraction towards women:

> After fifteen years of marriage, I thought that the marriage could still work, but ... I knew eventually I would have to leave my husband and that it was just a matter of time, and I would have to wait until my daughters were independent and, preferably, had left home. I began to feel that living as the *mère de famille*, the little bourgeois housewife, was just not me. I was becoming much more aware as a feminist. I was very happy with my growing-up teenage daughters, but I wasn't happy with where I was at.
>
> My overall perspective changed: it was a gradual veering around. Having come to the decision that I would eventually have to change my life, I suppose this opened a door, because thereafter I wasn't merely *attracted* to other

women but prepared to do something about it, to go a bit further – to see if they were attracted to *me*. My children were then fifteen and fourteen. I had been in love with my best friend for a long time, but although I had dropped several hints and gone away with her, had never got anywhere. Suddenly, out of the blue, another female acquaintance, Yvonne [not her real name], started sending out very powerful messages. She is a straight woman, and that caused a lot of problems because we were very, very involved, and it was a wonderful, and very painful, time for both of us.

The best, most significant, thing that came out of that relationship was that she forced me to say what I am. She said: 'Hilde, you're a lesbian, say it.' She said: 'There is nothing wrong with that, that's what you are, just say it.' And it moves me even now to talk about this, because that was the first time that I felt *accepted*. I had been so very lonely up till then. I had had no role models, I felt like a visitor from another planet, and she was the first person to hold out a hand to me.

She's still my friend; I love her very much and I'll always be grateful to her. However, I decided to cut myself off from her emotionally because I couldn't stand the pain any more. Probably because of the natural progression of the way I was going, I fell in love with another woman of my acquaintance, Zelda [not her real name], who was married and had children, but who had had some lesbian activity when she was much younger – a teenager.

This first lesbian relationship completed Hilde's period of transition from heterosexuality to lesbianism:

With Yvonne I had accepted that I was lesbian *intellectually* and *emotionally*. With Zelda I accepted that I was *physically* . . . I was very discreet, and as far as I know, none of my family or friends knew anything about this, but my younger daughter did guess around this time. She came home unexpectedly one lunch-time and caught me and my lover in an embrace. . . . I've never been able to discuss it with her, because we still have a lot of difficulties in that area.

It was difficult for both of us, especially for my friend, because her children were a lot younger, and if her marriage had broken up it would have been quite devastating. . . . As the children grew older they started to pick up signals. They were around the two of us a lot more, and my friend got very depressed and started to go to a local born-again Christian church, and they told her what we were doing was wrong – and so I lost out to God.

Problems with adolescent children can lead to the surfacing of deep tensions between partners. As a mature student Karen studied for a degree in English at Cambridge University. For the last two years of her course she experienced major problems with the younger of her two teenage daughters (J.). At one point, as Karen recalls, J. became extremely hostile towards Pat, Karen's partner:

> She tried emotional blackmail, saying, 'You choose her or me.' This went on for a couple of years. She went completely off the rails, and I was spending every night cycling around to pubs trying to find her because she wasn't coming home. Finally, I agreed she could be fostered for a three-month period just to give me a break. It was recommended – but at that point she eloped.
>
> I couldn't put the energy into the degree that I wanted to because I was worrying about her all the time. . . . When I sat my finals it was about three weeks after J. had eloped and was pregnant. She was only sixteen. I was in such an emotional state that I fucked up the exams and ended up getting an unclassified degree. I felt sad about that, because it was important to me. It created greater stresses within the relationship. Pat was very supportive of me but tends to be judgemental about the activities of my children, which causes conflicts within *me* because I'm not judgemental at all. I feel that whatever they do I've just got to be there and be supportive.
>
> I thought afterwards, it's a bit like wartime: at the actual time you are under stress, you bond together, but when things have resolved themselves you look around and notice all the devastation. . . . I now have a really good relationship with J. in many ways, but it didn't blow over. She just goes from one drama to the next, so she's a constant worry.

Initially, both daughters accepted Karen's relationship with Pat. It was, recalls Pat, when J. first came to live with them in Cambridge that the difficulties arose:

> I had always been very close to J. It was when she was about sixteen that she went through a very bad patch and decided she hated me. She told me I was disgusting and tried to hit me. It was very unpleasant. This went on for quite some time. . . . When she had the baby she didn't want me to see him at all at first, she wouldn't have me touching him. . . . so I didn't see the baby in the first couple of months or so.

Having co-parented both of Karen's daughters, Pat felt extremely hurt at J.'s behaviour towards her. Karen and her parents were also very upset and bewildered. Then J. arrived unexpectedly one day with apologies for Pat – and flowers.

Pat had originally wanted children of her own, but the experience has changed her mind: 'I can see all the problems they cause. . . . Sometimes I feel – not jealousy . . . but there's too much *dependence*, J. is too dependent on her mother. She can't cope with life.'

Writer Diane Langford experienced similar clashes between her daughter and ex-partner.

> They were absolutely at war. It was terrible and almost ruined my relationship with my daughter. My partner just didn't like children. I don't blame her for that, I don't particularly like them myself! But I did blame her because she knew that I had a daughter and they had got along quite well before we started living together. And then she started laying down all these rules – for instance, my daughter wasn't allowed to come upstairs after nine o'clock. The kid was ten or eleven years old, so it was a bit unrealistic.

In the early 1980s her daughter helped and campaigned for the London Lesbian Mothers Group, to which Diane belonged. 'My daughter was very supportive. She used to co-ordinate workshops for children and spoke at a conference in Leeds. It was huge. Women came from all over the place, about two hundred women and fifty kids.'

Ten years later, in a kind of reversal of Linda Semple's situation, Diane's daughter sold her story to a women's magazine. Headline: 'The day my mum told me she was gay!' She now has a child of her own and lives nearby.

Brenda Ellis and her second husband had always numbered gay people among their friends. Soon after he died (in 1984), her sons, A. and J., then aged eight and nine, asked her if she was gay. She told them she was. Her younger son then announced that he, too, was gay and talked of how he liked a boy at school, but Brenda believes that he was simply showing empathy.

> When P. [my partner] moved in, we went through elaborate rituals of pretending that we weren't lesbians, making up a spare bed in the front room. They [my sons] were totally paranoid – and still are – about me being a lesbian and coming out. I've got a great big poster from a gay magazine on my wall, but when there's a hint of their friends coming round, the poster gets turned round or moved.

Brenda's relationship with P. lasted 'on and off' for about six years. She moved in six months after they first met:

I started finding her clothes in my cupboards and eventually all of her stuff was in there. Next thing I knew *she* was there! My children did amazing things: like we came home one day and P. found all her clothes piled up in the middle of the floor in their bedroom. . . . We found it quite funny and just said: 'Tough'. They did like her and remained very fond of her. She was very good to the boys and really did love them, and gave them a lot of affection and attention. They always kept their home life, where they were involved with lots of our lesbian friends and babysitters, separate. They just didn't bring their friends around very much.

I remember the first time my son came home from school really upset because they'd said Martina [Navratilova] was a queer. He was about nine, and that was when he started getting paranoid about what was going to happen and how it would affect him.

They have always mixed with, and benefited from, my lesbian partners, who have usually been incredibly good to them, taken them on holidays, bought them clothes. I think they like it on that level, but don't want their peer group to know their mother is a lesbian. My son has been in a relationship with a girl for about a year and still hasn't told her, even though my [current] partner is often sleeping in my bed and his girlfriend is sleeping in his bed.

I think they are terrified that I will go to a sports event and have oral sex in the middle of a field or, if I go to the supermarket with my partner . . . my son works there and is terrified that we are going to start kissing. He says: 'It's just the way you look at each other.'

It would be interesting to compare the responses of children from a previously heterosexual background with those from the home of a woman who has, from the outset, lived as a single lesbian mother. It may be that some children find it harder to adjust to a changed domestic situation than to live in a lesbian household from the very beginning. One fourteen-year-old girl (Samantha), both of whose parents were gay, had found her mother's lesbianism harder to accept than her father's gayness because she had only discovered it relatively recently, whereas she had grown up knowing that her dad was gay:

It was such a shock when Mum first told me she was gay. . . . My mind went round in circles. I remember going into my bedroom and thinking: 'My God, my Mum's a lesbian!' I was so used to her being straight and Dad being gay.[8]

Similarly, Brenda Ellis believes that her sons' fears and hang-ups stem from their changed perception of her:

I was a heterosexual mum living with their dad, and that's how they saw it and wanted it. They have often bemoaned the fact that I didn't get a stepfather for them. My younger son still goes out with P. [my ex-partner]: they see each other fairly regularly, and I think she'll be a good friend to him when he's older.

A friend of mine who used to be a lesbian, came around to the house with a boyfriend for the first time. He hadn't been in the house five minutes when he started telling me that (a) the problems I had with my son were because I was a lesbian and (b) he didn't like lesbians. I was incensed, but very polite. He is never coming back into the house again. My son was outraged and has gone on about it ever since – that it was 'gross and completely out of order, how dare he? He knows nothing about our lives'. . . . It was the first and only time I have ever felt supported by my son.

Sharley McLean (seventy-two, Hyde Park Gays and Sapphics, former Terrence Higgins Trust counsellor, London) has a daughter and son who became accustomed early on to living in an extended family. This included a couple of gay male friends and Sharley's long-term partner, Georgina, who died in 1977 (see Chapter 3). Sharley's daughter has told her that she valued her childhood because of the variety of people involved in her life:

They were both quite positive about my sexuality. My daughter still is (we are good friends, always have been), but I have the feeling that my son has problems with it now. I was made aware of that when he was visiting England from Australia a few years back. . . . When he was in his teens it was no problem, but since the age of eighteen he has lived away from home, largely in the hetero world, and I think the Australian woman he married isn't very accepting – it's just a feeling I get . . .

I enjoyed the kids. Whatever mistakes I made bringing them up, I don't punish myself. I'm afraid they have to cope with that. . . . As teenagers I insisted they call me Sharley. I said to them: 'I am a person. I did not call you "daughter" or "son".' It was an argument which won the day.

Sharley married in 1945 and, although the marriage broke down five years later, she continues to share a house with her husband. However, they lead totally separate lives, with their own parts of the house:

We have had quite a difficult relationship throughout. We don't say a lot to each other. He is away a lot. I realize that it is a compromise, and economically it's easier. If we'd sold the house, we would not have raised enough for two different places. You have to make choices ... and I do get respites when he's away. The house feels quite different then.

Joyce Hunter lives in New York, with her partner Jan, a retired teacher. She has 'two wonderful kids who have been very supportive of me when they got old enough to understand about it. I am a very lucky woman'. She has five grandchildren. They all live in New York. Both her daughter and son were accepting of her sexuality from the start:

I told them to sit down. This was before I met my first lover. I said: 'I've got something to tell you', and I tried to do it in an age-appropriate way. I just said I was a lesbian. I said that it meant that I really care about women in a way that I should care about your father but I don't. ... I don't think they really processed it. It was 'OK, Mom, I got to go out and play ... ' [They were twelve and ten years old at the time.]

She had had a good relationship with R., her ex-husband.

He was a good guy. We were friends. I told him, and he said: 'I always knew', but I think he just *said* that. He said: 'I thought I could change you'. He was feeling bad that we would break up, but he was already having an affair. He said to me: 'Why don't we just stay together? I'll do my thing and you do yours and we'll stay together and still be a family.' I said: 'But you don't understand. I want a life, I really want to have a life.' ... We had a friendly divorce, around 1971. I couldn't stay in the closet any more, it was driving me crazy and I had to do something about it. I was depressed, too preoccupied with that to be a good parent.

Years later my daughter said to me: 'Mom, do you remember when you told us that you were gay? I already knew.' 'How did you know?' I said. 'One night,' she said, 'I came down to get something out of the kitchen and you were in there talking to your friend and you were telling him.' He was my only black friend during my marriage who lived up in middle-class suburbia. My husband was doing computer work there, so this guy was a good friend and kept me in touch, and I was telling him about it, so obviously she heard. ... My daughter is very close to us, a great kid.

For Joyce, the transition from single person to mother was particularly stressful. She had grown up in an orphanage with no constant, conventional role model:

When I look back on the relationship I had with my kids during their teens, they could talk about anything with me. I'd 'been there' and they saw me as very different. My son once said: 'Mom, I am really glad you are different'. He would come and tell me about problems with his girlfriends, even sexual stuff. I listened, I didn't give any advice, but he had somebody to talk it out with.

Once, I remember, before he started dating girls he had a relationship with a male friend, and he really loved this friend. It wasn't sexual, but he thought that if you loved your friend that meant you were gay. So we spoke about it, and I said you'll know if you are. We had this discussion, he was about seventeen. I said: 'You know, Mark, it's really OK to be close to your friends and to love them. If you fall in love with a guy and you think you're gay we'll all go out to dinner.' But he hasn't.

He works in construction as an electrical engineer. He once came home and said: 'I want to talk to you', so he's talking to me and my partner, and he's saying: 'You guys raised me to be soft.' I said: 'What's the problem?', and he said: 'Well, you know, I work in construction with all these guys. We went to the movies and I'm the only guy crying!' I said: 'Better than macho! Don't worry, if you cry you'll have less headaches!'

Del Dyer has twin sons in their teens. She also had a baby when she was eighteen – the result of a rape:

Although it can be painful, in some ways I think it's good to have the experience of being pregnant and hating every minute of it – and [then] being pregnant and really pleased about it . . . I tried desperately to have an abortion. I went to four different hospitals. They said: 'You are young and fit and healthy and there is no reason why you shouldn't have this baby.' I said: 'Yes, but I wasn't a willing party to its conception'. It was a boy and lived just over a week. It was eight or nine weeks premature . . . I didn't want it. At eighteen I wasn't ready to be a mother. I was just coming to terms with my own sexuality. I wasn't ready to start washing nappies.

My mother was a registered child minder and there was always at least one baby around the house . . . and I think that influenced me, unconsciously, to be aware of children. I have a genuine liking for babies and toddlers, especially now I am older.

Her twin sons were conceived in much happier circumstances several years later. She was thirty-two and had spent about five years contemplating having a child. Initially, she went to an AID [artificial insemination by donor] clinic. Then after four unsuccessful attempts to get pregnant, she tried self-insemination. She chose a gay acquaintance to be the father, and her ex-partner (Jane) is a co-parent:

> Jane said she knew somebody she could ask, a gay man she worked with and knew quite well. He agreed to be the donor and it worked first time. I remember at the time her saying would you like *me* to do it? and I said no, I wanted to do it myself. I think that has something to do with having been raped. There is a connection there: having control over something that once you had no control over. ...
>
> Jane was quite excited by the idea of me having children. Our initial plan was that I would have one and when that child was two years old she would have one, but as I had twins she decided not to have any. It was a very equal sharing of the financial and domestic areas. She was there from when they were born to when they were eight.

In the 1970s, while issues were being debated around class, race and pornography, Del found that *motherhood* was the single biggest obstacle dividing her from other women. The fact of having conceived children appeared to single her out from the majority of women in her two CR [consciousness raising] groups. In one group she was the only mother, a situation which she found a far greater source of *difference* than sexual orientation.

She doubts whether there was ever a particular occasion when she actually told her sons she was lesbian. Like Brenda Ellis's sons, they had grown up with gay people:

> Since I finished the relationship with Jane, they see their dad at least once a week and stay with him at weekends. They still see Jane on a regular basis. They go on holiday abroad with her, once a year. We don't have a close relationship now, it's quite distant, but we are still friends. Perhaps we wouldn't be if those boys weren't there – it's a link. I think there is a certain amount of respect for each other borne out of the fact that both of us have an interest in those children. Although we don't have a relationship any more, she still has one with them, and that's better than some people who get divorced.

Each boy has his own way of dealing with curiosity from peers at school:

> Darren is quite open about the fact that his parents are gay and that he has a co-parent. And he has paid the price for that because kids can be cruel to each

other. They say: 'You must be gay then'. Ricky keeps out of the way of those situations; whereas Darren is more likely to walk into it, because he *wants* to tell people that he was brought up in a different lifestyle. [Darren and Ricky are pseudonyms.]

Lesbian mothers, ever alert to the possibility that their children might be harassed or victimized at school, are only too aware of the need for discretion. 'Nicola' (ten), when interviewed about life with her two 'mothers', exemplifies this cautionary attitude:

'I've never told anyone at school and I never will. Mum asked me not to because she was afraid that I might get teased. I know that if I told my best friend she would only tell someone else and eventually all of my teachers and my headmaster would know that my Mum was gay. I pretend that Denise is Mum's sister and call her Aunt Denise'.[8]

But she sometimes feels isolated, the odd one out: 'I'd like to have a friend who also had a gay Mum. It would be someone to talk to and I could get things off my chest. Sometimes it feels like a room that is locked in my brain and won't open.'[9]

Despite – or perhaps because of – the growing 'outing' of lesbianism, instances of school bullying have almost certainly increased. Awareness, sadly, does not always guarantee acceptance or understanding. It is easy, therefore, to understand why some mothers feel the need to remain inside the closet. In the USA there are attempts, via education, to raise awareness and, in so doing, to help prevent bullying. A 1994 survey revealed that 1000 children had been born to lesbians in San Francisco alone. In schools across the USA children of kindergarten age are learning about the concept of homosexual families. New York City has adopted the Children of the Rainbow curriculum, a guide developed in consultation with gay rights groups, which urges teachers to discuss same-sex families with children as young as seven. Statistics on the West Coast population show that more than 30 per cent of anti-gay crimes are committed by teenagers. Consequently, many parents have welcomed the venture, believing that the earlier the subject is broached, the better.[10]

In the UK, people's heightened perception of lesbianism reflects, and is a partial consequence of, the higher profile given to lesbian relationships in TV soaps such as *EastEnders* and *Brookside*. And other popular primetime series, such as *Casualty*, have also not flinched from portraying lesbian relationships. In one episode a storyline focused on a lesbian mother whose teenage daughter is run over by a minibus. The mother and her partner, both deeply closeted, are shown visiting her in hospital. Before the accident, a scene takes place in which the daughter, resentful and angry, confronts the partner. 'You're not my mother,' she declares defiantly, adding: 'You're not my father either.' The situation is later resolved when mother and partner sit around the hospital bed and, probably for the first time, discuss their relationship openly in front of the daughter, thus helping to heal the rift between them.[11]

When Del Dyer and her contemporaries became pregnant, it was the 1970s and pre-AIDS. For the younger generation of lesbians in the 1990s, however, AIDS is clearly a crucial issue to be considered if opting for self-insemination. Gillian Rodgerson chose a close gay male friend to be the donor of her child:

> I had always wanted children, and initially I didn't have one particular man in mind, but ... I didn't want an anonymous donor. I wanted to know who the donor was. Beyond that, I didn't have any strong feelings about the involvement he'd have, because I figured that would be something I'd have to work out between the two of us. So my girlfriend and I thought about possible donors, and it is a funny thing thinking of your male friends in that light for their genetic material! ... We finally settled on a good friend of ours, and it took a while for me to screw the courage up to ask (I think he thought I was going to ask him to lend me money!).

Gillian recalls feeling 'tremendously embarrassed' at broaching the subject of an HIV test:

> I suspect that neither one of us has ever blushed so much before or since. Asking him to be our donor was daunting enough. I also had to ask him to take an HIV test, and that's a very difficult thing to ask somebody to do, particularly someone whom you know. Even though I know, rationally, that if he had tested positive it would not have been my fault, I would have felt very guilty, because he hadn't thought of taking a test before that. We talked about it, he thought about it, he finally got tested and was negative.

Three months later he had another test which, again, was negative: 'Then we looked at each other and thought: "Right, what do we do next?" ' After a lengthy search Gillian found a book on self-insemination in Camden Library. Her donor read the relevant sections and, at the second attempt, Gillian became pregnant:

When Sam was born he was badly jaundiced and put in an incubator. Fortunately, he was absolutely fine, but he was being fed through a drip. It was a terrible time, but I think it also cemented my friendship with Sam's father [X.]. It was tremendous to have him around, because my girlfriend, Bo, was going all through these things, there was me in a terrible state, and the baby . . . and X. could take her off to the pub after visiting hours and they could talk. That brought all three of us much closer together. . . . He sees Sam once a month.

Becoming a mother has been one of the greatest lifestyle changes she has experienced, and she admits that it has placed certain strains on her relationship with Bo:

Having a child is a wonderful thing but also very difficult, because you don't have as much time to yourselves. You are bringing a third person into your relationship, and for lesbian couples I think that the partner who is not the child's biological mother has to be a pretty amazing person for it to work – and Bo is, but I know that sometimes it is very hard. I don't think it's jealousy; I think it's just the fact that Sam and I have a physical bond. Bo and Sam have an *emotional* bond that's very strong. He just adores her. When he was a baby he recognized and loved her – but she wasn't breastfeeding him and he was very demanding. I fed him till he was fourteen months. He slept in bed with us.

You can't have sex without planning it, you can't go out spontaneously. It really does put pressure on your relationship . . .

I'm always happy to talk to other lesbians who want information or advice about donor situations and how to get pregnant. I think it's important to be open about it, because I know I had such a hard time finding information. . . . [Parenting] certainly has political ramifications. I see the upbringing that Bo and I do with Sam in some ways as a political project. That sounds so cold, but raising a son is a huge responsibility because of the power that men have in the world. . . . You do what you can. You set an example. Bo and I have the responsibility of being his example of what a loving relationship is.

Young children are often more astute than adults give them credit for, and will readily pick up subtle signals or body language. In 1994 Heather Cowan began her first lesbian relationship. She and her partner shared a house with Heather's six-year-old daughter, Abi, who is already becoming conscious of the existence of different and less conventional lifestyles.

They were in a house-share arrangement with another, younger couple; Heather recalls:

> As a child I knew nothing about sex, relationships, childbirth. I remember my mother giving me three books, when I was aged about eight, which were about 'The Body', 'where babies come from' and menstruation. The information was purely biological. Nothing about respect, relationships, trust. Homosexuality was a taboo subject ...
>
> I have friends in a wide variety of situations, and Abi never makes assumptions about people's relationships. She doesn't assume there will be a husband in the background. In fact, she's beginning to make an assumption that women will have girlfriends.
>
> My daughter and my friends' children are so *aware*. They know why their parents' relationships do or do not work, where sex fits in, that marriage is not the only kind of relationship. When I was a kid I believed that sex equalled love and love equalled sex: you got – or did – one, and the other followed. These kids know that sex and love are two different things which can (or not) go together. ... Abi is aware of a flurry of new women friends in our lives. ... She knows that man–woman relationships are neither the be-all and end-all, nor ideal for *me*.
>
> She's seen me suffer in an abusive relationship with a man, and she had a rough ride with that. For her the situation now is that much better. She continues to see the love and support that women can share.

Nonetheless, at her first school her daughter was subjected to frequent teasing from other pupils. The teachers were not very approachable or forthcoming, and simply told her to stop 'whingeing'. Before Abi moved to her new school in Plymouth, Heather explained her home situation to the headmistress. She had never come across a lesbian couple with a child before, but assured Heather that there would be no teasing – and this has remained the case. (Sadly, Heather's relationship has since ended.)

Many women opt for concealment and pretence as the softer, safer, less traumatic option. But for those in the public eye, the choice is a stark one: between openness and honesty – with the attendant risks to career and reputation – and secrecy, with the constant fear of being outed by a prurient media hungry for stories of sex, sleaze and scandal. In 1994 Sandi Toksvig, the Danish comedian and writer, decided to pre-empt the media by coming out publicly. Her partner, Peta, has three children, all conceived through artificial insemination. In a lengthy interview in the national press, Toksvig claimed to have delivered all three babies and to have equally strong maternal feelings for each one. She had never hidden the fact that her partner was a woman. As Toksvig explained:

> We want to be able to talk about it and be proud about it, but not bang drums. We didn't have children for political reasons, we did it because we loved each other. We don't lead a separatist life. . . . People say, what will you tell them when they're older? And I say, I don't know what they're going to ask.[12]

Diana Verity, the mother-in-law of the man who acted as donor for Toksvig's partner, publicly declared her disapproval of the arrangement, describing Toksvig as 'weird' ('If God meant two women to have children, he would have made it possible.'[13]). Verity's outburst received short shrift from columnist Lynda Lee-Potter. In a piece headlined 'Whose lives are they anyway?' she writes:

> Most mothers of grown-up daughters would, I suspect, feel apprehensive about the situation, but mothers with any sense would keep their mouths shut. Because being a mother doesn't give us any right to try to control or influence the decisions and behaviour of grown-up children.[14]

Toksvig's self-outing was a calculated gamble. She said she wanted to tell her story so that she and her children could live openly and without fear. Nonetheless, her decision to go public provoked a strongly adverse response from within her extended family, as well as from some of the tabloids. It was subsequently decided to 'drop' Toksvig as compere for the seventy-fifth anniversary celebrations of the Save the Children Fund (in October 1994), on the spurious grounds that (according to the trustees) her presence 'might distract from the events of the day'.[15]

Toksvig had apparently supported the charity for several years. As she said in a statement after the conference:

> It was apparently all right for me to give my time and energy, but not if I was gay. Perhaps there is a theory that in expressing my sexuality I have lost my compassion and concern for others in the world.[16]

The decision by the charity's council to drop Toksvig brought a vociferous reaction from her numerous supporters, including the Lesbian Avengers, who invaded the conference venue shouting and blowing whistles. Then, more than 250 staff at Save the Children signed an open letter to the *Guardian* condemning the move. Soon afterwards public pressure led to a climb-down, and a written apology from the charity was read out by Toksvig to a 5000-strong crowd at Stonewall's Equality Show at London's Royal Albert Hall.

Even before a lesbian has become pregnant, there is feverish speculation as to the rights and wrongs of the matter, with public figures ranging from MP Lady Olga Maitland to the Pope pontificating and sermonizing. In June 1994 an article in the Vatican newspaper vilified lesbian mothers who sought to become pregnant by AID. as abnormal and 'an aberration of nature'.[17] When, after her spectacular 1994 'swansong' at Wimbledon, Martina Navratilova announced that she was *thinking* about having a baby when she retired from tennis, this was enough to spark off a storm of invective in the right-wing media. In the *Mail on Sunday* John Junor fulminated about the possibility of 'some backstreet quack' fulfilling Martina's wish to give birth via AID. 'Won't he deserve for all eternity a front seat in hell?', he ranted.[18]

Then there was the widely publicized case in Virginia, USA, of Sharon Bottoms, the lesbian mother who regained custody of her two-year-old son after the state's appeal court reversed the judge's original decision. This brought a predictably venomous response from a Tory MP, the late Geoffrey Dickens, who described the case as 'a form of child abuse'. What seemed especially shocking was the fact that the original case had been brought by Bottoms's own mother, Kay, who was strongly opposed to her daughter's sexuality. The court concluded that being a lesbian did not constitute proof of parental neglect, and campaigning groups welcomed the ruling as a victory for all lesbian and gay parents.

Apart from the perennial issue of custody, the fear of rejection still deters some women from being completely open with their children, especially if they are going through adolescence. Jenny Wood (forty-nine, runs a white-goods business, Darlington) led an almost exclusively heterosexual lifestyle in Darlington for more than twenty years. In 1990 she decided to leave her husband and explore lesbianism. Her two daughters were in their late teens at the time, and it took about three more years before she felt able to come out fully to them:

> The response I got was really good. They'd been saying bits and pieces that led me to believe they wanted to know: they were asking without actually verbalizing it. And so in the end I took my courage in both hands – and felt I'd aged about ten years working up to it – and told them, and they were both fine. They would prefer me *not* to be [lesbian], but as far as they're concerned I'm the best mother in the world – and it's made life a lot easier.

I brought both my daughters up to be very independent and to be their own person. It seemed extremely important to me that they had a totally different upbringing to what *I* had. I wasn't at all happy with mine, and I made a supreme effort to take them to places, to give them a wider outlook on life. Never once have I pressurized them into having a boyfriend or getting married. They are so grateful that I never did that. I didn't want them to get into the same stuff that I got into – to have a life and regret most of what they'd done in it.

She has an extremely good relationship with both daughters. One lives locally with her own hairdressing business, and they meet up two or three times a week. The other one, also self-employed, lives in Leicester. They are supportive of Jenny both as an individual and as their mother, and they see her lesbianism as a side issue: 'They don't have a problem with it, in as much as I can talk about it and if I happen to be seeing anyone they will mention it. It is not a taboo subject any more.'

Like Brenda Ellis's sons, they like to keep the public and private sides of their lives separate:

I think if I was shown on TV carrying a banner at Gay Pride they'd probably have problems, but I haven't done that yet. I sometimes go to a women's demonstration up at the American airbase at Harrogate. It's a bit of a spin-off from Greenham, and they think: 'Why couldn't Mother just be a normal mother and not get involved in this sort of thing?' But they are quite proud of me and would prefer me to be a little bit different than totally normal and boring like a lot of their friends' mothers are.

Mandy (sixty-one, postgraduate student, Cambridge) was forty-one when she left her husband and two teenage children to live with her first lesbian lover in a cottage in East Anglia (Mandy is not her real name):

It was quite the most dreadful experience. It lasted in all about eight or nine months, which was long enough, leaving a home and a marriage of that length and going off with somebody who wasn't very supportive – she *knows* she wasn't – and I've not had any contact since.

My son was fifteen and my daughter eighteen, so they weren't little, but one has all the guilt about going and leaving them. I kept going back and doing things for them, but it wasn't the happiest of times. They were very supportive – they have never been *un*supportive of me – but with hindsight, it was quite difficult for them, coming to terms with me not being around and going off with a woman. They had to explain it to their friends. My son just coped with it – he liked the woman I was with – but my daughter couldn't bear her. She talked to a sympathetic teacher at school, who helped her through it.

It wasn't sweetness and light, I appreciate that now more than I did at the time. I think: 'Poor kids, what did I do to them?' There's the memory of little incidents – the look on their faces, that kind of *angst*. . . .

For me [the relationship] was almost an addiction – a whole new sexuality, and the first time I had ever been able to express it. Then one gets too involved and behaves in unacceptable ways.

In terms of motherhood, some younger lesbians prefer to keep their options open. Sophie Mills thinks that in time she would very much like to be a mother:

I'll give myself five years, then I'll have to start thinking seriously about what I'm going to do. If I don't have [children] it won't be the end of the world. The only thing I would *not* do is to have them on my own because, since I was about ten, I was brought up in a single-parent family. My mother did a brilliant job, but I just feel: 'No, thank you, not for me'. So I wouldn't do it unless I was in a really stable, secure relationship.

Savi Hensman believes it is important to have contact with children:

Nieces and nephews, the children of friends and so on – but . . . I don't think I'm someone who's felt a very strong biological or social urge to parent. For some people it's very important *physically* to have a child, and that's not something that I've felt. I think I would be as willing to adopt as to bear a baby.

Linda Semple has no family of her own but appreciates her 'extended' family, including a nephew and niece of whom she is very fond. She recalls one brief period of 'broodiness' in her mid-twenties:

I remember sitting down with my [then] partner and talking about it, and her saying: 'Well, it's your choice.' I went away and made a list of Items For and Against, and the Items Against were too many. So I thought: 'I'll get over this,' and a couple of weeks later I was over it . . . .

You begin to realize that you're thinking about [motherhood] for the wrong reasons – for prosperity, and for someone to look after you in your old age. . . . I mean, if lesbians want to have children, fine. There we were at Sappho with all that stuff about AID babies, but it wasn't for *me*, and I think a lot of women, if they can get over that broody period, will realize it's not for them either.

3 **d**ating and **r**elating

From her perspective as an AIDS activist, Sarah Schulman has said that no other group of people has been so *excluded from the dominant culture* as lesbians and gays. The lesbian and gay community has had to act *in loco parentis*: 'Our families propagate an official culture in which our lives are denied. ... No other group of people has been so abandoned.'[1] And yet there is a wider, more global interpretation of 'Family': a 'Brotherhood [sic] of persons or nations united by political or religious ties' (OED), a definition which is certainly applicable to lesbians, especially those who have dedicated time and energy to campaigning for lesbian and gay rights. Many of the women who talked to me have been – and in some cases still are – actively engaged in various campaigns, some connected with the AIDS movement (see Robin Gorna, Part II).

For others, however, different priorities and preoccupations have emerged in their lives. The personal and the political, once inextricably intertwined, have become separated out, the former tending to supersede the latter as relationships and social life have begun to take precedence over politics. But, as Emma Healey points out: 'Many women hanker for that sense of political identity that we strove for in the 1970s and 1980s; they see the lesbian community now as depoliticized and fragmented.'[2] At the time of writing, more than half of my interviewees were in long-term relationships. Not all live with their partners, and those who lived separately did so mostly out of choice rather than necessity.

In 1992 Sally Cline entered into a lesbian life partnership to which she says she is totally committed and which she finds 'fulfilling, challenging and fun'. She and her partner live in different houses – indeed, in different cities – an arrangement which gives them 'times of intense closeness and times of space and autonomy. We may not always choose to do this, but it appears to work highly satisfactorily.'

She has remained 'best friends' with the woman with whom she lived for nine years and with whom she co-parented three daughters. They separated in 1987, but 'we expect to remain close for the rest of our lives'. She also has a daughter and three stepchildren from her second marriage.

For many years she lived alone, and for much of this period she remained celibate. She has written a book on celibacy (*Women, Celibacy and Passion*, published in 1993 by André Deutsch). She has since redefined its meaning, believing in what she describes as 'passionate or sensual celibacy', a concept which she introduces into her life whenever it feels appropriate:

> Passionate celibacy is a form of female sexuality. It is the choice to be without a sexual partner for positive reasons of personal, political or spiritual growth, freedom and independence. Passionate celibacy is a sexual singlehood which allows women to define themselves autonomously, while still retaining a network of connections, rather than in terms of another person and his or her needs.

It is, she adds, a form of 'sexual practice', but without the power struggles of a sexually active relationship. These power struggles are supported by what she calls the 'genital myth', which she sees as highly inimical to the interests of women generally and of lesbians in particular: 'Women are coerced into thinking that genital activity is both necessary and productive for achieving loving relationships. ... Individual lesbians may enjoy genital activity, but coercion is proving disastrous psychologically.'

Savi Hensman met her partner, Sharon, in 1986 at a meeting for black and minority ethnic lesbians and gay men. They became lovers and moved in together soon afterwards. Savi then worked at the Black Lesbian and Gay Centre, and her partner was a community worker at another lesbian centre. In the early 1990s they began to live apart while continuing to meet up regularly. Both have friends in common and live near each other in Hackney:

> Both she and I have a lot of outside interests. I don't think I would have wanted to become involved in the kind of relationship where people's only interest was in each other. I think relationships of that kind can burn out quite easily, because they are very intense – and also rather selfish, in the worst sense, because they exclude everybody else. We try to support each other in doing what we regard as important, and in getting involved in activism of various kinds in the other areas of our lives.

Both have discovered definite advantages in living separately:

> For a start, there's something to be said for seeing a little less of the other person than you'd like. ... It gives a kind of freshness to the relationship that there otherwise wouldn't be. My partner now lives with other women in a Buddhist household, and I suppose for me it's highlighted the fact that she's a different person from me; we're not just halves of the same unit. That's been a useful lesson to learn.

Christianity is another part of her identity, but she has always had non-Christian friends, ranging from Muslims to atheists to people of other faiths:

> Being in a relationship with somebody who comes at life from a rather different perspective – some of the conclusions you reach may be similar, they are just worked out in different ways – that's stimulating.

Like many lesbians who have lived a 'single' or celibate life it can take time – and some psychic pain – to adjust to being part of a couple. There are subtle differences in the way in which most of us behave, according to who we happen to be with at any given moment, as Savi's experience can confirm.

> Meeting Sharon has had a major impact on my life. Parts of myself that I had shut off have been opened up, which has been painful as well as exhilarating. I have come to know more about myself. I can come across as very self-reliant and unemotional. In some places that's useful but ... I've sometimes found myself slipping into the role of the strong, protective one, and to acknowledge that I'm human and changeable has been important and useful.
>
> I've found it affirming to be loved and valued for who I am. There's also the risk of rejection that comes with that, and the feelings of vulnerability when there are problems with the relationship.

Becky is in her early twenties and a police officer with the Metropolitan Police in London. She too lives apart from her partner, J., who is ten years older and based in Berkshire, more than seventy miles away. Becky shares a house with her twin sister:

> I don't want to 'live with' someone at the moment because my work is my priority. The hours are shit ... I'm a single woman, I've got no children, no one

to go home to who's going to be worried that I'm four hours late home from work, which is what happened one night when we arrested someone.

They meet at weekends, commuting to each other's homes. In logistical terms, it's a flexible arrangement: 'It has to be. It depends on what the cash flow's like at the time – whoever's feeling rich is the person who does the travelling.'

Trend towards monogamy

Living alone but being part of a couple can mean the best of both worlds: more 'quality' time together combined with an escape route from the potential boredom factor of close daily proximity. Familiarity can, and indeed does, breed contempt. Oscar Wilde's sentiments are eloquently echoed by the prophet Kahlil Gibran, who urged: 'Let there be spaces in your togetherness.'[3] But what about monogamy? In the 1970s, to be a right-on lesbian feminist it was necessary to be seen to reject monogamy as a retrograde and outmoded concept. Experimentation and exploration of one's sexuality was regarded as *de rigueur*, and the slightest admission or exhibition of jealousy was considered ideologically unsound.

Throughout the 1980s and into the 1990s attitudes changed and non-monogamy among lesbians has lost the kind of social and political cachet that it once possessed. It has become increasingly 'unfashionable', as the emotional logistics of changing partners have often proved as problematic as the straitjacket that monogamy was deemed to represent. However, as young lesbians like Becky will testify, there is still a degree of pressure within the lesbian and gay community to get laid, almost as a way of affirming lesbian credentials:

> One person at work caused me severe mental heartache by saying to me that I should be sleeping around with people. Her attitude was: 'Oh Becky, make the most of it while you're young. You won't carry on pulling people for ever, you know.' ... I found big pressure coming from this one person to be wild, let go, be free. It caused me a lot of problems at the time, because I was just starting a relationship with my current partner.

Becky believes that the compulsion to go out and be 'reckless' stems from some lesbians' internalized feelings that they are freaks:

> It's a case of 'OK, I *am* a freak, therefore I'll behave like one, and so will have no respect for myself.' I dislike that sort of attitude because I always like to

think of a relationship as being long-term. I always enter into it with quite a lot of seriousness.

The only woman I interviewed who admitted to leading an ongoing non-monogamous lifestyle was Nettie Pollard. Nettie has a committed relationship dating back to 1973, but she and her partner have other relationships. 'This way of living can be complicated at times,' she concedes, 'but it's also stimulating and interesting.' She agrees that non-monogamy is not an easy option, but believes that that is no reason not to try to make it work.

Despite her transition to a more libertarian lifestyle, Jill Posener (forty, photographer, San Francisco) says she is now in a committed monogamous relationship, but remembers the time when radical lesbian politics decreed that non-monogamy was the norm – the accepted, politically correct expression of lesbian sisterhood (see Chapter 4). As she recalls, however, the practice dismally failed to match the expectations of the theory:

> We said that monogamy was a heterosexual way of keeping women subservient to men and we weren't going to play the game, but whenever one of us slept with another person's girlfriend, of course there was hell to pay. . . . It was all part of the gradual stripping away of real emotion, and although there was no leader, no 'Führer' telling us what to do, we all felt somebody else had more control than we did. I think we felt we were not effective politically if we had those kinds of emotions. That was the bottom line.
>
> I always lied, didn't tell my girlfriend that I was pursuing somebody else – too scared to. I would sleep with a woman and think of it as a mistake, then get interested in someone else and it would always hurt somebody. We're deeply jealous and possessive human beings, and I see nothing wrong with that.

In Linda Semple's experience, agreements to be non-monogamous often meant that it was her partner who had other relationships:

> I sat at home and bit my nails . . . so maybe I was not cut out for it. There's only been one time since I've been out when I've had more than one [concurrent] relationship. The individual people I was involved with were lovely and I had a great time, but I don't recommend it as a way of life. . . . If people are happy with open relationships, then fine. I suppose I'm a bit of a wet liberal about it . . . but I don't think it's any longer for me. I'm sure it's *age*. A lot of the young

lesbians that I know are so happy that they've got the *freedom* to go out to clubs, bars. . . . I always used to say when I was coming out that I appreciated the work that had gone before . . . but I didn't think that I absolutely had to, and I'm certainly not going to turn into a crusty old dyke saying: 'These young girls, they don't appreciate the work *we* did, they're too busy enjoying themselves.' Surely the only gratitude we want is the fact that they can go and enjoy themselves and have a fabby time, because that's what we are all working towards.

Because Wanda Goldwag had 'enormous amounts' of sex at a very young age, she has never particularly felt the desire to be wildly promiscuous since then:

By my early twenties I had had sex with forty or fifty women, then a ten-year period where I had sex with about three. Lots of them were one-night stands and casual things at conferences. Everybody was doing it – it wasn't a big deal, *I* certainly didn't think of it as a big deal. . . . As an adult (I didn't particularly see myself as an adult then), I have understood that it can be very destructive of relationships: it shouldn't have to be but it is.

Like Savi and Sally, Brenda Ellis has chosen to live separately from her partner. They live near one another in Brixton, South London. In 1989 Brenda began to suffer badly from arthritis, a condition which for her represented a major life change:

I started getting classic symptoms: sore wrists and lots of pain. I had never been ill in my life, never been in hospital. I went to the doctor, who gave me a test and said it was arthritis and would get worse. At the time I was with an American woman I had known for eight years as a friend, and we had just started a relationship. It continued for another six months and ended quite drastically. We had gone to the park for a walk on New Year's Day and she turned on me and screamed that she didn't want to be with somebody who was disabled, that I was ruining her life, crowding her lifestyle and the relationship was over.

She had been married, and her husband's daughter from a previous marriage was severely disabled and she had to do a lot of caring for the child. I think she had built up this huge resentment. I was completely shocked, because you never expect somebody to behave like that. But I've heard from other lesbians that it's very common, particularly for women with disabilities.

Throughout the following year Brenda avoided further serious involvements and decided that any future relationship would have to be with a woman who, like her, was disabled. Then along came Amanda, who is able-bodied:

> She only knew me with arthritis, and she is fine and we don't have a problem with it. She's made me much more mobile and more accepting, I think, of my disability.
>
> We both have separate lives. We have more differences than things in common, but we seem to get on incredibly well and want to maintain our independence. We see each other several times a week. When my arthritis is bad in the evenings – I have a lot of pain – the last thing I want is someone around. Although I would like somebody to comfort me, I haven't got any energy for them. If you are in pain you just want to be on your own. That's the only way you can cope. When I'm [feeling] bad I'm in a filthy mood, I want to be left on my own, I don't want anybody to talk to me, to fuss or touch me or be near. I don't want to have to worry about anybody else.
>
> It affects my sleep. I have to rest up at weekends. ... You work out your own way to live, another way of being. You learn what is OK for you, and people have to accept that. At work I tend to forget, because I am busy and involved [she works with the Greater London Federation of Disabled People].

Amanda is a gardener and a woofer (worker on an organic farm):

> She is also a country person, which I am not, so when she wants to go away for the weekend and walk in the country she just takes herself off. ... We have quality time together and think about what we are going to do when we see each other, rather than take each other for granted.

Since April 1993 Brenda has worked for the Greater London Federation of Disabled People. Several employees have disabilities, including another women with rheumatoid arthritis. Although it's 'quite nice' working with somebody who knows what she is going through, Brenda does not dwell on her disability. 'It seems *normal* to me, how I am. It's like putting on new shoes – you get in a wheelchair ... It's part of *me*, I don't even think about it any more. I drive the car and I use the wheelchair because I can't walk or stand for long periods.'

Through her work, and through being a 'disabled dyke', she has met other lesbians with disabilities.

I have also met some amazing women. The amount of diversity in the (disabled) community, it is a world that I had no idea about, even though I had been involved in women's politics and thought I knew it all. I never had any idea that there was a disability movement and that there were tens of thousands of people like myself campaigning, challenging, working towards getting access and improved conditions and better employment prospects for disabled people.

Lesbians, she stresses, are in the forefront of all this activity.

Most of the dykes I know who are disabled are out, although a lot of them aren't. Some are living in institutions or with parents who might not even know they are gay – and I found the same [situation] with disabled Black women. A lot of them are in the closet ... and they've got multiple oppressions so they just don't want to have to deal with it, it's just too much ... It is kept very private within the disability community, about who is out.

Lesbianism in a heterosexist society

However accepting of lesbianism *per se*, most straight people simply have no conception of what it is like to live as a lesbian. It is as if lesbianism is locked away in a vacuum, insulated from mainstream heterosexual social and cultural life, instead of being a valid social option freely chosen by a sizeable minority of consenting adults. The mere fact of their *acceptance* that lesbians exist at all is regarded by most liberal, forward-thinking hetero-sexuals as 'enough'. It does not seem to occur to them that lesbian lifestyles and perspectives might differ fundamentally from their own. Inured to the plethora of heterosexist images that surround them, straight people have to be continually reminded that there is considerably more to lesbian lives in the 1990s than separate, 'alternative' outlets such as bars or cafés.

Mary Jennings calls this phenomenon 'hetero homophobia':

It's like a complete and utter lack of understanding of what it means to live a gay life and be out. ... How do you deal with that? I took a [straight] female friend of mine to First Out [a lesbian and gay café in London's West End], and she said: 'Oh, this is fine,' as if it's OK, it's nice and what's the problem, you know? ... If you are out it's like – that's *it*. It's as if there's nothing *beyond* that.
...

> I think that being a lesbian is such a different life in so many ways. .... You have constantly to remind people, to *explain*. I just get so tired of liberal tolerance. I find it exasperating. I feel it's a sort of failure on my part, as if I'm not explaining things. ... It's not a barrier: it's a gulf, a black hole. A barrier implies something solid that you can deal with.

Perhaps it is the subversiveness evoked by the idea of lesbianism which elicits this mass myopia, this fear that governs and underlies straight people's desire to be seen as non-interventionist. Maybe it threatens their sexuality, their own private sense of self. But what they do not appear to realize is that by their very silence they are in effect condoning, and colluding with, society's homophobia. Silence denotes indifference, which in turn masquerades as tacit acceptance.

This indifference has been challenged to a degree by the spate of lesbian scenarios enacted in TV soaps, notably *Brookside*. Beth Jordache's lesbian liaisons started tentatively with Margaret, her neighbour on the Close, moved on to her steamy but short-lived affair with college lecturer, Chris, and graduated to a passionate kiss with blonde bisexual babe, Viv. The latter scene was censored in the weekend's omnibus edition, sparking off a mass 'snog-in' by the Lesbian Avengers outside Channel 4's HQ.

The sensitively scripted storylines and non-stereotypical character-ization has turned Beth into a powerful 1990s role model for young dykes. News of her prison sentence, following the guilty verdict for killing her abusive father, was greeted with 'real' protest from women's groups. Such was the impact of Beth's personality and her lesbianism, that her death in prison (in July 1995) was treated as the stuff of tragedy, accentuating her icon status.

Despite individual heterosexuals' claims of acceptance and empathy, when it comes to major 'life events' such as bereavement or separation, society continues to have no recognized legal or social framework, no 'safety net' for lesbians and gays. There are few, if any, officially sanctioned support networks to turn to at times of crisis or adversity. When a lesbian relationship breaks down, the resulting 'fall-out' can be overwhelming, the sense of isolation compounded by the more generalized alienation experi-enced by lesbians as a minority within the dominant heterosexist culture. An already limited social life may be further curtailed, especially if both partners have lived in a small town or rural environment with many mutual friends.

Because lesbian relationships are often perceived by the dominant culture as less serious or valid than their heterosexual counterparts, there is a tendency to underestimate the degree of trauma involved when a lesbian couple split up. Furthermore, because the option of divorce is not open to lesbians, there is often a great deal of 'unfinished business' to be attended to, of both a practical kind (joint ownership of property, division of possessions, etc.) and emotionally (e.g. a partner's co-parenting role).

Abusive relationships

Problems occurring within an *existing* relationship go similarly unrecognized, not only by heterosexuals but often by other lesbians. The last area of taboo among lesbians is *abuse*, a highly contentious issue that shakes up all preconceptions about violence being a predominantly masculine construct. Gill Storey was involved in a relationship that was both physically and emotionally abusive. Ann Wishart has experienced the latter form of abuse.

> I was dominated, totally submerged, within the relationship. I didn't realize I was. When I realized, I thought, 'Things have got to change' ... Socially and intellectually, I was strong, but emotionally I was a lot weaker. Therefore, I allowed myself to be manipulated ... What stopped me being politically active was the relationship and [the fact that] my partner was closeted. What made me politically active was making an active decision to leave that relationship. She made it very clear to me that she couldn't remain in a relationship with me if I was out to people, and you can't be very politically active if you are not out. I woke up one day and thought, 'I can't continue here ... I can't go through the rest of my life doing it someone else's way.' I wanted to do it *my* way. It was the first relationship I ever ended, and that felt incredibly strong.

Soon after moving from her 'politically correct' life in Brighton to the lesbian social scene in Sheffield (see Chapter 4), Bridget got into abusive relationships:

> I spent a lot of time doing things that I hadn't done for years, I suppose it was just a way of letting my hair down ... going out to discos, getting drunk, I started smoking again ... I got into very abusive relationships. I got involved with Karen [not her real name]. She was actually in a long-term relationship with another woman and I barged in and told Karen how I felt about her. ...

I felt, and have felt since then, terrible about splitting a relationship up, but Karen fell in love with me at the same time.

We were together for four years. We bought a house together and had a monogamous relationship, to the extent that she wasn't really happy about me keeping up close friendships with other women, even platonic ones. Another problem was getting enough time on my own. Karen didn't want me to spend time on my own, and that was often a bone of contention. . . . She was alcoholic. I don't think I was aware of it straight away, but it became obvious. She was horrible when she was drunk – violent and bossy. I did love her very much at the beginning, but our relationship was spoiled by all that.

It's hard to understand why I stayed with her for so long. Some of it was that I felt so bad about splitting up her relationship with her previous lover – I felt I had to give it a good go. Sometimes I used to wonder if Karen was just seeing how far she could push me, how much I would take. She used to torment me. I think she wanted to wind me up to a crisis. This happened regularly. I don't remember a lot of the details. I tend to block out things that are really painful. I felt I couldn't talk to anyone about it. That was to do with what I imagine was loyalty, but also not wanting to admit that I had made the mistake of choosing the wrong person, not wanting to justify why I had stayed that long, or to admit that things were going wrong. One day I woke up and realized that I couldn't go on any more. I wanted to cut loose from her, to walk out of the house and never come back. I walked out and . . . stayed with friends until I found somewhere else to live.

After that I felt that I wanted to find somebody who would make me feel loved. Because of the violence and aggression I had felt very *unloved* . . . and I had a relationship with Michael [not his real name] quite quickly after Karen, and the strong feeling was – here was somebody who wouldn't hurt me.

Now, I don't need somebody else to feel OK about myself . . . I am not prepared to tolerate intolerable situations.

The 1990s have seen the formation in London of at least two Lesbian Survivors' groups, one of which meets every week at West Hampstead Women's Centre. Pam, fifty and the mother of two daughters, was one of those who attended. She suffered constant emotional abuse from her partner, ten years her junior, throughout a two-year relationship:

She was jealous from the beginning and I should have known better, but when you fall in love with somebody you choose to ignore that stuff. She was terribly possessive, very rude to all my friends. . . . She wanted me to live with her, but my instincts told me definitely *No*. We used to see each other three or four times a week. She hated my children and was very jealous, so it wasn't like a sharing situation where I could involve her with them. They hated her. I was absolutely *torn*. It was an impossible situation.

The hardest part was the intimidation, the power that she exerted. She always wanted her own way. She was insulting and abusive.

The sole incidence of *physical* abuse occurred when the relationship was coming to an end:

I just wanted her out of the house and she refused to go. She was a martial arts expert. I went to hit her first, in pure anger and frustration because she wouldn't leave my home, and she threw me across the room. My ribs were broken and my kidneys injured. . . . My children were there, and watching the whole scenario. I was hysterical . . .

I couldn't call the police because, I mean, we're lesbians and very aware of how the police view us – and also, the fact that my partner was black made me not want to call them.

Afterwards, she terrorized me for two years. I'd be in a supermarket and she would come up to me out of nowhere. She'd obviously been following me, and she'd demand that I talk to her. I would have the choice of a scene in the supermarket or of having to go with her to her car and be kidnapped. . . . She lived the other side of London and used to sit outside my house in her car, sometimes all night . . . I changed my phone number three times. . . . She would show up at my workplace and insist that I come outside to talk to her. I had to go out to the car park, and she would force me into the car and take me off somewhere. My staff didn't know where I was for the afternoon. In the end I had to leave my job.

I was so traumatized that I hibernated for seven years, just locked myself indoors, had my phone permanently on the answering machine and became a hermit.

Pam has begun a new life as a designer, but the emotional scars remain. The sense of stigma that continues to surround woman-to-woman abuse creates feelings of extreme isolation, not only from heterosexual society but – and this is possibly the most distressing aspect – from the lesbian community itself: 'You can't broach the subject to other lesbians, it's too uncomfortable for them, so you start to blame yourself.'

The women in the Survivors' group who would otherwise be perceived as very strong in all other areas of their lives, suddenly find that they have become victims, their self-esteem totally undermined. It can take years to build up that inner confidence again.

Abuse can take many different forms: emotional blackmail, intimidation, rejection, sexual demands, any behaviour that causes fear. The abusive partner may resort to threats of suicide, as thirty-five-year-old Liz experienced in a year-long relationship with her ex-lover Grace [not her real name]:

> The emotional abuse probably started before the physical abuse. It was very subtle at first and ended up so that I couldn't step outside the house without her being there. She gradually got me away from my friends and my family. She was very manipulative.
>
> She would put me in a position where I would feel incredibly guilty about going out with an old friend, whether by saying: 'You don't care about me', or by threats of suicide. These became *attempts* at suicide if I persisted. She would have a go at slashing her arms and a half-hearted attempt at taking an overdose.
>
> Her level of violence would escalate. I got punched, beaten up. She stabbed me, strangled me, hit me with a bottle, crashed the car while I was driving it. If I was late home from work, that would spark it off. Or she would have a bad day at work, get angry with someone, come home and *I* would have to bear the brunt of that anger. I would never argue back, because I was so scared of the consequences. It would get to the point where it didn't matter what I had done: she would get out of control and I would get physically abused. I am normally confident and self-assured. That was totally reversed. It happened very insidiously.
>
> I am out to my family, but they didn't know my partner very well and didn't know what was going on – until it reached crisis point. I had been hit every day for a week, sometimes in public. She threatened to kill me: she had done this on a previous occasion, but this time I was terrified. Something told me that if I didn't leave I wouldn't get out alive. I just got into my car as if I was going to work, and didn't go back. I went to my parents. I had to leave the town I was living in . . . I left home, job, everything.
>
> Making the decision to leave and actually doing it was the hardest thing I did. I still loved this person and realized that she had a problem, and thought: 'Should I stay and work it through with her and help her? Will there be any difference at the end of it?' But I had to think of my own safety.
>
> I was in such a state of shock that I didn't work for six weeks afterwards . . . I used to think about it constantly. It was like watching a film flashing in front of me. Now, I am trying to rebuild my life.

> It destroys all trust. I am not as friendly and outgoing as I used to be. I
> certainly wouldn't enter into another relationship without being good friends
> with someone first.

Women who attend the West Hampstead group belong to a wide social and racial spectrum, with ages ranging from eighteen to fifty. Jean Cross, the centre's lesbian worker who runs the group, sees it as a useful first step:

> It's like that first stage with women's refuges – somewhere to go, someone to
> intervene ... but it's not been taken up in the lesbian community. Maybe it
> threatens our analysis of society, of *men* being the violent people. .... Here are
> these women – lesbians – abusing other lesbians, and what does that say
> about our view of the world?

In the UK, we have a long way to go before we can match the progress made in the USA. In New York, the streets and subway trains carry advertisements for organizations and helplines offering support for those experiencing violent abuse from same-sex partners.

In the UK, there exists a double standard, a basic devaluing of lesbian relationships by mainstream society. This is also evident in the event of the death of a partner (see p. 70). A kind of 'two-tier' system of official and unofficial response to crisis is thus created. There are notable exceptions, however, such as Relate (formerly the National Marriage Guidance Council). During the late 1980s, Relate extended their counselling service to include lesbians and gays, although they cannot guarantee to provide lesbian or gay counsellors, and their information leaflets refer, rather euphemistically, to 'relationship problems inside and outside marriage'.

MAKING IT OFFICIAL

In view of the lack of understanding shown by society as a whole, it is perhaps not surprising that many more lesbian and gay couples in both the UK and USA are choosing to celebrate and ratify their relationships via formal rites of passage, such as the secular 'affirmation ceremonies' performed by the Gay and Lesbian Humanist Association, or the Service of Blessings and Holy Unions conducted by the Metropolitan Community Church (see Gill Storey, Part II). The Lesbian and Gay Christian Movement has also been conducting services of blessing since the late 1970s.

In San Diego a priest at one of sixty Free Catholic Churches in the USA marries lesbian and gay couples. Co-pastor of the San Diego parish is Father John Rinaldi:

> Free Catholicism calls people to drop the judgementalism. . . . It's very hard for two gay men or women to belong to a church community where they can't be lovers, they can't be married, where they're denied the same rights as everyone else. I can't push people out of the door because they're . . . gay or lesbian. As a priest you're called to invite the world in, not reject anyone.[4]

Maggie Ford regarded her relationship with Ann, her late partner, as equivalent to a marriage:

> When I met Ann I didn't want to live with anybody, I didn't think I was capable of it. She convinced me that I was. She was right – I was – but only with her, because I really don't think I am easy to live with. . . . We belonged together. Marriage is a word that one uses to describe heterosexual relationships, but basically we got married. We were in many ways like two sides of the same coin, and now one part of that is gone . . .

Some couples generate and organize their own celebrations, advertising them in the gay press, such as the 'wedding' announcement Mary and Toria of Newcastle placed in the *Pink Paper* (4 November 1994). In the West Country interviewees Janie and Kim (see p. 96) held their own private 'marriage' party in April 1995. In more flamboyant fashion, both OutRage! and the Sisters of Perpetual Indulgence have helped to stage several lesbian and gay 'weddings' in Trafalgar Square. In 1994 the American state of Hawaii ran a campaign to legalize gay marriage.

Spain has become one of the most progressive countries in terms of lesbian and gay rights. Not only does it have an equal age of consent at fourteen, but around thirty Spanish cities recognize same-sex 'civil unions',[5] and in February 1995 housing rights were introduced guaranteeing a cohabiting partner of two years the right to inherit a tenancy or lease, irrespective of sexual orientation.[6] At about the same time, the Spanish airline Iberia, in response to public protest, amended its policy to include gay couples along with married or cohabiting heterosexuals, in its offer of reduced air fares.[7] (In November 1994 British Airways announced plans to extend cut-price travel perks to its lesbian and gay staff.[8])

In Germany's October 1994 general election, Cologne elected Volker Beck, an out gay member of the Green Party. Beck promised that he would fight to legalize same-sex marriages.[9] And in June 1994 Sweden became the third country in the world (after Denmark and Norway) to pass a same-sex partnership law. The law became operational on New Year's Day 1995, and on 2 January two Swedish women made history by becoming the country's first lesbian couple to register a legally binding partnership.[10] A survey a month later, however, revealed that a quarter of Sweden's civil marriage officiators had refused to implement the law. There are in any case certain drawbacks: registered partners do not have the right to a church ceremony, adoption or insemination. The advantages lie in parity of legal rights in the areas of property, inheritance, and so on.

Some argue against this kind of formalization of same-sex partnerships on the grounds that it simply apes the most reactionary and oppressive features of heterosexuality. Nettie Pollard believes that the idea of gay marriage, which is supported by Stonewall and even OutRage!, is a way of dividing people:

> People should be free to go through ceremonies if they like, but the message will be perceived as saying: 'Let us join in, we're as good as you are, we can be the same as you are,' whereas I would like to be saying: 'What kind of role does marriage play in society?' Or: 'What if there are two people in your life?'

Linda Semple takes a similarly questioning, non-assimilationist stance:

> I'm not a particular fan of Stonewall politics – you know: 'Everyone wants partnership legislation and the right to get married' – I mean, do we? Some people do and they should be able to, but I don't see it as the most important thing in the world.

THE DEATH OF A PARTNER

In the case of the ultimate loss, *bereavement*, the lack of any official back-up system soon becomes apparent, especially if one (or both) of the partners is closeted. With the emergence of AIDS in the early 1980s, it is an issue that has had to be continually and relentlessly addressed. The prevalence of AIDS in the gay community has generated a broad and diverse support network, from heterosexual women as well as from within its own ranks. At the same time, it has uncovered every last vestige of homophobia in families.

'Domestic' homophobia has of course always existed, often lying dormant until the onset of a major life event such as death, when it becomes fully exposed. Sharley McLean's partner Georgina, with whom she enjoyed a loving but closeted relationship for twenty-four years, died suddenly in December 1977. She had spent Christmas with her family, but failed to phone as arranged. Becoming increasingly anxious, Sharley phoned and was told, curtly, 'She's dead.' Subsequent calls to her partner's home were met with undisguised hostility and abuse. Letters and photographs had been discovered and destroyed. Georgina's parents refused to allow Sharley to go to her funeral and blamed her for their daughter's death (from a heart attack).

Sharley recorded her feelings in Women Like Us:

> I was too numb to do very much, walking around like a zombie totally unable to believe what I had heard. .... I went to the flat – I had waited too long, everything had been stripped, no trace of our things ... everything cleared out ... as though we had never been there.[11]

Immersing herself in gay politics helped Sharley to come to terms with the dual grief of losing her partner and the family's disowning of the relationship. First, she became campaign secretary of CHE and a year or so later, when CHE formed a 'breakaway' lesbian group, Sharley decided to stay on and 'fight' from the inside. 'Separating felt like apartheid and I am "anti" that, even today.'

She recalls an early lesbian conference where for the first time she was confronted by the ugly face of separatism: women who swore at her, calling her 'a fucking middle-class dilutist'. 'To me, they were – and still are – female fascists. Strangely, one of those women is married now and oh-so-middle class. Hypocrisy lives, OK.'

She continues, most Sundays and in all weathers, to turn up at Speakers' Corner, as a founder member of the Hyde Park Gays and Sapphics. In 1984 a long association began with the Terrence Higgins Trust. Her role at first was wide-ranging: co-founder of the women's group, working on the AIDS Helpline, running workshops on health education, distributing leaflets. Later she worked part-time as a volunteer counsellor and administrator of the Hardship Fund (since re-named the Small Grants fund). Although no longer a counsellor, as a speaker with the Trust she talks to schools, colleges, clubs, training networks, GPs. 'AIDS has had a traumatic effect on me. I have lost very close friends ... I avoid going to "Remembrance services", and funerals and hospital visiting have become an agony. I am there to visit X. and in the ward are two or three others I know.'

Coincidentally, Maggie Ford's partner, Ann, also died around Christmas time (1992). Both were out to their families, but had no lesbian or gay friends in the tiny Spanish village where they had made their home together. They had originally met back in 1979 when Maggie was working in the prison service and Ann had a job in a Manchester bookshop: 'It was the shop where I used to buy my books as a child. I used to go in there and browse, and eventually browsed more than books!'

They bought their first house together in Gloucestershire, and later moved to Birmingham when Maggie was posted to work in a prison there. After several years in the UK, they decided to go and live in Spain.

Maggie gave the deputy governor a year's notice and the following summer completed a four-week TEFL course in preparation for a new career teaching English to Spanish families:

> We had associations with Spain because Ann's parents had moved out there. ... And we liked it and bought a property there to get into the property market before they went into the Common Market, because we thought prices would go up – and they did. Then we sold it and bought this place in the mountains. ... We just loved it, it was such a change and so relaxing. A thousand metres high is like being on the top of Snowdon!

Two years later Ann became seriously ill:

> I asked her if she wanted to come back to the UK for treatment, and she said no, she felt she was getting treatment that was as good there as anywhere else. She had cancer of the ovary and it has been described to me by another friend as the silent killer, in that by the time you know you have got it it is often too late. She had a winter of chemotherapy, which didn't work, and then a summer of great improvement when she was seeing a healer. But it came back.

As a couple they had built up quite a large (but heterosexual) social circle through Maggie's students:

> I got to know a lot of people, and the support that we got was phenomenal. I never envisaged anything like that happening because, after all, we had only been there a couple of years. ... We never really knew *who* knew we were lesbian and who didn't. The agricultural community used to refer to us as the

'English sisters' and some people seemed to think that we *were*, so after a while we stopped saying well, actually, we are not sisters, just friends. If they're happy with that, let's leave it ...

It became more and more clear afterwards how many people did know about the relationship – in fact, most people seem to have done.

We both felt that being lesbian was important, but only a small part of us. *I* would have liked a [mixed] gay network, but Ann felt not the slightest need. She said: 'Why should I choose my friends because of their sexual orientation? I choose them if they are people that I like, and their sexuality is incidental.' By and large I agree with her, except that since I have been on my own it has been rather more difficult because there just wasn't anybody at all.

Within a few months of Ann's death, Maggie decided to try to make a new life for herself. After a long period with no access to lesbian or gay social life, she joined an international penfriend network:

I found being with people quite bruising, and the idea of meeting new people almost impossible, but I felt I could do it through letters. I thought: 'I am not going to feel like this for ever and I am going to want to make new friendships and relationships – close relationships.' I wanted a network in place for when I was ready to make another move, to take another step. That's what I've been working towards.

I would like to have somebody of some significance in my life, but I am rather cautious about it. I have been through various stages where I thought I had sorted it out and knew what I was doing and where I was going, but I have come to the conclusion that I didn't know at all. The major decision was to stay put, and that life should simply be allowed to *evolve* ... and to some extent I am finding out again who I am.

MAKING CONTACT

For lesbians who live in London and other cities or large conurbations, it is perhaps easy to forget that life elsewhere has not yet caught up with the sexual politics of the 1990s and that unenlightened, heterosexist attitudes continue to prevail. Life for the average young – or older – lesbian in King's Lynn or Ullapool can feel almost as isolated and bleak as it was before the lesbian and gay movement erupted in the 1970s. Conversely, in the teeming metropolis with its diversity of queer outlets, the lesbian and gay scene can be so all-absorbing that one can start to assume that this is a microcosm of mainstream society and that virtually everyone one meets is lesbian or gay.

As a means of meeting other lesbians, the personal pages have become increasingly popular during the 1990s. In both the UK and USA more women than ever before have been using the classifieds in publications like the *Pink Paper*, *Sheba*, New York's *Stonewall News* or the San Francisco *Bay Times*. In the weekly freebie, *New York Press*, there are columns for 'Women Seeking Women' and 'Men Seeking Men'.

Advertising is of course an option that has always been there. In the UK in the 1970s and early 1980s there was *Sappho* (monthly) and *Gay News* (fortnightly). In the late 1980s and 1990s, the *Pink Paper* (weekly) has dominated the market for women's classifieds, quite often carrying three or more columns of Women's Personals (also a telephone dating service, featuring an even greater number of ads). Many of these ads are far more sexually explicit and less restrained than those from earlier decades. Here are a few examples from January/February 1995.

> 'Dirty Dyke, 23, attractive, feminine, juicy fruit, lively, cheeky, drinker, smoker, seeks horny woman for ecstatic nights out/in' ... 'Gay Female, young 40, GSOH, enjoys wicked nights in and out, seeks similar' ... 'Student Nurse, boyish, cute looks, WLTM female for fun, late nights and pulse-raising experiences. Photo appreciated' ... 'DM Obsessed Utter Dyke, 23, law graduate, seeks totally dark and shiny Björk experience' ... 'Lesbian Couple, 25/34, adventurous, seek like-minded dykes for no-strings fun. Singles/couples. Photo/interesting letters get reply'.

Then there are those who practise SM.

> 'Bad Girl, 30s, highly educated, seeks a firm hand. Please help' ... 'Horny Young Dyke, with so much love to give, seeks same. Interests include beer and bondage' ... 'Slave Wanted. Fully comp or third party. Full MOT supplied'.

Such diversity is a mark of how much perception of this brand of 'blind dating' has changed. The stigma associated with advertising for a partner/ soulmate has all but vanished. Once regarded as the last refuge of the desperate, the Personals have developed into a massive, sought-after industry, reflecting the limited social scene for lesbians, especially those who are newly out and who may feel intimidated by the club and bar scene. The Personals have in some ways become a 1990s substitute for the old-style self-help or CR groups of the 1970s and early 1980s, and many women use them primarily for friendship rather than sex. Finding a lover or 'Significant other' is often seen as a bonus, an optional extra.

One of the first sources of Personals was Kenric, the nationwide organization for lesbians, which began in 1965 and proved a lifeline to women who thought they were 'the only one'. Women such as Hilde Morris who, like many of her contemporaries, was married with children, felt somewhat daunted by the prospect of moving from a predominantly heterosexual milieu into the lesbian subculture. After a very difficult five years of 'transition' (see Chapter 1), Hilde decided to join Kenric. She also began to look for a full-time job, with a view to moving out of the marital home after a year or two.

I'd be fully independent: that was the plan. My elder daughter was just finishing school and going to university, my younger one had just done her O levels, so it seemed like in a couple of years I could move out with less damage to them than before ... So in fear and trembling I wrote off to Kenric and got the newsletter. Kenric used to do badminton every month, on a Sunday, in Guildford, so I told my husband that I was joining a new ladies' badminton club. I was a very keen player at the time anyway ... I was absolutely terrified. I felt like I had this big red writing on my back saying 'Lesbian' when I walked through Guildford to go to this meeting.

Afterwards we all went to a gay pub and I was terrified that somebody would see me. It probably sounds very wimpish – but I'd been a pillar of the community, so to speak, for years: supporter of local scouts and guides, local schools ... I had everything to lose and didn't know if I had anything to gain, but I knew it was something I had to do.

They were quite friendly, but I didn't find anybody who took me under their wing, which is what I needed. In fact, quite the reverse. When we were in the pub one of the group started questioning me. Who was I? What was I doing? When I said I was married she almost started attacking me. I managed to face it out, but it was quite frightening.

I went to another couple of badminton afternoons, but I thought: 'I'm not going to meet anyone this way. I need to meet people like me,' so I put an advert in the Kenric newsletter. It went something like this: 'Married, 42, loves the theatre, walking, swimming, looking for companionship'. The first reply I had was from a woman who lives nearby, in exactly the same situation as myself – with children and a husband – and she's remained my friend ever since.

We exchanged letters for a long time before we met and we'd developed quite an intense relationship in our letters. We were both very needy, but the irony of it is that I went to a Kenric musical evening and met there the person who is *now* my partner *before* I met the person with whom I'd been corresponding.

I wandered around the block for at least an hour before I dared go in, and I was sitting there making polite conversation, trying to pretend that I was enjoying myself and all the while feeling very nervous, when suddenly the door opened and two women walked in. One of them stood and looked around the room with the haughtiest expression you can imagine – chin held high, *very* proud – and I thought: 'Ah, now the evening promises to be interesting.' I covertly watched her as she started chatting to people, not realizing that she was making her way towards me. We started talking and she said: 'Ah, you're the one who wrote that advert in Kenric, aren't you? The one who loves the theatre? I nearly answered that advert.' She asked if I would like to go out to lunch, and that was where it started.

Like Hilde, Jenny Wood had been married with children, and was recovering from an unhappy relationship with another woman when she decided to investigate the lesbian scene in the North-East:

I joined the Women for Women group in Newcastle. Any woman, lesbian or bisexual, who wanted to explore her sexuality, could go and talk in a safe atmosphere. It was interesting to meet lots of other women with experiences totally different from my own. I felt less isolated, and over the years I have got to know quite a lot of lesbians and have some good friends.

Some of the women who go are still married. Some identify as bisexual. A lot have been married before. It's just nice to meet other women who have *struggled* – some are still struggling, but some have come through it. It's very, very interesting to spend time with them and hear about their lives. I still find it sad that so many women have very low self-esteem.

For pre-feminist lesbians, social life in London and other major cities was confined to a few claustrophobic dives and clubs, such as the now defunct Gateways club in Chelsea. Diane Langford remembers regular forays to the 'Gates':

I had a girlfriend for a while who was about thirty-seven, and I thought that was so ancient! She had this motorbike and she used to take me on it to the Gateways. We used to go roaring round Marble Arch on this huge motorbike, it was wonderful!

Another Gateways *aficionado* was Del Dyer, whose early experience of gay social life was full of contrasts. She initially frequented the 'low-life' Huntsman Club in Berwick Street, Soho ('nothing more than a hole in the ground, an absolute death-trap because there were no proper fire exits'), then tried a group in Hampstead run by two women from MRG (Minorities Research Group, which started *Arena* 3, the UK's first lesbian magazine):

> The majority of them were well-educated professional women, upper middle class, and I just didn't feel that I fitted in at all. . . . They had social meetings once a month that were very closeted. sometimes in people's houses, sometimes in a pub – at the top of the pub of course, not to be seen by the general public in the lower bar. They had visiting speakers talking about lesbian history, and poetry readings, things like that. . . . I got my hair cut short. Then I started wearing men's clothes – shirts and jeans. They couldn't deal with that sort of cross-dressing.

As the youngest member of the group, Del was asked if she would like to appear in a BBC TV programme about gay women. She agreed, but although her face was filmed in shadow, she was recognized: 'People started talking in the flats where I lived and I had to move away from home.'

She felt more at ease at the Gateways because of its mixed clientele of women: professional, working-class, black:

> My initial reaction was shock, seeing so many women together in one spot and knowing that they were all gay. There was this role-playing image: one person would be dressed in a suit, shirt and tie with really short cropped hair; another would be in a dress, sometimes *ultra* feminine. You had to be one or the other. I remember somebody saying to me: 'What are *you?*' and I said, 'I'm not sure,' and they said: 'Not *sure?*' . . . There was a fascination about it. There wasn't much competition, perhaps a few seedy clubs where men were allowed in as guests, as I believe the Gateways did at one time.

Many of the original 'bar dykes' felt patronized and devalued by all the newly 'lesbianized' feminists of the 1970s, and resented this 'invasion' of their private space. The prevailing feeling among lesbian feminists was that a butch or male-identified persona was betraying women. Former bar dyke Beth Lambdon recalls the resentment this created:

> We were in the roles. They could pass for straight while we couldn't, and we had been the ones who had got the abuse, the ones who were out before

there was such a word as 'out'. I had very negative feelings about these feminists [telling me] what I should and shouldn't do. I felt I belonged nowhere. I was very cut off from the community in general.

Although Beth has gradually shed her butch image and become more feminist and politicized, she still empathizes more with bar dykes:

Most middle-class feminists have a tendency to look down their noses at you. When I started to go to women's group meetings, I found a great deal of prejudice. They were very class-conscious. I felt a second-rate citizen. They would use a lot of long words and not give credence to my views, because of my accent, and yet they'd stand around wondering why more working-class women didn't come along. . . . These women were privileged. They didn't live in the real world. They never had to think about things like who's going to look after the kids, because they could always hire a babysitter.

I used to get angry, I had a big chip on my shoulder at the time. . . . There tended to be a fair sprinkling of *political* lesbians who said they chose to be gay until patriarchy sorted itself out. It was all very well . . . but they would go back to being straight if they could find a man who wasn't as sexist as all the others.

Beth recalls a certain type of middle-class lesbian who went 'slumming'; middle-class women who

made a big play for working-class women and once they got them, ditched them and went after others. I've no idea what their motivation was. . . . It wasn't widespread, but common enough not to raise an eyebrow.

The only thing I did get from them was *sources*: I was shown where to find books and magazines. I haven't had the education, but I am reasonably intelligent and . . . I read everything, all the feminist and gay writing I could get my hands on – twelve years' back issues of *Spare Rib*, *Sisterhood Is Powerful*. . . . It is like being blind, and then you see and you can't be blind again.

Joyce Hunter was nineteen, married and pregnant when she found herself attracted to another woman, also pregnant and married. It was *circa* 1959, a time when the New York lesbian scene was as limited as London's:

'I don't know if I was in love, but I understood sexual attraction for the very first time. It was exciting and I wanted to be with her. After our kids were born we wound up having an affair for about a year. Then we broke it off. I got scared they might take the kids away. . . .

I moved upstate and started meeting a whole lot more women. Women would tag *me*. I got a job as a waitress and all the waitresses were lesbians. All the school-bus drivers were also lesbians. I was working in a restaurant in a mall, so I met these women and started getting really involved. ...

I would go to clubs, where they would get raided. Any time I walked into a bar I would just look for the exit first before I got comfortable. I never told anybody my real name. My kid brother used to call me J., so I just said my name was J. ... So all during my marriage I was with other married women, and it was easy to find people – not to have a relationship with but at least to have sex with. The women driving the bus were not married, but nearly all of them had had children. They were probably divorced, but they had somehow hooked up, so there was, like, this *group* of women. ... I think most lesbian and gay people are married and eventually get out. I hope it's changing – because if we could be who we are when we're young, then we wouldn't do this. It doesn't mean that we can't have families, but I don't think that we understood that during *my* time.

The advent of feminism in the early 1970s revolutionized lesbian social life and turned Joyce's life around in the process:

I met this woman in 1971 in a bar. We hit it off, it was the first time I really fell in love, it wasn't just about sex. She is still my very close friend today – we're like *family*. We were lovers for eight years. ... She gave me a book when we met, *Sisterhood Is Powerful*, and I told her I don't really read well. She said get a dictionary. So I got a dictionary and I read the book, and it was like, wow, there's another whole world out there and you could *be* somebody!

She said would I like to go to this dance at the Firehouse down Worcester Street, New York City. It was the first lesbian and gay community centre in New York. It was the first time I had ever seen so many lesbians having a really great time in a place that was not a bar, that you didn't have to look over your back for the cops ... I was so *fascinated* ... 'Who set up this party?', you know. Well, it was these activists, and that's why I got involved. It really changed my life going into that Firehouse. It was another whole *attitude*. I had felt robbed of my whole life, of who I was as a child and everything [see Chapter 1]. I also felt that way as a bi-racial person. I wasn't anything that was 'right'. I'm Jewish, I'm black and a lesbian, so, you know, it's like anybody could pick on me for any reason.

Despite gay writer Armistead Maupin's assertion that San Francisco was awash with girl bars,[12] Jill Posener claims that the lesbian bar scene in the 1990s is virtually non-existent.

The lesbians of the 1960s, 1970s and early 1980s were all bar-goers: we went into bars and that's how we had our social life. Things happen differently now. Nobody meets their lovers in bars any more, or their friends. Everybody meets them through political groups, or the 'clean and sober movement', which has kind of taken the place of neighbourhood bars. ...

Large corporations like ATT or Pacific Bell all have gay and lesbian groups – groups that are very physical, very open, where people meet their social partners, their life partners. You can pretty much be out in any American corporation, hospital, school, so that the bars were having a hard time surviving, people weren't drinking as much any more and were meeting elsewhere. ... Also, it's because we mix more. There are now men's and women's places to go to, and we go together. It's a different life, a different world now.

The trend towards a more mixed movement began in the mid- to late 1980s, partly as a result of the AIDS pandemic and also in the face of a more right-wing political scenario, which fostered a sense of uniting within the wider community against reactionary laws such as Clause 28.

In August 1994 Sophie Mills moved from Oxford University, where she taught classics, to take up an appointment as Assistant Professor of Classics at a liberal arts college in Asheville, North Carolina. She is one of several out gay members of the faculty there: 'There are two other lesbians on my corridor alone. The university has a policy against discrimination on grounds of sexual orientation, and (unlike Oxford) same-sex partners can be brought to university events without any difficulties.' Locally, there is one gay restaurant and three bars:

One is mostly for older gay men, one is a sort of paradigm gay club – smart and trendy with extremely loud music (not my scene) – and one which I do like: it's a bit scruffy but plays good music and mostly women go there. You can usually talk to people if you stand by the pool table in the back room.

Besides all this, there are lots of women's groups and activities. I'm in a women's choir, and a lesbian discussion group has been established by the partner of one of my colleagues. ... Asheville is not typical of North Carolina, which is squarely on the bible belt. Even at the university there is anti-gay graffiti, though it's often in answer to the activities of the university gay group – I guess it's the price you pay for free speech!'

While at Oxford she had chosen to remain partly closeted, as it was still very much a male-dominated environment where any discussion of one's private life was deemed inappropriate.

There have been lots of superficial changes and I think it will carry on changing, but basically it is a male institution and you knuckle under as one of the boys, which to some extent is what I did – occasional drinking sessions, which I quite like but is certainly not the whole *me*.

The city's centre had discos every Friday and Saturday night. It could be quite small and incestuous and one ended up meeting the same people . . .

Sheila Jeffreys lives with her partner, a lawyer and geographer, and their cats, in a very 'lesbian friendly' area of Melbourne. In her own street there are large numbers of lesbian and gay cafés and other businesses:

The fact that lesbian porn is being made in one of the premises along the street is a bit of a problem, but you get everything going together, I guess. I can't think of anywhere like it in London. You get women kissing in the street, passionately embracing. That's pretty impressive, so in that sense Melbourne's terrific, but . . . there are large areas of Australia that are relatively lesbian-free.

Before moving to Melbourne Jeffreys taught history at Hammersmith and West London College of Further Education ('mainly Mussolini, Hitler, the Russian Revolution, and so on'). She is scathing about what she calls the 'creeping lifestylism' of British society, about the preoccupation with sex, the separating of 'fun' from politics: 'You have to be having good sex, more of it and in different forms.'

One crucial determinant of lesbian social life is, of course, money. Because most men, whatever their sexuality, can still command higher earnings than most women, the much-vaunted Pink Pound is more applicable to gay men than to lesbians.[13] In London's 'gay village', centred on Old Compton Street, Soho, 85 per cent of venues are gay male. The remainder are mixed, which suggests the usual gender imbalance, with the guys vastly outnumbering the dykes. Not one venue is lesbian-owned, or lesbian-targeted. At other West End 'mixed' cafés, like Kudos in Charing Cross, women punters are very likely to be heterosexual chums of gay men.

All this is a reflection of most women's relative lack of financial clout. Many of these amenities seem to be more concerned about keeping up with current styles – and that requires hard cash – rather than offering 'something for everyone'. It's about the cliquish politics of gay male narcissism and navel-gazing rather than any genuine display of gay–lesbian altruism. It is, as Gillian Rodgerson points out, a scene dominated by 'young, white, metropolitan gay men'. Small wonder that most lesbians over the age of twenty-five feel alienated. There is little in it to draw them and plenty to intimidate them. London badly needs a new, efficiently organized lesbian and gay centre, where women are afforded an equal input. Losing the London Lesbian and Gay Centre in December 1992, following in the wake of Thatcher's axing of the gay-friendly GLC in the late 1980s, marked one of the lowest points in recent lesbian and gay history.

For older lesbians, Sappho and Kenric have continued to corner the market, while Venus Rising, one of the largest and oldest established lesbian clubs in Europe, sets out to attract a wide cross-section of dykes, and a correspondingly eclectic range of music. Club promoter Terri Murray believes there is no such thing as a proper 'mixed' club: 'Nothing that's 90% men and 10% women can possibly be deemed to be mixed'.[14] At the opposite end of the spectrum, Pumping Curls veers more towards lesbian chic and would doubtless be anathema to the likes of Sheila Jeffreys. It is run by DJ Maxine who says her club is 'not only for gay girls, it's for any women, younger women with money in their pocket who are not too hung up on political morals and values'.[15]

There are any number of women-only nights at gay men's clubs, like the Wow Bar in Wardour Street, and weekly lesbian saunas or jacuzzis in some of the city's health spas. Sue Wade, who runs the Wow Bar, believes in a lesbian economy, claiming that glamour and expense do not always need to be inextricably linked.[16]

Outside London, social outlets specifically aimed at lesbians are relatively scarce. Gay men, by virtue of being male, are part of the old-boy network and monopolize the commercial culture in towns like Brighton. Interestingly, however, when Chris Woods travelled around Britain for Channel 4's *Out* series he found that there was a much stronger sense of *community* in the provinces. Lesbians and gay men had 'a shared experience and a common inheritance'.[17]

OLDER LESBIANS

Not all lesbians enjoy clubbing, as is immediately clear from a glance at the Personals in the gay press. 'Non-scene' is almost as common a stipulation as GSOH or N/S. Other factors influencing lesbians' choice of social scene are age and mobility. Around a quarter of my interviewees were over fifty, three of them pensioners. Sharley McLean is a retired nurse with a small occupational pension. She is a long-standing volunteer with the Terrence Higgins Trust and also attends the University of the Third Age. Financially, she gets by. The biggest changes in her life are associated with ageing: 'physically slowing down, and other aches and pains . . . the realization that even in meetings with "Older Lesbians" most are twenty years younger than me'. She rarely goes to a cinema, theatre or concert because uncomfortable seats play havoc with her arthritis.

At seventy-two, she feels she is still in charge of her life, although the choices she makes are governed by considerations of finances, age or health: 'Within that perimeter I am in charge. I am alone but not lonely. I do not have to resort to mother's little helpers, booze or recreational drugs, to function.'

Brenda Ellis is only in her forties but her arthritis is so severe that considerations of access are always paramount and her social life depends to a large extent on the availability of wheelchair-friendly venues.

The generation gap among lesbians mirrors the heterosexual one, although perhaps to a lesser, more superficial degree. Dykes aged forty-five and over tend not to go in for tattoos, body piercing or the shaven-headed look. They are less inclined to seek out asthmatic venues or mega-loud disco music that wipes out even the most basic attempt at conversation. 'Hubbub to numb the brain so one does not have to think', is how Sharley McLean describes the latter, though she is not being deliberately judgemental, believing that 'you pays your money and you takes your choice'. Part of her own social life is spent with other Gays and Sapphics on a soapbox at Speakers' Corner in Hyde Park where, for more than a decade of Sundays, her audience has comprised all ages, types and nationalities, and where she has been 'chatted up' on several occasions.

In terms of actual relationships, an age gap can be part of the initial attraction: when in her sixties, Sharley had a brief relationship with an American woman forty years her junior. Jackie Forster cites a similar experience she had in 1992:

> with someone who thought she was a lesbian but who had never been on the scene before. It was horrendous – the age gap, political gap, the whole generation gap – and I was very cut up about it. I'd been celibate for a long while before she came on the scene, and I wasn't even thinking about a relationship.

Age is another aspect of lesbian *identity*. Wilmette Brown (forty-eight) is dealing with being 'middle-aged' and with the fact that she has not borne children:

I am also trying to relate to younger women, in the campaign [for Wages for Housework] and in general, trying to avoid harking back to the 1960s around people who weren't even born in the 1960s. I am trying to keep open to their experience. The things they take for granted we fought for. . . . Some see it as experience they can use and learn from. I think the learning has to be kept mutual, because I am always impressed by how younger lesbian women are much more forthright than we were. They don't expect to have to put up with what we put up with, and that's good. . . . They are also much less hung up about whether people are lesbian or bisexual or straight: they go in and out of the categories more than we did.

Wilmette strives to balance her campaigning and her personal life. She lives alone but has a partner and many friends, and is looking forward to old age and to 'becoming part of the movement of older people'.

Many of Jackie Forster's peers and friends have moved out of London, and she belonged for a while to AGLOW (Association of Greater London Older Women). About a quarter of the women are lesbian:

I have been to two conferences, and we all had the same basic problem of being alone and not having social contact, lack of money, pensions . . . and the sort of events that are offered now are so *noisy*, you can't hear yourself speak . . . and I was so relieved because I'd thought, you know, I'm back to square one – I'm the only one! We were all coming out with the same things and we boiled it down to the fact that we wanted bosom buddies; we didn't want to get heavily involved physically and emotionally, but it would be nice to have someone – or more than one – who we *really* enjoyed meeting up with, not because we *had* to. . . .

I love the arrogance, pride and self-assuredness of young lesbians today, but there isn't a *warmth*, I find, coming out of it. Now that could be the age barrier, because they are not meeting other age groups. We were a terrific mix: babies through to sixty-plus, and I miss that. I don't suppose they – never having known it – miss it, but I think it's an ingredient that ought to come back, because I'm still leery about *backlash* . . .

It seems to me the wheel is going full cycle back to the bar scene, because out of the bar scene the politics came; and then it was much wider and you didn't have to go to bars to meet other lesbians, you could meet them in meetings and organizations, and so on. But now where are they? It's bar dykes again . . . and this *slavish* following of America, which really gets up my nose. Why does everything have to be called Stonewall and ACT UP and OutRage!? None of these things represents lesbians. It's all coming from gay male politics

... and it's very *political*, the way we live, it's not just about having relationships and sex. That, to me, is not being analysed or even thought about at the moment. ... If *I* was in my twenties I wouldn't either, but because I was in my forties it was like wonderful fresh water, I was thirsting for it. But a lot of very young people were involved in those days; snow-crowned heads were very few and far between.

Like many older women Mandy (sixty-one) has found that getting older has brought with it increased self-confidence and a greater readiness to *challenge*, together with a broader world-view. One of her lowest points came in 1991 when, because of privatization, she was made redundant from her job as a carer with the social services:

I had been there about fourteen years. My whole service was cut out. It was very sad indeed. It was awful to have to tell clients who were almost friends that you weren't going to come any more. I used to run groups for elderly and disabled people and they were devastated. ... It was one of the most demoralizing things that has ever happened to me. I felt devalued, I felt my life was about to come to an end. I can remember saying to my partner: 'I suppose it's downwards to the grave now'. ... It was a horrendous experience.

Nearly four years later life has taken on a new meaning for Mandy. Her postgraduate women's studies course has enormously energized her, and she has rid herself of all negative post-redundancy feelings: 'I feel quite depressed on a national and global level, but on a personal level I have a feeling one can go on fighting.' The course helped put lesbian-related issues at the top of her agenda and provided her with a strong network of female friendships, lesbian or otherwise:

The government pays lip-service to helping women. It's up to women collectively, formally or informally, to get women's issues at the top of the agenda, and I think that is done through good female friendships. It's important that women *love* each other, look out for each other, don't regard each other as rivals.

Jackie Forster echoes this determination in her approach to the ageing process:

All through my life I've always been poor or very rich. I was on the dole, then earned a lot of money. ... I'm used to it, but there's the realization that I can't do anything about it, that I've got to go on living within the pension and housing benefit (I did have a small personal pension which I managed to pay for) ... and this change is an incredible perspective on life.

The blessed thing is that if you hang on in there's the bus pass – and things like the theatre. I can get concessions, but when people say: 'Ooh, I'd love to come with you', here am I being able to have stalls seats for about six quid and *they've* got to pay £20 or something so, you know, I was losing my friends fast.

I've become a voracious reader. I just *devour* books now, it's absolutely absorbing. Otherwise, I keep myself busy. I have a horror of ending up sweeping the front steps in my dressing-gown for something to do. It could happen very easily: 'Oh well, I suppose I'd better clean the front steps' ... and there are lots of elderly wrinklies where I live. I look out of the window and see it happening opposite and think: 'How *can* you?', and yet once upon a time she must have been a *vital* woman, out and about ... so I'm not going to let that happen.

Couples' profiles

1: IRENE B. AND IRENE D.

Irene B. was born in Liverpool but has lived in Yorkshire since the age of thirteen. She lives near Richmond, North Yorkshire, with her partner, Irene D., who originally comes from the Late District. Both are in their fifties, and in February 1995 they celebrated their thirty-fifth anniversary. In 1981 they gave up teaching careers to go into business together. They bought a private house in Reeth and converted it into a guest-house, a successful venture that lasted for ten years. Now Irene D. is a supply teacher and Irene B. runs the library and resources area at a secondary school.

Irene B.: 'I've been with Irene now since I was twenty-two and everybody knows we are together, and wherever we go we're treated as a couple. There's never been any need to make any sort of declaration or public stand or anything like that. She's always been accepted as my partner.

Our closest lesbian friends have been together twelve years. ... We've not had the opportunity to socialize up until now because we ran our own guest-house, but since we sold the business we're beginning to meet more lesbians ... but a lot of the relations seem to be short-lived. So we're more aware that we've become a little bit of a curiosity.

We met at teacher-training college at the end of 1958, in our second year. Our relationship started then. We were both at Bingley Training

College, in the same hall of residence. I'd had one short relationship before that . . . I never thought of myself as lesbian. You kept quiet about it, because you felt society wouldn't approve . . . I never knew there were such people as bisexuals! It was a very small world, I thought I was the only one. You kept it all under wraps. . . . I taught people for a number of years, and one of the things you didn't mention – you didn't want people to think, amongst all these other women, that you might be this odd character who fancied women, so you didn't say anything.

I find it quite liberating not to have to do that any more, even though I'm not what I call 'out'. Today it's a completely different atmosphere.

I went down to Essex for a year to teach . . . I'd already made plans to do that before our relationship developed. Then in 1962 I came back. . . . We were living in a flat near Shipley, a few miles from Bingley. . . . My family were all in Liverpool. . . . My father was a butcher and worked all his life in that trade. My mother was a shop worker. My father was very seriously ill, so they moved to a more rural area outside, and he died in 1966. She died in 1980.

Marriage pressures

When you went home at holiday time or to see relatives, or particularly if there was a wedding, it was: 'Your turn next', but you just warded off this sort of thing. . . . After you get to thirty they say things like: 'Ah well, you're happy as you are, aren't you?' They realize they're fighting a losing battle.

I'd gone from home to college and we lived in a hall of residence, so I've never actually lived alone, and even that one year in Essex I lived in with somebody . . . so from that point of view my life didn't alter much. I think probably the biggest change was having to think of somebody else other than myself. . . . You'd go somewhere and it would be: 'This is my friend Irene', sort of thing. Nowadays they would be quite open and say: 'This is my partner', or whatever. But again, as time went on, people began to accept. In fact, very often if I went by myself anywhere, the first question would be: 'How is Irene?', because people began to realize that we *were* a couple, not just two individuals sharing a house.

Irene is just nine months younger. It's certainly not been a case of meeting each other at twenty-one and there being no problems. There have been problems we've had to face. We've had two or three tricky phases, one within just a few years of us being together when I thought it was all breaking up, and another occasion many years later. We've always been able, after the initial closing-in and shutting-up, to talk things out. It's been far from easy, you have to work at things.

Above all, you have to talk about things that have come between you, things that are causing ill feeling or whatever ... and we do. Perhaps initially we don't. I'm the main culprit. I say nothing, just withdraw, but it always works out, and eventually we are able to talk through it. But I put that down to Irene, because she's the one who's always saying: 'You've got to talk about this'. If it was left to me, I'd clam up. I come from a family where there were never any rows. My parents had their disagreements, but never in front of us, so it was nothing I grew up with. When I first went home with Irene I'd only been in the house an hour when her mother suddenly erupted, *and* her father, and I thought: 'I can't stand this', but that's just the way the family were ... and the next minute they were talking to one another as if nothing had happened. That was something I wasn't used to and ... she would encourage me to say what I thought and felt. I've learned to do that over the years, but there are still occasions where it might be a couple of hours after whatever's happened that I finally open my mouth.

I've always been a worrier, I worry about things before they happen, and Irene isn't like that. So that's something else I've learned ... I'm more positive about myself now, *to* myself.

Teaching

In the 1960s and 1970s, on odd occasions when [homophobic] comments were being made in the staff room about an individual or situation, you just had to sit there and keep your mouth shut. In the 1970s Irene taught at a school where a member of staff was gay. In fact, we visited him and his partner, but at *my* school I can't recall anybody ... but that could have been keeping my eyes closed and not looking too closely for fear they might look at me. That's very much the stance I took then: because of the attitude of education authorities to teachers, you didn't draw attention to yourself in any way.

I have been a local preacher in the Methodist Church. But about five years ago something happened which drastically changed my attitude to the Church, so I resigned. I'm no longer a member of any church, but I still have a faith in God. ... Part of this growing awareness of my own identity has perhaps made me more – not aggressive but *self-assured* – and in one sense that's perhaps what led to all this conflict with the Church. Since all this happened, running alongside it was the vote in the Methodist Church about gays [1993]. Had I still been a member of the Church at that time, I'd have had to nail my colours to the mast then, because there was no way I could have sat through the discussions going on at local church level and said nothing. So even if this other trouble hadn't blown up, I'd have had to resign from the Church.

At the time when the vote was coming up, we said to each other that if we'd both been as involved in the Church as ten years ago, we'd have been in the position of having to say, in the small church meeting of village folk. 'Hang on, you're talking about *us* if you say that gays shouldn't be allowed to take office in the Church', but of course we were never put in that situation. By then we'd both left. To be honest, some of the time I felt rather sorry because I would like to have done that.

Irene D.: In the middle of the 1970s I worked in a school where there was a man who had come to work, just before me, who was gay and was clearly out. He lived very near the school with his partner, and obviously that made the staff more aware . . . I became quite friendly with one of the men staff who, in the end, obviously guessed [about me], and that was just him asking and me saying yes. And over the years that's happened on two or three occasions, an individual thing like that, but certainly not an 'announcement' to everybody.

My father certainly knew, simply because he had found a letter which made it obvious, but I don't think he ever said anything to anybody else. The rest of the family always accepted us as a couple . . . Family pressures – like 'When are you getting married?' – just fade away. That was much stronger for me than for Irene – but then I come from a large family with a lot of cousins, and so there seemed to be an awful lot of weddings and christenings where this became the issue, finally sort of stopping on my fortieth birthday. My mother rang me up distressed because she was worried about what I'd missed, but I assured her I hadn't missed anything that I didn't want to miss! She settled down, and I think that was the final comment.

The pressure to have boyfriends was very great – and it took a long time for me to accept my sexuality. My family was very male-dominated. It was very much 'leave school, get married', and it was difficult to fight against that. I used to talk at fifteen of how many children I'd have, and so on, but I could never actually see myself getting married, I could never see that as an end to a relationship.

An *only daughter*

I have two brothers, no sisters. That's been a real problem for me, particularly as one brother had only one child, and then there's been a long gap and my younger brother, who's fifteen years younger than me, is just having his family now. So in that interim I've had remarks like. 'They're not really grandchildren unless they're your *daughter*'s children', that sort of pressure – very pointed ... I didn't feel tempted [to succumb to it], not really.

I look back at school and can see the sort of crushes that were more than just crushes, that I wouldn't have acknowledged at that time. I realize now it was more than just a *crush* on the head girl; there was definitely something *there* that I chose to ignore ... I can remember very clearly thinking. 'This shouldn't happen, I shouldn't be in love with a woman', and having to go through all that. I doubt whether I used the word 'lesbian'. For a long time you think you're the only one.

Double *life*

There were times when you were conscious that you were leading a double life. You'd want to say and do something that was a natural part of your relationship, but you'd have to be careful – somebody might see you or notice, or a look might pass between you and you'd think, you know, 'Don't do it'. So I think it was very much an acting, a covering up ... Things said, like. 'It seems more sensible to be buying a house together than paying out rent.' Since we met people who came to stay at the guest-house, who were obviously lesbians, that's become easier and we worry much less than we used to.

When I left college I stayed up near Bradford, living in with an old lady when I first started teaching. So Irene and I had a year apart ... She came back up and we had a year in which she was living in a flat and I was still with the old lady, and then we decided to get a flat together. As Irene said, temperamentally, we were quite different, and so there was that adjustment – of two people living together and coming from different backgrounds. My father was a miner, my mother worked in hotels. She married very young and, I think, did a lot of growing up herself while I was a child: she was just seventeen when I was born and so it was a very volatile background. And living with somebody like Irene meant a big change for me, but a change which in a sense I was ready for, because I was always the one, within that large group of extended family, who could just get into a corner with a book and cut myself off from it. So just living with one person was a relief, but also the whole business of caring for and working with someone else in quite a different relationship, I found difficult at first.

I trained to teach history, but when I first started teaching I taught general subjects. I taught in two eleven-to-sixteen schools, then had a year out and did a course at Leeds University, came back and taught RE to eleven- to eighteen-year-olds, and then drifted into pastoral work as a deputy head. . . . The third school I went to was an all-girls school. We had a German student with us in the Language Department for a while, and she and I got quite friendly. I realize looking back that she was a lesbian and had probably recognized in me what I hadn't recognized in her. I left during the year she was there, and I remember her coming up and saying: 'I'm going to miss you very much', and I realize that obviously there was 'something' there – and from the comments that were made by the staff about her. . . .

On another occasion we took some sixth-formers on a field trip to Amsterdam, and there had been some conversation about one of the girls in that group and another girl in the sixth form: she received a letter every day, and it got to the point where I just couldn't bear the comments. So I collected the post and left hers under her pillow, because I felt that she was having to put up with too much.

At that stage I was in a junior high school, in the senior section, for quite a short time. And one evening Irene picked me up after school in the car and next day, when I went in to take this particular group, a girl called Penny said to me, 'Do you know that Miss B.? . . . She's awful, she is,' said Penny, and then proceeded to tell me all the awful things Irene had ever done, but I never confessed that we lived together.

No labels

I'm not very happy with labels. Once upon a time, if I was hanging a label on myself, I might have included 'Christian'. But now, if someone says to me, 'Are you a Christian?', I hesitate longer than if they say, 'Are you a lesbian?' . . . I think it has always been a problem being a lesbian and a member of the Christian Church. We have always been very uncomfortable with various parts read from the Bible, like Leviticus and Romans. Once we sat through the most terrible sermon, so homophobic it was unbelievable. It was the first time we had come across it so strongly in the pulpit. We didn't walk out. There has been so much we have sat through over the years, where we should have walked out, but in our twenties and thirties we didn't want to draw attention to ourselves. Now, we would probably stay and take him to task.

Working together

Irene B.: We had both done twenty years' teaching by then. . . . We sold our house and put all our money into buying this property in Reeth. My mother had died and there was money from the sale of her property, so we just sank everything into the business. We started from scratch. We had very little to fall back on again. People were saying we were very brave. We were saying: 'No, we're crackers', but we wanted to do it and we didn't make a lot of money.

We both enjoy cooking, also it was something Irene wanted to do, because she'd had a taste of it – her aunts had had a guest-house in the Lakes. . . . We've done things we would never have tackled had we still been in teaching with good salaries: if you want something fixing you get somebody in, usually a man! Well, we've had to do all these things ourselves, so that's been quite good experience for us.

We had a few lesbian couples and gay men to stay, and we made good friends of some of them. We still see two in particular, regularly. It was rather nice to feel that you could offer accommodation to gay couples without them feeling self-conscious. . . . We've stayed in places where we've booked a double room and when we've got there it's, 'I've put you in two singles, I think you'll be more comfortable in those'. You feel like screaming . . . but we weren't advertised as specifically gay, or women-only. After the first year, it was word of mouth and very little advertising. We met a lot of very nice people of all ages and both sexes. That suited us rather than offering something to one set of people.

We worked very well together. Irene is the one with the organizing ability, and I can get on and do things: if I see them I'll do them. There was never any conflict of interests. We were both working for the same thing.

Irene D.: I didn't want to be in teaching until the end of my career, and thought that I would like to do something else. The combination of living in the country and running the guest-house seemed the ideal thing for us to do. Financially, it was a gamble, and particularly as our finances meant that in the end we bought a house which we converted into a guest-house rather than buying a completely new one . . . and moving away from the environment in which we were happy to a completely different one. . . .

I don't think we ever envisaged going back to teaching. The idea was that we'd give this a try: there were just the two of us and if it fell flat it wouldn't really matter. We set ourselves five years, and we did ten and enjoyed it very much. When we moved and worked out our finances, it became obvious that our season was going to be Easter to the end of October. So we needed some [income] to keep us going during the winter. We moved in the September, and in the November I started doing supply teaching and I've done that ever since, each winter.

The variety of other people's reactions was interesting . . . I think we'd sat for so long and listened to teachers who'd wanted to be out of teaching – and even now I do get irritated when I hear them say: 'I wish I could get out of this job', because so many of them could . . . but not everyone's prepared to take a risk, and it *was* a risk. There's the pressure it puts on a relationship, because you've got to be able to rely upon each other. And there's the 24-hour-a-day thing. . . . We coped better than I thought we would. There were problems, but we are quite different and we comple-ment each other. And by then I think we were very much aware of each other's strengths and weaknesses . . . and therefore we could work together.

I think we grew a lot closer, although it was difficult. I mean, we were worn out, tired and they were long days and stressful days. Perhaps before, it would have been 'put up and shut up' for a while, but you couldn't clear off and do something else. You had to learn to work your way through problems.

Irene B.: You couldn't carry on an argument because you were having to deal with members of the public who had paid to come and have a nice holiday in your house. So you can't go around looking miserable . . . and therefore you quickly patched things up. Any disputes we had never lasted long. If we hadn't known that Mr and Mrs Smith were coming down for breakfast in half an hour possibly they might have developed more.

Division of labour

Irene D.: I did the planning and the booking. You kept the accounts. Irene cooked breakfast and I served breakfast. We cooked dinner between us, and Irene waited on dinner.

Irene B.: We just followed our own natural interests. I automatically got on with painting, decorating, whatever, simply because I enjoy doing that.

Irene D.: And you hate ironing!

Irene B.: And I hate ironing! . . .

Irene D.: The only people in our social circle were involved with the Church and when we came to Reeth our membership was transferred. We were both local preachers, and so we were involved in all the churches in the Dale. Our social life – what there was of it – mainly took place in the winter and was geared to the churches, apart from friends back in Bradford.

Irene B.: Swaledale, particularly, is a very, very close community and we feel quite strongly for young people there because it is very much a farming, heterosexual community, and anything which doesn't fit in would almost be eradicated. So we were never aware of any lesbian or gay people.

Living together

Irene D.: It's only recently that we've analysed [our ups and downs], and even then only very tentatively. Part of the problem, I think, was accepting *my* sexual identity. The sort of hetero pressures had been there all the way through, and there have been men that I have known and been closely involved with. . . . I think Irene was always worried that I would leave, and that I would leave for a man, and perhaps that is the root of our problems. Deep down I don't think I ever thought I would, but it's taken me a long time to get rid of that particular pressure and to reassure Irene that there's no way that I would do that.

Irene B.: It was harder for me, not being *sure*. Our relationship was harder at the beginning because of that. At the back of your mind there was that little nagging doubt . . .

Irene D.: We've never discussed monogamy. I could certainly never have coped with an open relationship. . . . We wouldn't have been happier with a 'free' relationship, coming and going. Perhaps I would have felt differently? . . . but it hasn't happened like that, has it? At the times when it was rough, you decided to stick with it. I think there was a time when you might have gone but you decided *no* . . . and the fact that you stayed and stuck it out . . . I'm glad we did!

Irene B.: I think the main thing about our relationship is that it didn't really start off as a sexual relationship; it started off as friendship that grew into a sexual relationship and, therefore, we've had that basis of friendship all the way through . . . and because we weren't actually living together for at least two years, we had a chance to grow as friends, to get to know one another, which I think is a good foundation.

Irene D.: We try to tell the young ones. . . . When Irene told this young gay woman friend of ours, she was absolutely floored that anybody could be together so long. And so whenever we're introduced this is what comes up. We try to say that right back at the beginning we never envisaged anything lasting this long. I mean, you just don't. We knew then that we wanted to be together, it was as simple as that . . . and so it's very difficult to say what is the 'secret': it is that we have just grown together over the years and that we do love each other and—

Irene B.: We're so sort of easy together. It sounds a bit sort of—

Irene D.: Like two comfortable armchairs, doesn't it?

Irene B.: It sounds a bit boring and dull . . .

Irene D.: But it hasn't been, because the relationship has changed—

Irene B.: In a way, it's better now than it's ever been. Whether that's to do with the fact that we've made more contact with other lesbians? . . . and we're more open about our relationship—

Irene D.: We're more confident in ourselves – and in all ways there's an ease of being together in company, now, that once upon a time – there might have been a strain. We share a lot. Sexually it's still alive, very much alive and changing, and the whole thing – the whole relationship—

Irene B.: These friends we met who came to the guest-house – we've been very friendly with them and through them we've met other gay people—

Irene D.: And been to a kd lang concert!—

Irene B.: So we've made some contacts down there, and then – with having more free time up here – we've made more contacts through J. and W. [two women who run a restaurant together. J. had taught in the same school as Irene D.]

Irene D: I'm still not happy about the school situation, certainly not in the school I'm working in, because it's an ex-army school, and so you have all the problems of racism and homophobia, which are very strong there. And I certainly think for young people in the school situation it's very difficult still. . . . There are times when I compare what it was like for *us* and I think: 'Good, things have got better', and then you read things in the *Pink Paper* and you think: 'It hasn't really changed underneath'. But as more of the young ones show that confidence and pride that so many of them have got, then things have got to change, but I think it's a very long-term thing.

Irene B: For us, it's almost like a second childhood, because we're starting a whole new scene. . . . There's magazines to read and you can buy them in WHSmith, there's no secrecy about it, and we're meeting lesbian women who are quite openly out. It's lovely to see it, we're very pleased for the young ones that it's got to that stage. . . .

On the other hand, I hear tales of homophobic attitudes and behaviour and in a sense it's got to be harder for them than it was for me, because as long as I was careful there wouldn't be any of this. But they'll have all the support of the other people who are out and won't feel as if they're the only ones, with nobody to turn to and talk to should they need to. . . . There is a community spirit, even if it's just in the town of Darlington, or in the village of wherever.

Irene D: I think people's attitudes at the grassroots . . . If I can go back to this Methodist Church's debate – one of our ladies said to us, 'Some of these gay ministers are nice, but I don't think *we* would want one' – and that is it, isn't it? I think we are accepted because we've been a couple a long time, but the minute that we say, 'We are lesbians', then, 'Well, no, you can't be, because we *know* you'! So many people, you see, don't . . .

2: JANIE AND KIM

Janie and Kim are lovers. Janie is twenty-three and studying education at university. Kim is thirty-five, Canadian and a PhD student, researching special educational needs. They live in the West Country.

Kim: I always knew from a very young age that I fancied girls. The first time I kissed a girl was when I was eight years old: I knew that was what I wanted and had crushes on females all the way through my life. . . . I had heard the word 'homosexual' bantered around, and spent a lot of time in my teens in sports and stuff and was teased about that because it was very unfeminine. I wasn't very feminine at all, and so was teased a lot about that, and just didn't fit in with my high-school friends. As I got older – fifteen, sixteen – I realized there was a word for it: *lesbianism*. And I looked it up in the library and spent a long time thumbing through dictionaries. . . . When I was seventeen or eighteen and became involved in hockey – and there were a lot of lesbians in hockey – I realized that was probably what I was. And when I had my first relationship at twenty-one, I *knew* that was what I was. It was never a problem.

Janie: It wasn't such a clear-cut process for me. I knew I was never going to get married – for a long time that was a problem, because I really wanted children and I couldn't sort of square it with myself that it was all right to have children and be a single mum. I thought it was best for children to have two parents. I'd never met somebody who was outwardly lesbian. During that time I was living on the Isle of Wight and it was quite a closed, conservative society. It was a gradual realization. I've always had crushes on women, and then I went to boarding school at sixteen and felt things a lot more strongly. My matron was gay, she had a partner – and so did my headmistress. I guess that was when I realized. And then I was having a relationship with a girl in my class, and I said this to my mother, said I was gay. She was washing up at the time and didn't make any response. She's always said that she never heard me, but I'm sure she did. So I spent two years thinking it wasn't acceptable in my family. Then I fell head over heels in love with an older woman and told my mum again, and it all came out in the open. Since then she's been fine.

I'm out to most people, probably because I'm a bit younger than Kim. So the people I meet now, at my age, are mostly out as lesbians; whereas I think people of Kim's age – it's a different generation, you're more wary, aren't you?

Kim: I don't think it's an issue, because from the age of seventeen or eighteen I was in a very closed community of lesbians within my sport. My hockey coach was gay. Our team was known as Marina's bunch. She was also the Olympic coach and our assistant coach was gay. So I knew that was there, it was just a *given* – and all the older women were gay, and it became part of my life. If I played hockey, lesbianism was there. I suppose you could say I was raised in that 'cloister' – like being in a closed nunnery. . . . And then when I was at university it started coming out in all the other teams.

Janie: I found out at boarding school. Although it wasn't 'gay-positive', it was all women – a lot easier.

Kim: It was never a question of me having to come *out*, I just felt either that people would assume it, or that I didn't feel I needed to say it.

Janie: Kim looks quite manly! A lot of people think she's a boy.

Kim: But it's not something that I consciously think about – yes, I'll dress myself as male. I just dress the way I feel comfortable, and if I put a dress on I'd look like a man in drag – which I did look like at my brother's wedding. Female clothes don't fit me, for my build or my persona, but I've never identified myself as male . . . I'm quite shocked when someone says, 'You're very dykey looking.'

Identity

Kim: I identify as lesbian. I've never had a hetero relationship. As I get older I hear what people are saying about homosexuality and I think, 'God, they're talking about *me*.' So I get very angry, but maybe that's because I'm a lot maturer now and can cope – if there's an argument there that I can become involved in … but, I would identify myself as just *me*. I'm Canadian, although I was born in the UK. I was seven when my parents emigrated, and so I've lived most of my life in Canada. So I don't associate myself with any sort of class system at all, although my father was a very successful businessman, so I guess we were what you would call upper middle class. Lived in a good neighbourhood, a pool in the backyard.

Janie: Kim doesn't understand class at all. I've been brought up very much on class lines – riding holidays and boarding-school sort of upbringing – and I guess that's important for my identity. Although I don't particularly like being upper middle class, it is part of me. I define myself as totally lesbian …

Kim: But you're more of a *radical* lesbian, aren't you?

Janie: I don't think either of us fit into the radical lesbian –

Kim: No, but *you'd* be quite happy to shout it from the rooftops. … I don't see the point in that.

Janie: OK, so we both define ourselves as absolutely lesbian, but it's not the key thing in our identity, is it?

Kim: It's part of the whole –

Janie: Neither of us has any great need to push our sexuality onto other people.

Turning-points

Kim: My very first relationship lasted four years. That ended because my ex-partner decided that she couldn't cope with being a lesbian. Even the word 'lesbian' scared her. So she ran off to Australia and married an Australian … and that was a big turning-point for me. … Then I went to teacher's college, and I never thought that being gay was an issue. When I was teaching, it did become an issue, because all of a sudden you become the single teacher in a staff room and all the married teachers want to pair you up with all the single male teachers. And if that doesn't fit they've always got someone's son or cousin, or some relation that's single, and 'Wouldn't you two make a perfect pair'. That becomes difficult, because then they want to know what you did on the weekend, and for my weekends it was always hockey with all my lesbian friends – I was always with women. So I sometimes found myself making things up . . . but one of my closest teacher friends figured it out. Before I met Janie, I hadn't been in a relationship for six years.

Janie: I guess I realized that it would be quite a struggle to have the life that I want, to have children. I don't think it will be too difficult teaching-wise, although I obviously have to decide whether or not I want to come out. I got quite upset when one of the teaching staff at my school got married and we had a big 'do' for her . . . and I felt really sad that even if I did come out in the staff room it's very unlikely that anyone would ever recognize that I had a personal life, that I might want to have a sort of marriage. I knew that they wouldn't recognize it in the same way that they'd recognize a straight marriage (see p. 68).

The other thing I've experienced is not having any guidance as to how a relationship should progress. Straight girls of my age have got a whole series of magazines and advice pages and people to talk to – family, their mums and aunties and straight friends – about boyfriends. As a lesbian I'm very open with my mum, and she's very accepting and likes Kim. She accepts us as a couple, but she feels she can't give me advice, even over the simplest thing. So there's no one I can talk to about the relationship, because we pretty much share the same friends, don't we?

Kim: There's no way I would ask them, because they're pretty dysfunctional anyway. So the only people I could turn to are my gay male friends, and they haven't a clue either.

Janie: I find it quite difficult, because there are no set conventions to work with or against – about how long you should be in a relationship, when you should move in together – nothing like that, no framework, which I find quite scary. . . . It would be easier for me if I was in a straight relationship, because I would have the getting-to-know the parents, getting engaged, married, having children – it's a very structured thing – whereas with lesbians, people seem to be going in and out of relation-ships all the time. There are no rituals that mark the beginning and end of them.

Kim: What has set me free in a roundabout way, though it's terrible to say this, is the death of my parents [in 1991]. They never ever knew, and it was like a sense of freedom. It was just like, I can finally be who I am and not worry about hurting them . . . and not disappoint them. Although maybe I should give them more credit – maybe they would have accepted me, although I doubt my mother would have. So that was a big turning-point for me, and since then I have been more open about who I am.

Janie: I've had quite a big change in moving to the West Country, because I was free of the shackles of the Isle of Wight where there are no gay clubs. I've found that I embraced the lesbian community and then moved away from it. At first I was very excited about having a community that I could call my own, and I was very into women's coffee shops and talking with lesbians and reading lesbian books. But I found it a very tight community, and in some ways I was going from one sort of restrictive place where I couldn't be gay, to another sort of place where, if I let myself be drawn in, I was being very stereotyped. Gay men have got a wider choice of stereotypes that they can be.

Kim: I didn't like that circle and would not be involved in it, it wasn't part of me at all. . . . I looked at them and thought: 'What a bunch of no-hopers'. They were a sad collection of very sad, lonely, angry women. . . . A place where lesbians gather is called Desert Hearts, and it should have been called Desperate Hearts . . . I mean, you went downstairs into the 'pit', underground, and had to walk through a straight bikers' bar where everyone knew what you were, where you were going. It had a rough, dirty, grimy element to it and I didn't like it at all. And then you went into the bowels of the earth – you know: 'Keep away from everybody', that's the message I was getting from that.

Janie: I find that the lesbian community isn't open, it's very much stuck in the 1970s. And just as the feminist movement is stopping people from entering it because it has such a narrow agenda, so the core of the lesbian community is rejecting people with different ideas. Like bisexual people would be shunned by the lesbian community.

Kim: The thing that bothered me about Desert Hearts was that it was a women-only disco. . . . Because my brother is so pro-gay and so pro-*me* (he's known about me since I was seventeen), I really resent the fact that I can't take him to something like that.

Janie: I like all-women's do's.

Kim: But there was a real hatred for men there. I've seen what happened when a poor guy got lost and came down thinking it was a bar or disco, and all these angry women just descended on him, when all they had to say was, 'Look, this is a private party, you're not invited' and send him upstairs. But there were four or five of them with clenched fists ready to have it out with him. I just think, you know, we have to work with men. OK, lots of women have reasons to hate men, but it just festers, I think.

Janie: Kim is more partial to making friends with men than I am. I don't like men.

Kim: I don't really like men either. It just so happens that all the people I'm around happen to be men. When I first came to my postgraduate house, there were eight of us: two of us were female, so I had to get along with six men ...

Janie: I'd like to go somewhere with no men, I'd be very happy to live somewhere – I guess, anywhere with just women would be separatist – but somewhere which didn't go along with *all* those separatist ideals.

Campaigns/issues

Kim: I haven't been really active in anything: Bristol Pride in 1994, the first time ever. ... I've always supported gay pubs and clubs, and now there are all these magazines coming out, and I do buy them. I'm thinking of the Pink Pound now: why should I spend my money in a hetero club where I don't feel comfortable? I should go to a gay club. So I'm really thinking in that regard now, more so than ever before.

Janie: I've always thought the Pink Pound is undervalued, and if we got together more and talked about it as a community a bit more, I'm sure we could make significant advances. ... Kim and I went to Bristol Pride, but I didn't like it because it was raining and it was held in an arts centre, and it was full of loud music and smokers who were putting their cigarettes out on the carpet. And that for me is a typical example of how the gay and lesbian community excludes people. I don't want to be in a place with loud music, and I couldn't be in a place with that much smoke, so we had to leave after a few minutes.

Kim: It was too crowded ...

Janie: And it attracted a specific sort of person. Practically every stall was sex aids.

Kim: Yes. For me, there's a whole subculture to it. Maybe I am naïve, but I really think things like that give the straight, homophobic person that extra ammunition to say: 'See? I told you they were all perverts.'

Janie: Although the only thing that really binds the gay community together is our sexual interest, there's a lot more to people than that.

Kim: It has to be more than that. Because I come from a sports background and I'm athletic, the Gay Games really intrigues me. I was asked to participate when I was in Canada four years ago and I didn't because I was scared, scared that friends of my parents would see me. But how realistic is that? . . . being spotted out of 100,000 people? But that was how uptight I was about my parents finding out, and feeling that it would ruin their lives and my dad's business, and things like that.

Janie: I'd like to see us being represented at different levels, especially some recognition within the hard core of the community that there are a lot of people out there – increasingly, Kim and I are coming into this category – of professional middle-class lesbians who aren't on the scene because the scene excludes them. And I think it's really important that we do everything we can to promote lesbians who are that image.

Kim: I'm sure in London you have clubs that cater to them, because back in Canada we do.

Janie: Mmm, dinner clubs and things.

Kim: I don't like to be seen as *only* a lesbian, you know, shaved head, Doc Martens, dungarees . . .

Janie: When people think of lesbians that's what they think about, because the rest of us don't push ourselves forward. It's important that we recognize the whole range of people who are lesbian. We have to get away from this idea that you have to hate men, be vegetarian, and like cats . . . I mean, there are all these rules that are written into being a lesbian, and it's very hard to challenge them.

Kim: Lots of lesbians in Canada and America have *dogs*!

Janie: I think Jeanette Winterson is an excellent role model for lesbians, and kd lang. . . . but as a younger lesbian I got an image of people going on marches and the Greenham Common women, and it wasn't an image I could relate to.

Kim: My role models were always professors, highly successful women who were very well off, top in their field, all lesbians and . . . I strive for that.

Janie: I wish I'd had that. I think young lesbians need role models like that rather than thinking they have to stomp round in DMs and shave their heads, although they might still go through that stage, as I did.

Social life

Kim: On 1 July 1994, I moved into my own one-bedroom Georgian flat, which is not too far from where Janie lives.

Janie: It's a bit too damn close to where I live! I'm not ready to live with somebody yet and not ready to have Kim just down the road, which she is.

Kim: So we have set boundaries, which I'm not allowed to cross. As long as I keep to my side of the street, then I think things will be fine. I realize Janie needs these boundaries, so I respect them and that's not a problem for me.

I'm living alone now. I used to live with a group of people. When I lived in Canada I was living by myself, so it's back to that again. My social life is quite quiet. We're both very busy – Janie with her college and me with university. . . . If I go out I usually go out with my two male gay friends to clubs. Janie doesn't like loud music and smoke. I only go out once in a while, and Janie does a lot of babysitting on Friday and Saturday nights anyway.

My aspirations? To finish off my PhD and to get a job in a university, either in Britain or, preferably, in Canada, because job prospects are better. The lifestyle certainly is a lot better, and the pay – and the climate . . . I'm very interested in children's education, especially in kids that have social problems, educational problems. I'm concerned for the education in this country: the more I do research here the more I'm concerned about what will happen to these kids in the future.

Other interests? Athletics. . . . My main interest is Janie.

Janie: Soppy sod!

Kim: Finances are a big concern for me at the moment as I'm living off the savings that I acquired from my parents' estate, and the more I take time off to do this PhD, the more I see money going out the window. I can see myself having to do a part-time job just to try and cover some of the bills.

Janie: I do a lot of babysitting to supplement my meagre grant. I rent a room in a family house with a single mum and two daughters. . . . . I look after her little girl who's seven, and she's spent quite a few days with Kim and myself. We've taken her on trips and stuff. . . . I have never hidden my lesbian books, and my landlady vacuums my room, so she might have seen them. It's very difficult to tell. I have had problems getting accommodation before because I've told people I'm lesbian, and they've just said no, so I didn't actually tell my landlady that I'm gay. Somebody needs to publish some sort of manual for lesbians that's not a sex manual. There's 'what lesbians do in bed' books and lots of soppy romantic literature, but there needs to be some sort of guide to living together, commitment ceremonies, etc. What you need to do legally, stuff like that.

Kim: A hard work guide to lesbianism.

Lesbian futures

Janie: My main interests are babies and cars. I'm determined to have a large family, and I've got very, very cross because of this debate about lesbians and children. I'm crazy about babies and my main aim in life, I'd say, is to produce children. My other concern is cars and pollution and stopping the building of roads.

Kim: It's a mixed bag. I see some things that are quite good, and then I see there's almost like a Victorian era here about sex and homosexuality, and I think back to Canada, where it's really carefree.

I think it's good that all these magazines are coming out, and that people like kd lang and Melissa Etheridge have got the guts to say, 'Look, I am gay and it's no big deal.' And it's been good when Martina's come to Wimbledon with her entourage of lesbian women and lovers. . . . It's good for people to see that. And Jeanette Winterson.

Janie: Yeah, Jeanette! . . .

Kim: We went to see her talk about her new book, and she was very open about her relationship with Peggy Reynolds. And Peggy Reynolds was sitting right there, so that's hopeful, too. It's good to see that lesbians are coming out and saying, 'Yes, and this is my partner.' I mean, I work in a department where there are two lesbians in a relationship, living together, and they act as if they don't. They feel they need to put on this persona that, you know, they're just good friends.

Janie: When they go on holiday together they both pretend that they happen to be going on holiday to different places at the same time.

Kim: Then one of them comes back with horrendous stories about all the young men she's picked up. It's ridiculous.

Janie: As a lesbian I've found I can live quite happily and without too much trouble as long as I'm reasonably careful. The whole thing about Jane Brown and the press exploiting her lesbianism worried me a great deal, especially as I'm going into teaching – and it angered me as well. I don't like the way lesbians are portrayed in the press, but I think many different groups are portrayed badly in the press. Whether you're black, working class, upper class or disabled, the press will pick on that as something different and exploit it.

I'm fairly hopeful about the future for lesbians in the UK. I think we've just got to do our own thing: if we want children we've got to have children; if we want a career we've got to go ahead and have a career. We shouldn't expect people to do too much earth-moving for us.

When I think back to what life would have been like if I'd been born fifty years ago, it would have been very difficult to be lesbian, but I think most people have got no real cause for complaint about being a lesbian in this society. It was much, much worse for people who came before us. We know people who were forced to – felt they had to – get married, who now have children and a husband and realize they're lesbian, and are in a desperate situation; whereas today more people realize early on they're lesbian because it's more of an option ... Having said that, for Muslim or Sikh lesbians, it's obviously a lot harder.

I did get quite involved for a while in the whole lesbian lifestyle. And I enjoyed that, but, as I said, I felt very pigeon-holed ... There's a lot more to both of us than just our sexuality. We're people with a whole range of interests and characteristics, of which lesbianism is just one.

Some people who identify as lesbian feel the need almost to accost you and tell you of their sexuality, in the same way that people with very marked political views will come up to you and almost try and convert you, or people with a particular religion will push that at you. And although I can understand why they feel the need to tell people, I don't think it's a particularly clever way to go about getting straight people to accept us.

Kim: Another thing about lesbian culture, is all the heavy drinking and the drugs. I mean, where I come from there was a lot of heavy drinking, and I got confused and thought, 'Is that part of the hockey environment I'm in, or part of lesbianism?' I was getting these signals when I was seventeen or eighteen, and they all smoked. I'd never smoked, because I think it's a filthy habit and it ended up killing my mother, and I didn't feel it was the proper thing to do to my body because of the athletics ... and I was never a heavy drinker.

Janie: It's very difficult to be a lesbian and be teetotal.

Kim: Mmm. Very difficult ... and since I've met Janie, I rarely drink –

because Janie doesn't and I don't like to drink alone . . . And it's funny, all my friends are taken aback now, especially my lesbian friends are like, why don't you drink any more? What's wrong with you? Why are you having orange juice? And they really pressure me. It's almost like it's part of the culture . . .

Janie: That culture which can oppress just as much as it can free . . . Kim's got a cat!

Kim: Yes, I've fallen into that slot – 'lesbian with cat, vegetarian'.

Janie: I don't like cats. I like dogs.

Kim: My cat is politically correct – her name is kd which causes great amusement when I take her to the vet . . . The neighbour next door asked me if she was the first gay cat . . .

I have to admit that I do get a bit paranoid sometimes. It's very difficult as – much as I love Janie and want to hold her hand and touch her in public – I get very nervous, because I'm not sure how people are going to respond, and I don't want to be shouted at.

Janie: It doesn't bother *me*. I think it's very important for two women to walk down the road holding hands, not being sensational about it, but just to show people that you can be normal and happy and fulfilled, and just happen to be lesbian as well.

Kim: This is my fourth relationship – and this is the first time I've gone out with someone who knows who they are and can express themselves. The others – L. felt she didn't like who she was and couldn't live that life, S. was the same way, and number three was an absolute disaster. So this is the first *out* relationship I've ever been in.

Janie: We're both very happy to be lesbian, aren't we? I wouldn't want to be straight.

Kim: I've never regretted being lesbian, and if I died tomorrow I'd wish to come back as gay. I don't think I'd ever want to be straight . . . I like who I am, what I am.

Janie: Yeah, we both feel very happy and content with life, don't we?

Kim: *Now* I do, yes. I've had a few rocky years . . .

Janie: We're both quite happy just tootling along being ourselves.

Kim: Maybe we should be out there showing people how happy we are?

Janie: Well, let's get out there kissing in the rush-hour traffic!

Kim: It's raining, and there's too much smog!

Janie: All right, let's watch the news instead . . .

disaffected dykes

The Women's Liberation Movement acted as a catalyst for changing lifestyles, as many women made the decision to move from heterosexuality into lesbianism. For thousands of Western feminists, lesbianism came to represent a positive political statement of their resistance to male-dominated society. The Women's Movement provided the ideal route for female sexuality to be explored and reassessed in the context of a society where the ascendancy of male-defined values and methodology had remained largely unchallenged. The early years, in particular, were heady, historic times whose repercussions were far-reaching in terms of women's autonomy and self-esteem. Alternative life experiences and choices were suddenly perceived as viable, and traditional assumptions of heterosexuality questioned.

Women, *en masse* were rushing out of the closet of patriarchal confinement, and at the core of this phalanx was a huge contingent who were beginning to identify as lesbian: women whose previous life experience or 'incarnation' had been primarily heterosexual, but who were undergoing what amounted to a process of transformation. A process so intensely powerful that, for many women, it felt almost like a religious conversion.

As in all such sects or groupings, admission was free, but in some cases there was a heavy subsequent price to pay. The price of belonging or 'joining' frequently entailed the subjugation of one's own feelings and psyche to the collective decision-making of the group. Sisterhood became so powerful as to seem almost infallible:

> There was too much pressure to toe the party line. It was a thrill to finally have a forum to talk about the pain inflicted by men. The years of keeping silent about male oppression were finally ended and we were reveling in a

community of women. The brutality we inflicted on each other in the name of political correctness was only meant to 'cleanse' the community of 'male' standards.[1]

From the vantage point of the 1990s, the lesbian feminism of the 1970s is seen by many as a Utopian construct, in which practice failed to live up to theory. Like all concepts of *community*, whether predominantly religious or political, the idea of *sisterhood* was a highly seductive one, but one which, ultimately, proved to be largely unworkable. Lesbians are not, and never have been, a homogeneous group – any more than any other oppressed group. To link them in this way is to deny their reality as diverse, complex human beings.

It was the American writer Adrienne Rich who in 1980 promulgated the idea of a 'lesbian continuum', based on solidarity among women and resistance to patriarchy rather than on sexual identity or genital behaviour.[2] At about the same time in the UK, the Leeds Revolutionary Feminists defined a political lesbian as 'a woman-identified woman who does not fuck men. It does not mean compulsory sexual activity with women.'[3]

Women who did not subscribe wholeheartedly to the *theory* of political lesbianism began to feel further marginalized. This sense of alienation led to feelings of frustration, disenchantment and, in some cases, self-blame, as Paulina Palmer explains:

> The dogmatic insistence on political correctness and group-allegiance which it generated proved irksome to many women, while the principles of political commitment and self-sacrifice which it fostered, though inspiring in the abstract, were in many cases too extreme to be practical. The difficulty of maintaining such high standards of behaviour either alienated women or, if they were sensitive souls, plunged them into an abyss of guilt and self-criticism.[4]

Palmer goes on to cite Sigrid Nielsen's autobiographical essay, 'Strange Days', in which Nielsen recalls the origins and growth of her disillusionment while working in radical bookshop collectives in Edinburgh. Nielsen listened to other disaffected women, mostly 'refugees from split collectives', and could not at first accept that there might be isolation built into the idea of the community. But Nielsen's own sense of isolation was very real, indeed profound and far-reaching, permeating both public and private areas of her life. Voluntary work was seen as synonymous with social life:

but though we worked for the community, we did not work as a community. ... Many women contributed more than their share. ... But it was difficult to know exactly what your share was or when you had given it.[5]

For these women, community signified 'surrender: of identity, of personal taste, of privacy'. Solidarity degenerated into claustrophobia and burn-out:

We were trying to live an ideal future into the present, and we had cut ourselves off ... from the past and from people outside. ... We lived collectively and worked collectively; we always had an audience. But we were not used to living so close to other people, and so we overworked, and put everything important into the work, in order to keep ourselves private.[6]

This deliberate disjunction from external influences and stimuli is redolent of what can and often does happen in many religious cults. As in these cults, albeit to a lesser degree, there was the constant underlying *fear* of daring to question the 'received wisdom' of the group. Indeed, as Nielsen's experience has shown, it appears that dykes' disenchantment stemmed less from the separatist movement *per se*, and more from the collective process which it engendered and with which it was inextricably bound up:

We found it hard to respond to each other and easy to compete in subtle ways ... the work was not connecting us with other women, but cutting us off. ... I lost friends over ideological quarrels, and I missed them badly, but I could not tell anyone about my feelings without casting blame: on the women who were gone, or the ones who were still my friends but seemed to think I was taking it all too hard. I began to understand some of the things the disillusioned had been saying to me.[7]

Bridget is thirty-five, a single parent with one son, aged four. Her involvement with the lesbian-feminist movement began in the early 1980s via visits to Greenham Common and an interest in peace issues generally. She also belonged to the *Outwrite* (feminist newspaper) support group. She was based in Brighton, first as a student and later working in a wholefoods co-operative. She lived in various types of accommodation, including a mixed housing co-op and, eventually, a lesbian separatist house. Her engagement with lesbian separatism was a gradual process:

I became aware of certain books, saw *Spare Rib*, and there was a women's centre that moved to a room above the shop where I was working. A series of things happened and made me aware of the Women's Movement, and a big part of that was seeing women who were probably lesbians or feminists, seeing what they looked like and feeling that I could identify with that. I wanted a relationship with a woman for a long time before I actually stopped having relationships with men.

There was always that potential there. In my heart I don't think I'd seen myself as heterosexual ... and so what the feminist movement did was to make it easy for me to feel OK about having relationships with women.

However, most of her memories of lesbian feminism are very negative ones:

There were too many rules and no room to be yourself, to dissent. At the end of the day I didn't know what my own mind was. It was almost like swapping one set of rules for another, and in some ways it reminded me of religion. I was brought up Catholic, and there were parallels, similarities ... I didn't realize how unhappy I was at the time. Looking back, I wonder how I could have managed to accept it all and not resist it and see the harm it was doing me.

It felt so good belonging there that I didn't want to be rejected and kicked out, which I thought would happen if I spoke my mind. I wasn't facing up to the fact that it was not very sisterly. A lot of cruelty went on, victimization. If someone was friendly with a man, she would be rejected, and I was aware of other issues like racism being very important. It was taken to such an extreme that I – and others – felt that unless you had double or triple 'oppressions' you were nobody, nothing. Disability and class came into it as well. There was that phrase 'hierarchy of oppression'. People weren't taken on their individual merits.

At least one other woman felt the same as me. We lived in the same house. We have gone over it again and again, trying to make sense of it. We feel quite damaged by it. ... No men were allowed through the door, not even family members. Boys were not welcome at a lot of events. One night we had a fire and firemen came in and it was such a culture shock.

Since that time Bridget has totally changed the direction of her life, moving from the south to the north (Sheffield) and having a child with a man. She feels a close bond with Thomas. Before he was born, she regarded everything male as 'horrible, repulsive. ... I didn't have the courage to be open in my own mind, to think anything different. There was the very strong feeling that even if you happened to work with men, you were a traitor in some way.'

Bridget later gave up her job with the co-op because she was working with men which was very much frowned upon by the separatists:

> I pushed a lot of my feelings and doubts down. . . . I felt it would be difficult to bring up a boy, because I would want to suppress the male side of him, try too hard to make him into some perfect anti-sexist boy, which I knew just wouldn't work. Now, to me, Thomas is lovely as he is, all sides of him, and I don't feel I want to mould him into some ideal child or man. I just think that if he feels good about himself, then he will be fine as far as I am concerned.

Had it not been for the Women's Liberation Movement, Bridget doubts whether she would ever have had the courage to leave the closet. Nonetheless, while acknowledging the Movement's crucial role in enabling her to recognize, and act on, her lesbian feelings, Bridget now feels more pain than gain from the experience: 'In time I might mellow. I am still recovering.'

Someone else who, by her own admission, has moved from one extreme to the other, is Jill Posener. Jill, another 'defector' from lesbian separatism, emigrated to San Francisco in the mid-1980s, a change of culture and environment which represented a personal watershed, a symbolic journey. It is an experience which has more than matched her expectations. John D'Emilio writes enthusiastically about gay politics and community there: 'For gay men and for lesbians, San Francisco has become akin to what Rome is for Catholics: a lot of us live there and many more have made the pilgrimage. . . . For gay men and lesbians, San Francisco is a special place.'[8]

Jill's made her first inroads into the lesbian and gay community at the end of the 1960s, via CHE:

> They were the only organization that I saw listed anywhere. They were based in Great Windmill Street, Soho. That was my first appearance where there were others like myself. For men it had a much greater purpose, because it had a very strong campaigning element in relation to laws. The 1967 Act had just been passed, so there was still a lot of legal activity, but for women it had no real virtues whatsoever. There was a CHE women's group, but they meant nothing to me. I was very uninvolved. I didn't know about GLF then. I wish I had. I think the idea of outrageous men scared me, although later, all through my life those were the men with whom I have had most in common and most empathy. But at the time men dressing like women – flamboyant, lavender costumes and make-up – were just not part of my thinking.

She was deeply involved in the lesbian feminist movement for almost ten years, from 1974 to 1983:

> I couldn't understand how any woman could be heterosexual. I lived quite a lot of the time in Radnor Terrace [South London] in a women's squat. It was a very angry, potent period of time, when I defined myself as a separatist, when I couldn't consider working or living around men. Burned all my posters of Jimi Hendrix, broke all my Elvis and Bob Marley records, and regretted it ever since. Didn't write to my father for two years.

Like Bridget, she recalls inwardly rejecting the unwritten, but rigidly enforced, rules of her community:

> I had been tormented and terrorized by the small-mindedness, by the venom, of feminists who had their agendas, and if you didn't fit the agenda then you had to tout your party card ... And what's so shocking to me is that *I* was one of those women. .... I think of that whole period as like a lost weekend. They were formative years, but I regret them.

Anyone even remotely acquainted with Jill Posener would find it hard to understand why such a self-assured, outgoing person took so long to become aware of precisely what was going on and how it would affect her. She explains:

> Because I was *afraid*. I was part of the community. There must been thirty or forty women living in this one street at one time. Everybody knew what everybody else was doing. I was doing theatre with Gay Sweatshop, I was beginning to take photographs, I was kind of *public*, so I had already made myself a bit of a moving target.
>
> But to live in that community was to abide by its rules. ... We all denied that we set them. I liken it a little bit – and I don't want to be too extreme here – to the Stasi, the East German system. Everybody spied on everybody else.
>
> It wasn't as if we were in terrorist cells. We were not like the Baader–Meinhof or the Angry Brigade: we weren't bombing things, although I think many of us came very close to taking that kind of step – but we did as much as we could without causing physical pain. We graffitied, we lay down in front of court houses, we occupied newspaper buildings ...
>
> I was in torment throughout the 1970s. I said and did all the right things, but inside I was cringing. .... I felt deeply unhappy. I was running with the pack, and

part of it was, like, wanting to prove to the pack that I was good enough to belong, good enough to be part of the front runners. ... There was this euphoria when you did something that got the approval of the pack. You felt as if you'd won a lottery.

Looking back, Jill sees her engagement with lesbian separatism as a kind of addiction:

There were many highs, but they were accompanied almost inevitably by dreadful lows. ... And I was terrified about being middleclass. You'd go to a disco or something and there would be working-class women at the door with tins, saying: 'We're collecting for the working-class women's holiday', and if you were seen not to put money in the pot you would be ostracized or condemned in the Women's Liberation newsletter. I used to read the newsletter desperately hoping that there would be no mention of me. I'd think to myself: 'Wait a minute – I'm a confident human being. What's going on?' And we don't talk about it in those terms. We're very generous to the feminist movement of the 1970s. We're very 'closed mouth' today. We don't discuss it often, those of us who feel damaged.

I would hope that there were many other women who had a much healthier relationship to their particular part of the women's community. But I lived within a very small community and one which felt very attacked, so that it felt as if we were the last line of defence. We used to barricade our doors. Local men and boys would come down and hurl bricks through our windows. The police would regularly try and clear the squat. So I lived with a siege mentality. When you were loved by a woman in that environment, whether it be the love of a friend, lover or compadre, it was a heady, glorious, drug-like feeling – and to *break* from that ...

In some ways she was so 'politically incorrect' that she had no choice but to quit. By questioning areas around lesbian sexuality, for instance, Jill so scandalized certain people that they rejected her.

During the years of her involvement, there would be frequent interviews in the press or on TV:

There'd always be some public outlet for one or other of us to speak, and we'd always say: 'We do not like heterosexuals in any way whatsoever. We do not objectify women.' We'd say that sexual attraction was the least of our concerns; we were sisters who loved each other and that looks weren't important ... and every time I said this and heard this, part of me inside was *dying*.

It was deemed 'politically incorrect' to admit to finding another woman attractive, and also to evince desire for a woman who looked different from one's own physical type or persona. Jill used to get bored with going out with women who looked like she did:

> You see, my ideal of a beautiful woman is a *femme*, and that was a completely unacceptable way to be in the 1970s. Skirts and make-up were out. I used to look at images of women from America in the 1950s and my mouth would water.
>
> I ran a women's disco for a while. I once played 'Brown Sugar' by the Rolling Stones. This woman came and scratched the record and ripped the needle off. She said: 'You can't play this, it's about the rape of a black woman.' I said: 'I think it's about the *honouring* of the black woman Mick Jagger was involved with.' There were songs all over the place that I couldn't play. ... A whole bunch of them would come up and say: 'What are you doing? You can't play this.' I didn't have the self-assurance to stand up to them and say: 'Leave me alone', because this was my gang. ...
>
> It wore me down from very early on, but I didn't say anything, because where could I go? ... Everybody knew who you were going out with. These days the equivalent would be unsafe sex. If you are having unsafe sex everybody's, like: 'What the hell are you doing?'

It was a time when not only fashion and music but sexual behaviour was monitored. As Jill recalls, butch–femme role-playing was strictly off limits, and sexual practice – 'if you were having any sex at all' – was expected to conform to lesbian-separatist theory:

> I'm getting really down and dirty, and perhaps I shouldn't, but I remember once a woman said to me – we were in bed and I wanted to make love to her and I put my fingers inside her, and she hit me, pushed me away and said this was totally male-identified. If a woman said that to me now, I would say: 'Wait a minute, there's some echo from the 1970s here ... '.

For Jill and other fugitives from separatism, their involvement in lesbian-feminist politics was an utterly ambivalent love/hate experience, characterized by the extremes of fear and joy:

> I suppose what happened was that I didn't get a lot of joy out of my lovers, so I got joy out of graffiti, out of political actions, and I took risks. I have been badly hurt physically, I've been jailed – I'm not proud of that, I think it was the drive for bigger and better activities.

After a notorious rape case in which the perpetrator, a Queen's Guard, received what was widely considered to be a derisory sentence, Jill was among a group of women who scrawled 'Sack the Judges' in massive red lettering on the Queen Victoria statue outside Buckingham Palace:

> We got stopped by the police, who then let us go . . . and when we came back to Radnor Terrace there was this kind of hero's welcome. We were tough and I wanted to be the toughest. I guess it was my way of getting approval.
>
> The other way is that I became a vegetarian, because that seemed to be the thing to do – and I'm a lifelong meat-lover. . . . Everything that means something in my life I tried to eradicate.

Despite Jill's subsequent *volte-face*, she concedes that her days of being a radical dyke did offer positive gains as well as pain:

> I'm not someone who is wanting to condemn the entire era as a terrible mistake, because I think that we advanced theoretically – and on a very practical level – what feminists were willing to do, the risks we were going to take. And we kept the issue of women's choices very much in the public eye. No apologies for that. In that respect, I remain as militant to this day.

The 1990s trend towards lesbian SM is anathema to old-style lesbian feminists such as Sheila Jeffreys, because of its associations with role-playing and butch–femme, which she regards, with unequivocal distaste, as totally beyond the pale. Jeffreys sees the popularization of SM sexuality as part of a growing movement towards eroticized dominance and submission, a movement which threatens the very foundations of lesbian feminism. It is a theme which she explores in *The Lesbian Heresy*, her controversial analysis of the backlash against political correctness and of what she sees as the adoption of patriarchal practices within the lesbian community.

In my interview with her for *Diva* magazine in 1994 she had this to say:

> I still think it's damaging to the cause of lesbians in that very old-fashioned, hostile stereotypes are again being pushed in the gay media – and of course, it's getting through to the popular media. . . . kd lang and Cindy Crawford didn't come from nowhere. . . . It was already in what Madonna was doing in the *Sex* book . . .
>
> Whatever happened to positive images? . . . Now, the extraordinarily hostile images, of abuse and oppression, are coming, apparently, from our sisters within those gay cultures! And that's very damaging for our lives.[9]

Jeffreys emigrated to Australia in 1991 to take up a lecturing post at the University of Melbourne, where she is one of the few out academics. (She is Senior Lecturer in Political Science.) She has found party politics in Australia to be less right-wing, more libertarian, than in the UK, but fears the growing evidence and influence of lesbian SM. In state capitals like Melbourne and Sydney it is increasingly evident, both as 'popular entertainment' in the Hellfire clubs ('where SM sex acts are acted out on stage by volunteers and everybody pays seven dollars to go and watch'), and in the gay media:

> You see women's naked bottoms in black leather, lacy stockings, all that kind of thing. You see them in hetero culture now – in women's magazines, in the fashion industry. .... So the *values* of the SM industry are spreading, even if there are not huge numbers of people actually practising it – and that affects the culture. It affects how we can feel and what we can do in the world.
>
> People need to understand that they will get the society they are helping to create in their personal lives ... people will get what their vision is. And if their vision is handcuffs, black leather, eroticized dominance and submission or even nasty, tacky, old-fashioned masculinity and femininity, that is the world they will get.[10]

Replacing pride and positive images is 'a celebration of oppression and the effects of that oppression, as if that is something to be proud of.'[11]

The backlash against feminism is a product of the growth of right-wing politics in the Western world during the 1980s, and Jeffreys cites a parallel backlash within the lesbian community, as gay male politics and values are prioritized and feminist values undermined, even jettisoned. It was a decade marked by 'a privatising of the *person* ... a taking-back of whole areas of life to try and make them politics-free'.[12] The personal, she suggests, is no longer political. In *The Lesbian Heresy* she urges women to be heretics and reject current trends, arguing for the reclaiming and rebuilding of a sexuality that is positive and egalitarian and 'free from the pressure to love the boot that will kick us into submission'.[13]

Refuting the notion of a sexuality that is irrational, fluid and constantly changing, Jeffreys believes that it is possible to *deconstruct*

> who one is attracted to and the ways in which one is attracted. .... Like – I am one of those thousands of women who left heterosexuality and became a lesbian, never really having considered it. If one can make as dramatic a change

as that ... then we as feminists can make changes about eroticised subordination.[14]

What Jeffreys fails to concede is that, given this 'social constructionist' theory of sexuality, it may indeed be equally possible and valid for certain woman-identified women to revert at some point to heterosexuality (see Harriett Gilbert, Part II).

Her previous work, *Anti-Climax*, was a diatribe against the (hetero/ sexual) revolution of the 1960s and the ways in which it had exploited women. Critics of both books have accused her of having moved too far in the opposite direction, of having excised the sex from lesbianism, a criticism which she counters by claiming that it is possible to have fun in 'progressive' ways rather that 'reglorifying and legitimating masculinity and femininity'.[15]

Throughout the changes which she bemoans, Jeffreys has remained a staunch lesbian feminist. Indeed, her intransigence appears, if anything, to have been reinforced by all the hype surrounding *lesbian chic*, a trend which Jeffreys regards as a travesty, a betrayal, of grassroots political lesbianism.

Like Jeffreys, Julia Tant despises the *lesbian chic* trend and deplores its saturation coverage in the mainstream media: 'There was a definite social context to feminism in the 1970s, which these feminists haven't a clue about. Most of them are hetero anyway – just playing at [lesbianism], doing it at other women's expense, and that does piss me off.'

One significant change that has occurred since the 1970s is the absence of CR (consciousness-raising) groups. It is a phenomenon that has all but vanished, consigned to the annals of feminist history. In the autumn 1994 semester, one academic friend of mine, who teaches a university women's studies course, made reference in a seminar to CR groups, and was chastened when one young woman student asked, 'What are they?'

Wanda Goldwag can confirm this shift of emphasis:

CR groups seem to have disappeared off the face of the earth – also Women's Liberation conferences, at which you could discover you were lesbian because everybody else was screaming abuse at you and you were with a small group of people who you realized were *like* you. I personally can do without that sense of unity! I had a lot of unhappy times during Women's Liberation conferences, realizing that they saw me as a threat – and that whole ethos which wanted to pander to the straight press by saying: 'No, no, we're *not* lesbians' when actually, of course, about a third of us were out as lesbians and another third turned out to be lesbians. I went to one of the first lesbian conferences (at Warwick University), and that was one of *the* most liberating experiences for me, because suddenly I was in a feminist environment in which it was OK to be a lesbian ...

There was a period when the Women's Movement was getting very bad publicity and a very bad press about being lesbian-orientated, and they were trying to say that they weren't. The same thing happened in the States ... and so although I always thought of myself as a feminist, I didn't think of myself as heavily part of the Women's Liberation Movement. At the time I would have said my loyalties were with the *gay* movement.

It is probably no coincidence that many of the women who were involved in and committed to these groups in the 1970s and early 1980s have since gone into counselling or psychotherapy, as practitioners, clients or both. It is a trend which in the UK mirrors wider political and economic changes: from a more altruistic, caring, pre-Thatcherite society to the individualism and self-interest of the 1980s and the mass insecurity and disenchantment of the post-Thatcherite 1990s.

For some women, the disappearance of CR groups and the fragmentation of the Women's Movement has left a conspicuous void. Others, like Jill Posener and Bridget, have moved on, absorbing, appropriating and experimenting with new ways of thinking, new ways of *being*.

It is not altogether surprising that they began to feel threatened and tyrannized by the radical lesbian faction of the Women's Liberation Movement. Invested with all the stereotypical connotations of man-hating Amazons decked out in dungarees and DMs, separatists are the women who have always been held responsible for giving lesbianism 'a bad name'. It is perhaps understandable if their rather hidebound attitudes and tactics, their refusal to countenance theoretical 'grey areas', alienated many lesbians as well.

However, it is easy with hindsight to attribute blame and, in so doing, to risk jettisoning the ideological baby with the bath-water and to overlook the particular circumstances – the social and political context – in which the lesbian-feminist movement evolved. It was a time when it was very necessary – indeed, crucial – for lesbians to find and develop their own sexual politics and private campaigning space, to be able to organize separately from men after years of being intimidated or silenced by masculine privilege. Furthermore, throughout history it has usually been the mavericks, rather than the moderates, who have brought about lasting change, who have been the ones to achieve the most tangible gains in a particular cause or movement. Christabel and Emmeline Pankhurst did not set out to court personal popularity, and neither did their successors, the separatists of the 1970s, nor the Greenham women in the 1980s.

Indeed, it is important to stress that the gains accrued through lesbian separatism vastly outweighed the kind of negative experiences alluded to here. My aim is not in any way to condemn the Movement *per se*, but rather to record and illustrate some of the more problematic and largely unforeseen consequences of that whole ground-breaking era.

It is not possible to build any new revolutionary movement without a certain measure of political fall-out, and lesbian feminism has had its quota of detrimental side-effects and delayed reactions. Those women who were its casualties, and who ultimately rejected its more extreme tenets, may be likened to certain self-styled hippies of the 1960s who, during the late 1970s and 1980s, adopted different lifestyles, both physically and spiritually. While some sought continuing nirvana in religious cults such as the Bhagwan Rajneesh's movement (the 'Orange People'), many metamorphosed into materialistic Establishment clones in suits and shoulder pads, exchanging ideals of peace, love and meditation for power-dressing and the practical pursuit of 'serious money'.

In the case of the lesbian-feminist movement, many erstwhile activists subsequently opted for a more balanced lifestyle, one which embraced sex and fun as well as debating and campaigning. Others abandoned most of the politics in favour of the fun. However, unlike the fading of the hippie dream, the retreat from lesbian separatism was accompanied by *fear*, the kind of fear engendered by certain women who continue to identify as lesbian separatists, as Jill Posener recalls:

> I can think of a few women who, if I see them coming, I will cross the street to avoid, because my heart starts thumping and I feel like I'm in the headmistress's study. If I were to confront somebody who I felt had been part of that, they would probably be shocked to know that they had instilled that fear in me. I don't think that anybody would have intended that. Strange, strange times.

Unlike Jill and Bridget, Del Dyer always distanced herself from radical lesbians, convinced that separatism harboured a fascist element which she found dangerously worrying and unpalatable. In the late 1970s she started to meet women who were separatists, and felt very 'separate' from them:

A lot of people said it was because I had sons ... but if I'd had daughters I would have felt exactly the same. Some of the women I met were completely barmy. ... The toilet [at the Women's Arts Alliance] was in a terrible state and they said it was because they couldn't find a female plumber! In the interests of hygiene, I don't see the logic in that.

It is interesting how the word 'radical' has acquired different connotations in the 1990s from its usage in the 1970s, when it was employed primarily to denote revolutionary left-wing politics. The OED defines it thus: 'Affecting the foundation, going to the root (*radical change, cure, reform*); (of surgery etc.) seeking to ensure removal of all diseased tissue ... ' (my italics). In referring to her appropriation of, and empathy with, the radical sexual politics of Berkeley, California, Jill is not talking separatism but sex. Her life in the 1990s has changed beyond recognition since the days when she was out daubing graffiti on billboards and protesting about pornographic images that debased women. In San Francisco she recalls that the extent of such 'radical' sexual politics was overwhelming. It started the very day of her arrival there in September 1986.

I was staying with this friend and she said: 'We're going to the strip show tonight.' I said: 'What do you mean?' I'd spent the 1970s breaking porn-shop windows in London. I'm a person who threw cans full of garbage into porn shops and they had to close down – that's *my* history. I was one of the few people arrested and actually convicted on the Reclaim the Night march in 1978 ....

We went to a lesbian strip show. I was pretty shaken by it: here were a bunch of dykes watching lesbians take off their clothes for them and putting the dollar bills down their pants, and I thought: 'You know, it ain't so *bad* – to see women doing that.' ... There was a black woman there, whose name I've now forgotten, who was a very famous San Francisco icon. It was exciting to see a black woman *empowered* like that – and she was empowered, no question about that. That was the night I met Susie Bright and her lover. For me that was a transformation and a liberation of the kind that I hadn't had since my very early days as a feminist.

This, surely, is the ultimate paradox: that the concept of 'liberation', the cornerstone of the Women's Liberation Movement, should be associated with two such polarized lifestyles. When Jill Posener talks about living one life publicly while, privately, trying to be 'true to herself', she sounds like a pre-feminist lesbian locked in the closet:

> When I moved to America and started living in San Francisco, I began to find
> a way of having the public and the private merge, so as not to experience that
> terrible conflict.

Another major source of change for Jill lies in her attitude towards gay
men. Back in the mid-1970s she worked with the Gay Sweatshop theatre
company as a photographer and writer:

> But I sought conflict with the men I worked with, because I didn't see men as
> my community. From a very early stage I had reinforced the position in myself
> that men were the enemy and their being gay made no difference to that.

In separatism's uncritical and relentless prioritizing of women, the
slightest indication of empathy with men and male-defined values was not
merely discouraged, it was proscribed. As Nicci Gerrard wrote in a piece
encapsulating the contradictions of political lesbianism: 'inviolable belief
in a single right course combined with evangelical fervour can become an
austere regime, where scepticism and ambivalence are swept aside in the
passion for clean change'.[16] Interestingly, Gerrard's observations were
published in 1986, the year that Jill Posener left the UK to live in San
Francisco.

From her newly 'radical' stance in the 1990s, Jill Posener regrets adopt-
ing such a circumscribed view. As she settled into her new, more
hedonistic, Californian lifestyle, she recalled the suppression of her own
instinctive feelings of warmth and affection towards gay men she had
known in the UK in the 1970s:

> All the men whom I'd known and worked with and *loved* deeply but couldn't
> express it, because when it came to making choices between lesbians and gay
> men, you knew which side of the fence you had to be on. And the men I'd
> rejected were now dead from AIDS and I wanted to get them all back for a
> day. How could I have been so *stupid?* . . . I will not make that mistake again, of
> excluding people from my life because of their gender, their race, their
> sexuality.

Even the men in her own family – all 'good guys' with gentle non-macho
credentials – were once in a sense demonized by her:

> I once said to my father: 'All men are rapists and if you're not a rapist yourself,
> you get the benefit of it.' My father, of eighty years old! . . . And he looked at

me with a kind of horror and sadness in his eyes, just sat there looking at me as if: 'What am I gonna do to reach my daughter?' . . . I now feel very 'resolved' with my father. We've developed a wonderful friendship – and my two brothers (one older than me, one younger) are terrific people. Both of them live in Berlin.

The only women from the lesbian-separatist movement with whom she remains in contact are those who have made similar transitions to her own. Women like Sue O'Sullivan, a former lover and 'one of my dearest friends'. Sue, a writer and founder member of the *Spare Rib* collective, now lives in Australia, where Jill went for six months before emigrating to the USA.

Emotionally and psychologically, Jill is 'well and truly recovered' from that period in her life:

thanks to America, San Francisco and the love of some very, very good women over there, and some people who took the blinkers off. It was like waking from a very deep and nasty sleep. I wish I'd known of anybody else who felt like me. Presumably, all of us were isolated. If I'd had the guts, in the early 1980s, to run an ad saying: 'Those of us who are disillusioned, let's get together and talk', we might have been a lot happier earlier.

She had remained fiercely loyal to a community from whom she had begun to feel increasingly estranged. The extent of differences was finally revealed in the debate around lesbian SM. Jill's massive shift from her campaigning role in the anti-porn movement to a libertarian, pro-SM stance was perceived by many women as a blatant betrayal, and led to her ostracism.

She had been questioning areas around SM and had obtained a copy of Pat Califia's *Coming to Power* (the SM 'bible' for lesbians in the USA): 'Although much of it had been shocking and horrifying to me, the unadulterated glee and pleasure with which she described sexuality was something that I had not experienced.' With all the zeal of the newly converted, Jill began to raise these issues in various forums, including a Jewish women's conference where she was accused of being an anti-Semite, Nazi, fascist and misogynist. Outside London's Lesbian and Gay Centre leaflets were handed out warning other women of the presence of SM lesbians there (the decision to allow SM groups to use the centre was a hotly contentious one before the LLGC closed down in 1992).

Jill then decamped to Australia and subsequently moved to the USA where, for the first time in her life, she feels she has found a genuine home:

> The West Coast is as its reputation implies – live and let live, QED. I know there are women who are fiercely opposed to SM who live in the same city as I do, or over in Berkeley, and we don't meet, we have nothing to do with each other.

Her girlfriend, Suzie, works for the AIDS Foundation in San Francisco. They have a home together, two dogs, two cats. In her work as a freelance photographer, Jill has worked for magazines – gay and straight – designed book covers and collaborated with Susie Bright on a controversial book about the pioneers of lesbian photography (published by Cassell in 1995). The knowledge that they worked together for two years on *On Our Backs*, the lesbian pornography magazine, has long been the subject of impassioned debate among the lesbian community in the UK. Jill remains unperturbed:

> I did it consciously and actively and with every intention of pursuing and exploring a whole area that I had deprived myself of. And after a while I got tired of working there and it's over with, although I still think the work I did around lesbian sexuality is some of the best work I've ever done . . . . It wasn't about trying to go in the other direction because, even though I had shouted: 'Porn equals rape, porn equals violence against women', inside of me I had never quite believed it. I had always had questions, but those questions could never be raised.
>
> We used to walk through Soho tracking down porn shops, and a whole bunch of prostitutes or sex workers would come out and scream at us: 'This is *my* job, *my* workplace and you're depriving me of business.' And what answer did we give to them? 'You're self-oppressed, you don't understand, you're in hock to the man.' But we never offered any alternatives, and to this day I believe that sex workers are far more in control of their lives than most workers in a canteen or office building. And I do not believe the sex industry is a cause of women's oppression. Fifty per cent of the sex workers in San Francisco are lesbian. ... The reality is that they're putting themselves through school because the sex industry pays them very well, or they're raising their children, sending them to private schools.
>
> There are other women working at the lower end of the sex market who are drug addicts and who are not long for this life. You only have to look at

the Roddy Doyle's TV series, *Family*,[17] to see that most women *not* working in the sex industry have that kind of life also. This is not about women in the sex industry, but about women in this *society*, and I think we took an easy aim, an easy target.

Now fully involved in Californian life, Jill experiences a kind of culture shock each time she visits the UK. She returns twice a year, mainly to catch up with friends and also to visit her family in Berlin: 'There is a small-mindedness here and I don't feel I belong. America, for me, is this feeling of space, expansiveness, independence.'

The one thing that has not changed about Jill Posener is her *image*: she regards herself as a lifelong butch. And Suzie, her girlfriend, she says is very definitely a femme. They have been together since July 1989, and Jill recalls her first impressions of Suzie:

She had lipstick and nail varnish on and was wearing a very tight black dress, and the idea that this woman was a lesbian was so *exciting*. . . . She's completely a woman. Both men and women are attracted to her.

I've looked like this since I was eight years old, and what's so delightful is that I don't have to compete with men for this woman's attention. In some ways, butch is a kind of third gender – you know, we're not quite women, not quite men. But it has nothing to do with gender *fluidity*. If somebody told me I had to wear a dress, I'd rather go to jail.

I don't dress butch like 1950s girls did; I don't wear men's clothing. I have that kind of androgynous 1970s look, so I fitted in quite well then. But what we couldn't do was to have women who looked like my girlfriend or Susie Bright.

These were the original 'lipstick lesbians', closeted and marginalized by their own sisters, their existence denied, consigned for a long time to a kind of social and cultural wilderness.

Jill is a staunch member of the Democratic Party, though less politically active than she used to be. Her main preoccupation in the 1990s is gays and immigration, an issue which she believes that the American lesbian and gay community has so far failed to address, but which has become increasingly important because of the legal ban on visitors who are HIV-positive.

Although she does not yet have full residency rights, living with her partner in the USA has given Jill a sense of family life, of community – these very things which she lacked during her childhood and which, again, in her twenties, she feels she missed because of her radical politics: 'I could still do with more work and more money, but I have a happy family life and a woman whose love is dear to me, and those are my political and emotional priorities.'

When she first moved to Sheffield, Bridget rebelled against the kind of prescriptive lifestyle she had experienced in Brighton:

> I had one long relationship in Brighton. We didn't socialize very much. It was all hard work and no fun, so I went the other way: all fun and no hard work. I got involved with different types of women in Sheffield: they were less dogmatic, more down-to-earth.
>
> I have been back to Brighton about three times. The last time I went, the summer of 1992, I went around looking at some old places and remembering things, which was a good thing to do – a way of exorcizing [the past].
>
> The most important thing for me at the moment is being with Thomas, bringing him up. I am interested in home-educating, not because I want to create some sort of genius, but I would like him to have the freedom to ... be away from all the restrictions and limitations that school imposes on children. I have hopes of finding other people who are interested in the same sorts of things, so that we can get together.

Bridget describes her financial situation as 'pretty dire'. Like Thomas's father, she is on income support, supplemented by sporadic earnings as a freelance writer and campaigner: the sort of work which fits around her life at home with Thomas. Before this, she was involved in a government scheme in Sheffield, running a community print shop. She and a woman co-worker set up courses in printing, computer graphics and desktop publishing, but despite their success in establishing and building up the scheme, it was axed due to government and council cuts.

She has a strong network of women friends, most of whom have children. What she would most like is to be involved in an extended-family type of network where she would have contact with other adults and children:

> I'd like to live independently, but closely and supportively with like-minded people. I value my privacy and being able to shut my own back door and keep other people out when I want to.
>
> I also feel that I am undergoing a very long process of trying to discover what I really feel about things, instead of going along with one dogma or another. Just trusting myself and having the courage to say that something

feels wrong to me, even though the people I am with may not feel that way.
... I don't feel that I belong with any particular group.

With the apparent shift away from the self-obsessed individualism of the 1980s, the need to *belong*, to feel part of some wider group or network, has become an increasingly powerful one. Paulina Palmer explains how attitudes to the concept of *lesbian community* have changed, from the 'celebratory' stance of the early 1970s, born of naive and idealistic expectations, to a revised, more pragmatic approach. From the idea of a *unified* category of women to a 'loose-knit assemblage in which differences of race, class, age and ideology are recognized and accepted.'[18]

Black and working-class women, she stresses, 'have made a significant contribution to this shift of perspective, by criticizing the racial and social narrowness and universalizing tendency which characterized the lesbian feminist movement's concept of sisterhood. This change in outlook was accompanied by a new mood of moderation which reflected the political conservatism of the age'.[19]

There is no doubt that since the early 1970s the lesbian community in both the UK and the USA has moved on and changed shape, and will doubtless continue to develop and mutate, perhaps in a more flexible form, as we move towards the twenty-first century. Writing in 1988, Sigrid Nielsen was optimistic but realistic about the future development of a lesbian community.

A community can never be created: not through hard work or in any other way. It must simply be recognised and respected. It cannot be exclusive, like a club or a class. It is an opportunity, a place to make things happen, not a favoured state or a promised land. If its promises are to be trusted, they should be few and very down to earth.[20]

It is an evolving process which must take its course, and whose consequences cannot be predicted. From the ideal of a close and intense group of activists 'sacrificing their lives for one blinding flash of change', the 'real' community ('large, diverse and scattered') has been gradually emerging.[21]

II

Different Directions: Interviews

forty-one, minister, Metropolitan Community Church

I was born in London, where we lived in rented accommodation. My mother has a nursing background; my father was an engineer, a surveyor. When I was three years old my parents decided to move out of London. They bought a plot of land and built their own five-bedroomed bungalow in a village near Sevenoaks. When I was thirteen we moved to a smallholding, not to be worked in a farming sense but it gave space for my brothers to have their motorbikes and myself to have my ponies.

I went to a local village primary school, and then to a grammar school. However, my schooling was cut short when I was expelled. There was a catalogue of various things – typical behaviour problems. I was diagnosed with acute depression and spent the next couple of years in and out of hospital. I began in children's wards and ended up on adult psychiatric wards.

At that point I was taken into care as being beyond parental control. I wasn't doing anything criminal, but I spent a great deal of my time running away from home. My mother came and picked me up from about ten different police stations all over the country. In those days, much like today, I don't think society really knew how to deal with somebody who is either very unhappy or doesn't *fit*. And so I was put in care and was in a remand home for three months, then an assessment centre. During this time I became a Christian, and whereas up until then I had been going back to juvenile court every three weeks and refusing to acknowledge their authority, following my conversion I decided to try living at home again.

Although he died when I was seven, my father was a violent man and emotionally oppressive too, and my depression and behaviour problems were thought to be a result of that. I wasn't aware of my sexuality, or of any lesbian feelings, at that point.

I returned home at fifteen, and at sixteen I went off to college in Kent for two years where I did a course in preliminary residential childcare. I'd met a woman of twenty-three through some mutual acquaintances. She worked in one of the local towns, but her parents lived in Wales, and she invited me to go and stay with her and her parents for a long weekend. It was during that time that I had my first kiss with a woman. That was undoubtedly my first lesbian awakening, but I certainly didn't know, or use the word 'lesbian', and didn't consider myself homosexual, simply that I happened to be in love with another woman.

When I was eighteen I went into nursing, entirely for the wrong reasons. It was Orpington Hospital, where my mother worked, and every Christmas they did a pantomime. I was madly in love with the ward sister, who always played the principal boy, and I decided that if I went and trained there I would get closer to her. I continued to be very attracted to her. To my amazement, I ended up loving nursing and completed my training without any problems – and that brought me to twenty-one.

At this time I was struggling very hard, because I had the dichotomy between my faith as a Christian and my Church telling me that homosexuality was wrong, sinful and evil, and consequently I was believing that *I* was. I was doing what they expected of me and had become engaged to a missionary. Although that sounds terribly heterosexual, the fact was that he was in Africa, I was completing my nursing training, and so for the two years that I was engaged to him I only saw him for two weeks out of the whole two years [1972–74] and had a very close friendship with one of the other nurses.

So there was this whole *duality* of my life. There was what really fulfilled me emotionally, and what everybody else *expected* would fulfil me emotionally. I just saw myself as a woman who liked other women. I didn't give it a name. My conditioning was coming very strongly from a fundamentalist Christian Church, and so I was very sheltered from much of the Women's Movement at that time. They were not the circles that would be encouraged *at all*. I was taught by very strong peer pressure within my Church that [feminism] was wrong.

When I was fifteen I had asked a friend, who I knew to be a Christian, where she would recommend that I attended and – perhaps unfortunately, with hindsight – she recommended a Pentecostal church. I joined a local congregation and was very susceptible to their teaching. I was also desperately trying to change my life, to change this need always to run away from things. I was swept in and indoctrinated – brainwashed – into believing that spirituality meant a particular, 'acceptable' Christian lifestyle. And, for a woman, that meant that I must subject myself to a male.

Women were taught that men were heads of households, which my head was probably accepting as a teaching, but my heart wasn't. It was always a struggle and didn't seem to come naturally to me. In many ways it prevented me being a friend to anybody, because people were seen only in terms of *souls* and another soul on the 'notch' belt. Friends had to be 'middle class and respectable': this was the underlying teaching.

During those ten years I had three serious relationships which, of course, were lesbian – it's just that I didn't name them as such. I did find that I couldn't go through with the wedding planned for January 1975. I went and stayed with some Christian friends I knew in Manchester, and there began my third relationship. We became lovers, but then her conflict between us and the Faith – we were attending the church locally – prevented her from continuing the relationship.

It's playing a game: all your friends and acquaintances within the Church know that you are close friends, but it's almost as if nobody wants to know the *truth*. ... It came to a head for us when some friends of hers were coming to stay, and she said I'd have to sleep in the spare room while they were there. I just couldn't understand that, it didn't make sense to me at all, and shortly after that she decided not to continue our relationship. That was about 1978 and I had been with her for two years.

The sum total of my life was the tension between my Christianity and my sexuality. I was always wanting to put the Christianity first, and my sexuality, which was far more than my sexual *activity*, was always there and part of me. I had applied to the Birmingham Bible Institute to go and study, and a member of the congregation sent me a letter informing me that if I took up my place they would inform the college that I was a homosexual. And in many ways that did me probably the greatest favour of my life, because it brought my relationship with the Church to a crisis. I left and returned to London, and felt too ashamed to pick up with the local church.

I began working for a nursing agency and was sent to work at the National Theatre. And at this point I first came into contact with people who identified as gay – [in particular] a gay male, I think he worked in catering. He offered to take me somewhere where women – lesbians – met. I was terrified, but went: it was a pub in Vauxhall and I found it just amazing. I couldn't identify with it at all. It seemed so weird and offbeat to me, but one of the women, K., offered to show me some other places that women went to. I took her up on it and ended up in a relationship with her for three years.

More than one or two people in the Church had known about my sexuality, because I had 'confessed' it. They had at different times been trying to heal me, cure me, change me, forgive me. I was never actually tied down, but everything else that happened in *Oranges Are Not the Only Fruit* was my experience. Part of the brainwashing is that you believe you are doing the right thing for God. It was dreadful, it destroys people. It's very difficult being a recovered Pentecostal . . . I would never go back. I may have left the Church on the issue of sexuality, but I could not go back to that sort of fundamentalism for a thousand different reasons.

Leaving was a big change. It was also one of the worst and saddest experiences of my life, because I was so unprepared to meet lesbians that I had no information to make informed choices about relationships or anything like that. I ended up in the battered-lover syndrome and spent two years and eleven months out of the three years trying to get out of my relationship with K. I did break it off several times and then there would be cut wrists, suicide attempts and emotional blackmail, as well as physical violence to me. I was hospitalized twice.

I was completely unprepared for the world of women. My understanding of women was that they obeyed their husbands. There is a slight counter-balance to that, in that my mother's influence taught me that women did not need to be dependent. But that in itself was quite interesting, in that she had stayed in a violent relationship herself. He died, and I feel that she has spent the rest of her life – and our childhood – trying to compensate for that.

Within about a year of the relationship with K. ending, I bought my own pub. I did it because the sort of places that I'd been going to didn't, I feel, address the needs of women that I could identify with. They always seemed very sleazy – apart, of course, from the Gateways, which was smashing, but it was a *club* and I had the dream of a *pub*, where people could drift in and out. So I bought the freehold and transformed it from a strippers' pub into a women's bar. It was in Redchurch Street, between Bethnal Green and Shoreditch. I changed the name from the Crown to The Alternative.

I was the sole proprietor and had no financial backing. I think I was turned down forty-nine times. Nobody was very interested in a 29-year-old woman who didn't have a man with her and who had never stood behind a bar in her life. So that was a bit of a non-starter. Then I was trying to raise finance . . . and it was just no, no, no.

Immediately before, I had my own business with a partner – in office equipment – and had sold my 50 per cent to his wife and was therefore interested in a new business . . . I opened the pub and one of the local papers reported accurately my words – I could *die* now – I remember saying that this was not a pub for lesbians but for *ladies*! So when I did come in contact with the Women's Movement I was really quite opposed to it, because the idea of women in dungarees . . . didn't appeal to me at all. At the beginning I just didn't swallow the whole feminist thing. This, I wanted to be very clear, was a pub for *ladies* who happened to like other ladies . . . I attracted a whole load of women out there who also did not relate to the dungaree image.

It was an ideal spot for all the Kenric types. I am not against them individually – lovely people, a lot of them – but they were your middle-class professional woman who is closeted at work. I think that is one of the fascinating things – that there is this whole Women's Movement and then this enormous number of *uncountable* women, lesbians, who are living their quiet lives, going out to places, contributing to our society without any recognition.

I suppose I found it fascinating that at different times in my life I have moved within those sorts of circles. However, it was the experience of owning the pub that played a part in politicizing myself. This came about because I was open seven nights a week, and the pub would be absolutely teeming on Friday and Saturday nights and maybe Sunday lunch-times, but the rest of the week could be quite quiet, and I would have a group of regulars who were very young women. I was struck by the fact that these women would come in every night straight from work, sit through the evening with maybe three halves of lager and talk about nothing but relationships. The sum total of their lives appeared to be going to work in order to come *down* somewhere where they could just be with other women. There seemed no direction to their lives. I became so angry that young lesbians had nowhere, no choices, and it reminded me so much of the fact that I had been completely unprepared for a lesbian world and fell into all sorts of traps . . . It began the anger I felt about a system that didn't allow them to broaden their experience, that seemed to be stopping them, and that there was nothing – and nowhere – for them. That's when I became political and began to read up on issues.

Part of the frustrating side, for me, was that they hadn't been empowered to articulate how they felt, so it only ever came out in terms of talking about the last time they'd all got drunk or the last girlfriend they'd had. . . . The older ones were more out, or leading more flexible sorts of lives.

When I first got the pub it was full of male lorry drivers, so they were none too pleased when I started cancelling the strippers! One of them continued to come, but that was because he was actually a transvestite and he thought the changes were wonderful. On special occasions he would bring his wife as well, and he would be cross-dressed. . . . I used to say that men were welcome as guests and there were two rules for the men: one, 'You don't chat up the women', and the second one was: 'If you don't know what I'm talking about then you're out anyway.'

It was well advertised in the gay press and I also got the co-operation of the local police. This was quite hilarious – you begin with a provisional licence until you go to court, so that you can trade from the day you purchase, and I think I had about two months of being open before having to go for my licence application. I remember worrying about whether or not I should tell the police the sort of pub I was turning it into and decided, just before the day I was due in court, that I would go and see the local licensing police, and went along taking with me a copy of *Capital Gay* (it had a write-up on the pub).

I walked in wearing a skirt and high heels (I was very much a lipstick lesbian in those days) and said, 'I think you know I am going for a licence tomorrow. Have you seen *this*?' I opened it at the page, the licensing officer read it and that was fine. It then turned out that he and a colleague had had a bet on whether or not I was a lesbian and . . . they actually *knew* I was. And this was all to do with the fact that the police had prosecuted my former lover for the final act of violence, and therefore I am down on police records as a lesbian, which *personally* doesn't worry me but helped to make me aware of just how oppressive our society is, and how many lists and statistics are kept, without our knowledge, by the police. It also helped me feel that if they are going to keep a list of homosexuals then I want to be on every one!

Ironically, the women who radicalized me were the ones from the Metropolitan Community Church [MCC], and it was through discussions with them, in the pub, that I was able to find a new church 'home' and to start to get together the whole of my life – my faith and my sexuality. The MCC is a wonderfully aware and open Christian Church. It is quite the opposite to a fundamentalist system, which is very much a closed group. One of the most exciting things was just to sit with other women and share stories, experiences. This is where I was able to listen to other women's struggles and the oppression experienced by so many, and it was through these debates that I began my path into feminism, recognizing feminism as an authentic option for the world's survival.

After a few months of soul-searching, I became a member of the Church [in 1984], and later I would hold discussion groups in the pub. So the pub itself became more of a political base, and I became aware of all these new (to me) terms like 'consciousness raising'. . . . Only later did I sell the pub in order to go to college and study theology, so the two ran concurrently for quite a while.

Becoming a minister was an enormous step, but it was also a sense of coming home. It was what I think I had always had a feeling I was *about*. I had always had a sense of *calling*, and this fulfilled everything for me. It just seemed right and natural. It was a place where I could be a whole person, and that means that I was strengthened in the rest of my life as well. I will self-identify as a Christian, a woman, a lesbian – all of those things in any order you like.

I was ordained in September 1993. I am not called a priest – I could choose to use that word if I wanted to, but I choose not to. . . . In the United Fellowship of Metropolitan Community Churches (UFMCC) you do your training, including a minimum of one year's experiential training, and you are then licensed as a clergy person. Before you can be ordained you have to serve as a clergy person of good standing for three years, with evaluations, and go through a board.

For me, one of the biggest issues has got to be that men and women are still having enormous pressures put on them through their sexuality. Our young people are not equipped in the same way that their heterosexual brothers and sisters are – for adolescence, and for life choices. Therefore, an enormous amount of my time will be spent listening to people's horror stories of how our society seeks to alienate them from the cradle to the grave – it covers the whole gamut of age ranges – because our childhoods are denied us.

The response [to AIDS] from the gay community has been totally remarkable and has shown just what strength there is in these men and women who have been so disadvantaged through their upbringings and yet have proved themselves to be a community of enormous strength.

I have supervision for any counselling work that I do, and I have had to develop coping strategies for dealing with my own potential burn-out. I still experience all of the emotions that go with it: the futility, the anger, the sadness, the loss of very special people, and I hurt at the pain of others who are having to grieve and mourn.

Ninety per cent of my congregation is homosexual. Twenty-five per cent is probably lesbian. . . . Some of the younger lesbians are not out to their parents and are terrified of them knowing – and these are eighteen-year-olds in the 1990s! I've worked with several people on ways of coming out to parents if they choose to. I think it's a good idea to prepare a pack of positive information. If you come out to your parents, how can you expect them suddenly to take it all on board when it's taken *us* years to? And we are forced to look at the issue – *they* can choose to sidestep it and pretend it's not happening, and many will do that for a while. Nonetheless, there'll probably come a point when they are inquisitive. And when you think that all of the stuff *we* could ever find out was in the dictionary that labelled us 'inverts' or whatever, then I think it's a good idea that there's some material that is accessible for them when *they* want to see it – positive, basic stuff.

Although I was clearly a late starter, the Women's Movement has had an enormously beneficial influence upon me. The methodology, which includes the analysis, the justice, the integrity, the sharing of stories, the redistribution of power, all these things inform the way that I now live my life. It is through becoming part of this movement, and seeing the parallels with which I believe authentic Christianity can make changes in our world, that I can have a sense of harmony in my life. The duality is gone, and in its place is the opportunity to allow myself, a Christian lesbian, to be within a mutual relationship with all sorts of people.

When I was young, it was always society telling me that I couldn't be who or what I was. Police, social workers and doctors said I wasn't normal to be so angry as a young teenager. My Church said I wasn't normal not to desire a man and marriage. Closeted women said I wasn't normal to want to be open about our relationships. Within unhealthy lesbian relationships I was told that I was not normal if I didn't expect to have to take other people's violence. Society told me I wasn't normal as a lesbian. The Women's Movement showed me that I could reclaim my self and my values, and begin to express my own sense of normality.

I still want to listen to other people's views, but that listening no longer means that they have the power to control me or to corrupt me into their own image of what or who they think I should be. I continue to change in all sorts of ways, but now it's on a voluntary basis.

Harriett **G**ilbert

forty-six, writer/broadcaster/journalism teacher

I am the oldest of seven children. My father was a solicitor and crime writer, my mother was his partner's secretary and stopped working outside the home when they got married. I was born in North London and we moved to Kent when I was three. I was educated at the French Lycée in London until about the age of twelve, then went to boarding-school in Kent.

I thought, ridiculously, that university was a channel which led to a conventional marriage and children, that I would be stuck in a rut which would lead me to the kind of life that I absolutely didn't want. I can't think how I got this idea. My parents weren't too keen on me going to drama school, which is what I decided to do instead. I went to the Rose Bruford College of Speech and Drama in Sidcup. I went there because they did a teaching diploma as well, and it was the only way I would get my parents' approval. The teaching I hated. Many years afterwards, when I saw one of those signs with a little boy and a little girl crossing the road, I used to feel physically nauseous.

I knew very soon that I was not going to be an actress. The impression I had was that it was having a director shout: 'Look sexy, darling', and just being passive. I thought: 'This isn't for me', but what I still love is the whole theatre *world*. I dislike theatre people, they can be extremely irritating, but it was the first time I'd come across such a mixed group in terms of class and educational background. It was un-snobby about everything, not even *intellectually* snobby ... and there is enormous sexual tolerance towards people's various sexual ways of being – and I partly hung on in there because I was giddy on all this.

There were several out gay men in my year – no women that I knew of, but I fell passionately in love with A., a fellow student who was a woman ... it went nowhere, but not because she said: 'My God, a lesbian, how awful!' Several other students knew, but the problem was that there were fewer role models then. It was only afterwards that I read Colette, for instance. I knew there were gay men in the theatre and a lot of male actors were gay. ... It had a kind of glamour associated with camp and style, whereas dykedom then certainly didn't.

So you had (a) to say you were abnormal, or different, but (b) to say you were rather grimly and unstylishly abnormal – but it's far easier to come out as *stylishly* abnormal. I don't think people made it hard for you, in the sense that they would have discriminated against you particularly, it was just hard in terms of your own sense of how you did it and how you lived with this persona.

I started reading Simone de Beauvoir, but what I read far more avidly was Radclyffe Hall, Colette and Vita Sackville-West, and anything about or by Virginia Woolf – not for their feminism as such, but just for *ways* of being lesbian. I am ashamed to say part of it was to do with trying to find a style that I could feel happy with, that didn't feel like a downtrodden Sister George victim figure. Maybe I am *not* ashamed to say that, but I have only just realized that was partly what I was doing.

I am fairly certain now that A. had had physical relationships with women, she just didn't want one with me. I was miserable, but I think I was miserable about a lot of things. I was miserable because I had no idea what I was doing with my life, and because I think a lot of people in their late teens/early twenties are, and I was quite a slow developer.

When I finally left college, I moved up to London and went to live in – not a squat, but a curious kind of illegal housing somewhere in Putney. I decided I really needed to find the Gateways. I had seen The Killing of Sister George in Sidcup, and so I knew that this club existed. I trolled up and down the King's Road trying to find where it was, and also thinking that half the women in King's Road must be lesbians on their way to the Gateways. I eventually got taken there.

I knew quite a few gay men. One day, in 1969, I was wandering down Putney High Street and met a guy I knew. I was looking for work and he said: 'There is an employment agency you might find very interesting, my dear, because there are two dykes running it.' So I went, and indeed had a very long relationship with one of the women who worked there, Billie [not her real name]. I worked for her at the agency. She was always getting me the best jobs! I used to go off and work as a temp at the BBC ... I can't remember how many weeks I had been going in there before she asked me out – it wasn't long.

I was with her seven years. We lived together. She left me for another woman. The relationship had been disintegrating for some time. It was very devastating . . .

I thought of myself as primarily lesbian but potentially bisexual. I had lost my virginity as a very deliberate exercise when I reached twenty-one and thought. 'This is a bit ridiculous in the late 1960s . . . ', but also because – I was quite convinced at that point that I was lesbian – I didn't want somebody saying to me, 'Oh, you just *think* you are because you've never had sex with a man.' And I didn't even want somebody saying, 'What, have you never had sex with a man?' So I slept with X. This was a very unfair thing to do to this poor guy. He was a nice guy, quite pretty and the only *clean* heterosexual man that I knew. He actually washed his clothes and wasn't utterly disease-ridden. It wasn't too difficult – I smoked a lot of pot and persuaded him to take me to bed.

I saw him a few more times . . . I didn't give it a chance to be successful as sex. I didn't really *want* it to work, and I wasn't conducting any fair experiments at all – I wanted to get it out of the way. Within weeks of that I had met Billie . . .

I didn't exclude men from the future. I flirted with men *and* women . . . It wasn't until the mid-1970s that I defined myself as feminist. I used to model for life classes, and I was chatting to one of the students, an elderly man, and we were having an argument about something and he said: 'Oh God, don't tell me you are one of those women's libbers?' Until then I had quite deliberately thought: 'I don't want to be.' I said: 'Yes,' because there was no possible answer except Yes, and I thought: 'Oh well, I suppose I am then.'

Not long afterwards I started getting involved in doing work for *Time Out* magazine, which is where I came into contact with serious thought-out feminism – and a lot of lesbian feminists, far more than heterosexuals. But I still think that among lesbians, feminism developed less hectically, less fast and less desperately than it did among heterosexual women, because there weren't the same day-to-day issues of oppression – obviously not in personal relationships.

It's very interesting when I think of my hard core of friends who are lesbian – a number of them are now celibate. I think all of them would still *define* themselves as lesbian. It's amazing how many of them are not in relationships . . . How does one define celibacy? I have one friend who thinks if she has not had sex for a fortnight that she is being celibate. She has high standards – or low standards!

My relationship with Billie finished around 1978. I then had a longish fling with another woman, a social worker, which broke down because she was involved with a man as well and she kept putting him first, up with which I will not put. She told me she was having this affair with someone else, and kept saying it was about to end. It just dragged on for months, and I walked out on something that was finished. I then started an affair with a man I had been working with. I don't know why – I didn't consciously plan it – but I also started an affair with a woman shortly afterwards. I think I was trying to test something out.

I was an extremely inefficient bigamist. They both knew about each other, there wasn't any secrecy. I just found it difficult having sex with two people in the same time frame. I always felt as though I was betraying somebody or other ... The woman was happy for it to carry on, but the man wasn't. I couldn't anyway, and I eventually finished the relationship with the woman and am still in the relationship with the man, Robin.

In a perfectly neutral environment I would call myself bisexual, but I am well aware that in some sense it depends on who is asking me and why. It depends on what direction the flak is going to come from. In some situations you put yourself in the position of where you are going to get the most flak, so you are not thought to be avoiding it ... I can imagine circumstances in which I would identify as lesbian, which would be a bit like a mad political act, it certainly wouldn't be particularly truthful – and I wouldn't to someone who *was* lesbian, because I think they would, quite rightly, say: 'What kind of a lesbian can you conceivably call yourself?'

I think I am bisexual for the reason that I am as liable to be attracted to somebody of one sex as of the other. My radar still operates like that, even though I am supposed to be – and, indeed, am – monogamous. And were this relationship ever to end, and were I lucky enough to find another partner, I have absolutely no sense of what sex they would be.

Robin doesn't like me calling myself bisexual, because he says every-body 'hears' bisexual as a sort of swinger, like 'I am available' and 'How can you conceivably be a monogamous bisexual?' And in that sense, to him, I guess I'm not ... He hopes I define myself as heterosexual, although he is well aware that in a way that is dishonest of him, because he is equally likely to be jealous of a *woman* around the fringes of my life as a man, so he knows perfectly well why I define myself as bisexual.

He is married to someone who knows about our relationship. I don't know how systematically I have done this, but I have still guaranteed some kind of marginalization in my life and – it has to be said – vast quantities of disapproval, because, of course, to be a feminist woman having an affair with another man is not a very sound position to be in. I've forgotten now what an abrupt change it was, but I can remember having dinner with

Robin in a restaurant quite early on in our relationship, and our feet were touching under the table. And when the waiter came towards the table I can remember thinking: 'I mustn't pull away', because all the time I'd been with my long-term woman lover, in public, it was always that sense of it being an act of defiance to still keep your feet tangled under the table and to still hold hands in the cinema when they shone the torch down the row. I suddenly thought: 'This is absolutely expected, this is how we are *supposed* to be.' I was very aware that it was just so much easier. There wasn't anything I could do that I wasn't doing before. It just didn't have to be a great sort of *gesture* every time. It was a phenomenal difference.

There was relief – and guilt, of course, like: 'Why should it be so easy?' – and then *anger* at all heterosexuals, who had always had it so easy. I had never ever felt any anti-heterosexual feelings, or even felt particularly angry at homophobia, because I have constructed for myself a life where it is very easy not to be straight. So I am not a very angry person about the way life is, because I have made sure that life . . . has been quite congenial to me.

I had a very knee-jerk, bad reaction from one or two lesbian friends, like: 'Traitor' and: 'How can you do this?' That, by and by, dwindled. I can understand it, I probably was a bit defensive, but I didn't think they were behaving unreasonably. They were annoyed that I was having an affair with a *married* man.

We have agreed to disagree. It's like I have friends who are Tories. I think there are relationships you have [where] you know that in certain areas there is no point in getting into an argument. Other lesbian friends of mine were never at all ghastly about it anyway.

I was quite angry if somebody who I suspected was trying lesbianism on as a political garb, then implicitly, or in print or in person, started trying to tell me how to conduct myself as a lesbian. It's not a major aspect of the feminism I've experienced, but it's certainly there. . . . That I did feel quite annoyed about because – I suspect I am that awful thing, a liberal with a small 'l' . . . I believe in pluralism, in tolerance within limits. If I had wanted those kinds of rules I could have stayed within my parents' set of rules. There was a perfectly good set there, and it wouldn't have got me into so much trouble. I do find that kind of legislation on how one should behave sexually, irritating.

When I first encountered feminism I was so busy and fascinated by the whole new structure of thinking that I probably got quite doctrinaire – because in a way it was such an intellectual pleasure, suddenly seeing the whole world reshaped once you'd started thinking from a feminist perspective, that it was quite easy to start laying down the law, whether in writing or among friends. So I have become more tolerant. I think I am reverting to a kind of laziness, but this is more the *real* me. The fervent one was probably less natural, but I did enjoy it, I quite liked arguing positions through to their extremes. I am now laxer and think Utopia is not realizable.

My biggest engagement with feminism has been via reading and writing rather than running crèches or marching or going to conferences. I did march for the right to abortion. . . . I have done one bit of activism – I was a founding member of the women's committee of the Writers' Guild. This was late on, around the early 1980s, and there were still members of the Guild – older women, by and large – who said: 'This is a disgrace: I'm not a woman, I'm a writer. We can't have positive discrimination,' which just made me laugh, because I thought all this had gone. But it's very easy to live this protected life where you imagine that things have changed because they have among the people *you* meet and . . . none of the men you meet overtly thump their women or shout at them or say: 'Where's my fucking supper?' . . .

I think I was an *excited* feminist, the *ideas* excited me and they still do. But it is at that point where ideas start to sound like a programme for living, and to be turned into rules, then I think – they are not meant for that, they are too complicated.

WORK

I have never worked hard like I have done in the last five years. I am very lucky because I can get work, but it is a constant tightrope: all the freelancing I do could stop tomorrow. I work within areas where they are retrenching, and it's not so much that feminist activity or thought or debate is a luxury but that the *energy* isn't there.

Also, . . . I was interviewing Katy Roiphe when she was over, and there was a point where . . . I am interviewing her for the radio and I feel very impatient with her and I think: 'Oh, for goodness sake yes, yes, yes, *but* . . . ', and I realize I sound like a middle-aged harridan and am exactly the sort of woman she can't bear. And I don't know who's right. I think I am partly right, because a lot of what she and Naomi Wolf, for instance, are saying is very simplistic and is ignoring a lot of writing that has gone before; but at the same time it would be odd if they just accepted what women twenty years older told them – why should they? I think there is a sense that one generation of feminism is tired and doesn't know where it is going any longer. The only thing it is active around is pornography.

I think this whole censoriousness about sexual representations is ill-conceived, but I am now bored with it. I think if all feminists can get agitated about is whether or not there should be Page Three girls, it's come to a very sorry state . . . so maybe my generation has just run out of things to say, and the younger generation is saying things that I don't find very interesting because I have heard it before. I'm aware it's a terrible thing, it's like saying: 'Call that pop music?' – but it's true, nonetheless.

AGEING

I think I made decisions that got me where I am: 'This is why I am here rather than somewhere else'. I feel that it's [my] personal choice, in the sense that I don't feel: 'Oh gosh, how did this happen to me?' . . . But – I am working harder than I want to – I am getting too old, I can't work through the nights any more. I don't want to have to be worried like this, I don't wish to hit sixty and work be dropping off and have no means of supporting myself, which is extremely likely to happen. . . .

The biggest change is hitting forty and, instead of seeing yourself as progressing from birth to something, you see yourself as progressing from where you are towards death. . . . I definitely feel I am over the brow of the hill: not in any particularly bad sense – it's just an interesting change of horizon. The horizon is death, and I think of all the things that have altered since the late 1960s/early 1970s, that is the *most* . . . I will probably start writing fiction again. What has also changed is that I no longer think I am going to write *the* great novel of all time. After your thirties, some edge to the ambition just goes.

*J*ackie *F*orster

sixty-nine, founder of Sappho, director, London Women's Centre, breast-cancer survivor

It was 1970, I was living near Marble Arch and had joined the CHE group 4, which was a good mix of women and men. We had the idea to talk at Speakers' Corner, and as I was living nearby they would congregate in our house. Out we marched with a vacuum flask and the kitchen steps, and that's how I came out – getting up those steps and bellowing away at Speakers' Corner.

Those of us who weren't talking used to stand around the steps and hurl insults at each other so the crowd would come, and then we would vanish. I remember I was to Lord Soper's left, his sacrosanct spot, and suddenly there was this rush of people. I looked round and they all came rushing because it was a *woman* who was *white* . . . and I was told by Jill Tweedie that I was the first woman to speak there since Annie Drummond and the suffragettes. So there's a wonderful link.

I was nervous as hell, but when they heard what I was talking about – when I was saying, 'You are looking at a *roaring* lesbian who is alleged to do nasty things with girl guides' – their mouths fell wide open. But they stayed and we did a tremendous lot of trading behind the steps, because there were people from abroad who couldn't believe this, and so we introduced them to CHE . . . and we did that every Sunday for a very, very long time.

Personally, *inside*, it took much longer, because I had my first lesbian relationship in 1958 – that's when it started – and I really didn't come out until 1969/70. It's a great process of convincing *yourself*. From then on there was not really any problem. My parents were dead, my brother and sister-in-law knew and, of course, I was working in *Arena3* and Sappho and meeting a lot of lesbians. And there was always encouragement to get us to come out, and I still urge people, because of the *relief*, you know, when you've got to the other side. . . .

I'd moved into this house near Marble Arch with my lover Babs . . . and my sister-in-law came up to visit. Babs was showing her around, and there was this enormous double bed in the bedroom. . . . We had to sit down and say, 'This is the way it is.' She didn't take to it very easily and sort of guarded her children from us, which was pretty stupid. We both found – and it goes on still – how endlessly *dull* heterosexual couples are, so there wasn't any sense of worrying whether they approved or not.

My niece knows (she's a tremendous ally), so does my nephew (he doesn't know how to handle it). My niece is twenty-six and was born on my birthday, so we call each other twins. She comes along to lesbian do's and brings her chums, and there's absolutely no hang-up at all. She's very at ease with it, didn't go through any of the agony *we*'ve been through. She knows her own sexual identity, which is very straight.

There was a most gorgeous man [in CHE] called Vivian Waldron, and he was a very senior civil servant. He'd retired, so he *could* come out. He was talking about all the agony, the years of suppression . . . so I said: 'OK, Vivian, if you do it I will too', and having been in the theatre for years I could project and get the crowds around. There were two other women in the group, Jenny and Jo. Jenny got up and spoke, and so there were the two of us, with completely different things to offer – so much better than everybody getting the impression being a lesbian was like *me*, poor darlings.

I was always . . . *shaking* up those steps. We never had a handful of people there – it was an *enormous* gathering. A marvellous group called the Fanackerpans made it their business, when new speakers arrived who they didn't know, to go for them. The art of it is that you deal with them, get laughs or reactions, but you have got to keep talking to the others who can't hear and keep the narrative going. . . . It's rough the first time, till you get that technique. When we went to have a cup of tea at Joe Lyons, the Fanackerpans would come and join us and say good and right-on stuff.

I refused to be *gay* all along the line, because it was such a heavy male imprint. And so I always talked about myself as a lesbian, because I thought the more it's talked about the more it becomes like butter, rain or whatever. I developed into being a lesbian feminist through the Women's Movement, and then about late 1970s/early 1980s the lesbianism wasn't that important any more, so I became a *feminist lesbian*, opening up much more towards *all* women's causes and injustices, and so on. Never 'gay'. (I can't take 'queer', it's a highly pejorative word.) 'Dyke' I found very hard – it was my conditioning, I guess, that this was a great heavy masculine type of woman, this was the symbolism of the dyke for me – but now I have no problem with 'dyke' and reclaiming it. . . . It's just the repetition and the familiarity, it doesn't have any nightmares about it at all. But I can see women still insisting they are *gay*, and I think, 'Oh no, it's a betrayal,' all this dominance by male gayness which is quite alien to lesbians. ... It depresses me the amount of time lesbians are spending following the male gay patterns. I just wish they'd do some thinking about the *lesbian* identity.

I wasted over thirty years of my life having a heavy heterosexual phase. Maybe from the outside I should be bisexual, but after my first lesbian affair I went back to the straight scene, screwed men, knew I had been in love, completely loved in a way I didn't ever find with men. And then, when I found my second female lover, I just knew *this* is the way I am ... so I've never had any kind of fling-ettes with men since the early 1960s. The mould was set – that was Babs and we were together ten years.

I was in my forties when it all hit me, and I should have been having a little rose-cottage existence, waving off the children to careers, and so on. Even though I was having a relationship with another woman I didn't *like* being lesbian – I still thought it was dirty. And it was only through meeting other women and this whole marvellous digging around and consciousness-raising in lesbian feminism that I really *un*learned every-thing I had been brought up to believe, and thought, 'This is a load of *rubbish*'. And the relief, the release, was marvellous. ... All these fuzzy thoughts and things like 'You mustn't appear to be too bright because men won't like you' and 'Don't talk too much' and 'Be nice' – all that was such a terrible straitjacket on me.

And then, talking with feminists [who were] saying: 'But you don't have to be loved by everybody – find out what your identity is, share it,' it was like a real breakthrough, and after thirty-three years as a so-called straight. ... It was as though I had remained half alive all the time, and I am now a whole person. And I just think that if I had stayed straight with all the inhibitions and improprieties about it, I would have missed *so* much.

I can't deny the middle-class background. What was instilled in me by my parents were *injustices* – that's what really gets me up on my hind legs – and I haven't let those go. Certainly, in the early days when I first encountered the bar scene, which was the Gates and male gay clubs – they were sleazy and people weren't on the level – I suppose I was a snob about it and thought, 'I don't really like this.' So that hasn't let go, and I think that causes distance between the way I act and the way other people act. I would not climb down or go back on that just to please the general scene.

My father was an army surgeon. My mother was very much wife and mother, and very beautiful. I spent the first six years in India in the Raj days. I then came back and went to a 'home' prep school, then two public schools, and then did a stint at commercial college. They were very much British Legion, Red Cross and public service, which wasn't stuffy at all . . . so the kind of joining in any battle against injustice, the uniting for lost causes, is quite natural to me. I was a prospective Liberal candidate for Cheltenham, and it seemed natural one should take up the lesbian and gay movement, and the feminist movement, because the injustices are so unbelievable. And their wonderful zest and laughter and sharing – and *growing*.

WORK

I'd worked all my life. Theatre, then prime-time TV on BBC's *Tonight* programme. . . . Eventually I got to the stage where I couldn't go out covering events, because everybody wanted my autograph. I then took the plunge and went to America and, after a lot of nail-biting and agony, got on the TV shows I wanted to, and then met this amazing *breed* which I call the third sex. I mean, American women were like something I'd never seen in my life. They made their decisions about what they wanted to buy and where they wanted to live, and the men went along with them. This was the mid-1950s, and there wasn't a whisker of feminism about then. But I thought: 'Oh, they *are* bossy and overbearing' (terrible conditioning we'd had here). When the old feminist philosophy and words such as 'role-playing' and 'patriarchy' came along, I was ready to absorb,it, and had the examples of these women, with amazing freedom and licence, but very constrained at the same time.

When I was over there waiting to hit these TV shows, the English Speaking Union [ESU] asked me to go and speak at Boston. They said: 'We understand you are very well known in Britain. I longed to see Boston, because I was based in New York – foul city. So I left on the train, and was thinking what on earth am I going to talk about? So I thought I would do the TV programmes I'd done about the British, avoiding the ones that used a lot of close-up . . . and the technique on the [BBC] *Tonight* and *Highlight* programmes was the juxtaposition of the visual against what I was saying – a visual reporter, not a talking head.

At the ESU they were used to lectures, so they were all sitting there with their eyes closed. Died the death . . . but in the last ten minutes Mrs Humphries on the tea urn and Mrs Muller on the coffee urn opened their eyes to look at their watches, looked up and saw what I was doing and choked, which woke up the other women. So the last five minutes were hilarious. . . . There was a scout there for a lecture bureau called Columbia and she said: 'You must sign with our office'. I said OK, signed the contract, came back here, forgot all about it and then this massive envelope arrived in August saying I would tour, and these tickets for trains and planes came out like Christmas decorations.

I did women's clubs, conferences – the whole lecture circuit. This lecture bureau would book all these, and they had agents all around the States who had their areas. It was the most amazing system. . . . Very good money. I used to go back every autumn and tour. . . . I had a collection of themes – herring fishing on the North Sea for twenty-four hours, Paris fashion shows, hunting, Queen Charlotte's Ball . . . I would try and suss which they would go for.

Apart from that, I'd fallen madly in love with Babs, and Kate Millett's *Flying* is absolutely what I was going through – you know, this outer calm and, inside, this turmoil and who could I talk to? . . . It was an astonishing experience. And travelling these *huge* distances, and learning about America, their language and their thinking – each place was different. I owe a great debt to America for having made me wake up. I was never polite. I was emphatic and adamant, because that's what Americans said you must be . . . and then having this incredible transformation into women . . .

In the early 1960s I ended up in Canada and stayed there for about four years, in Toronto, doing TV there. My sister-in-law pupped for the first time – she's the only woman in her family and I'm the only one in mine, so I had to come and be supportive. The child arrived, and before that I had taken a producer's and director's course on telly and had got a job with a CBC [Canadian Broadcasting Company] afternoon programme. But while I was in the UK there was the most enormous upheaval . . . and everybody I knew was fired or left. A friend of mine whom I was replacing said: 'Don't come back, you probably will find you don't have a job, stay where you are.'

I listened to her . . . and went and worked for Border Television, and wrote a provincial page on the Lakes and Borders for *She* magazine. I did that for about two years, then went back to America because of having met Babs in Canada. She'd moved to America, and we were meeting up again with all this terrible pond-hopping. Babs came over to England and we set up house in 1968, just when everything was breaking in London – the GLF, the Women's Movement, very early tendrils like Juliet Mitchell and Sheila Rowbotham. Perfect timing for what I call my informative years.

I was still hanging on to men through GLF and CHE. I was on the executive committee of CHE, GLF was beginning to fold, and it was very much male-dominated politics, which I didn't question, and nor did any of the women – we joined CHE because what else was there to join? Then it was the Women's Movement because, having heard Juliet Mitchell talking and the way the whole meeting was unstructured, it was like a foreign language, but something said: 'I must learn this, learn what they are talking about.' And so did Babs. So we went back to another meeting, and, again, there was this astonishing jargon going on.

The lesbian scene was monthly meetings with *Arena* 3, where you came up against a complete *antithesis* ... I mean, they didn't care a bit about whether we were being oppressed by men: they were just looking for another woman, or they wanted to come out as a couple and have a beer and a chat. ... so it was trying to get the two things together in *me* first, which was drinking in all this feminist stuff, banging away about it to lesbians – and yet it was the lesbian *actuality* of not relying on men emotionally, financially, physically. Ti-Grace Atkinson said it beautifully – that feminism is the theory but lesbianism is the practice ... but it took an awful lot of talking and listening and writing and conferences and stand-up rows. ... A lot of verbal screwing used to go on, but it was women *boiling* with this energy – whether lesbian or straight – but not finding the words for it, and that's what started the shouting.

I think the most influential group was Women in Media [WIM], working with these marvellous Fleet Street wordsmiths – and women on radio and TV. Very, very articulate women. They had their male connections and they *could* find the words, and there was the concept – all of which came out of WIM – of 'Why aren't there women newsreaders?'

The huge climax in 1974 was the Sex Discrimination Acts – three Green Papers, three White Papers. ... To learn all that House of Commons technique and all the Private Member's Bills: this was a world we'd never thought of, that we'd go streaming into the Houses of Parliament and tell them what should go into the Act – and be listened to. A lot of lesbians came too, because Sappho was very much involved in all that, and it would get into the magazine and then people would come to the meetings.

Then we had the brilliant idea of fielding the first women's rights candidate, in 1974: Dr Una Kroll, a wonderful deaconess, bless her. So here we were fielding a candidate, finding the deposit, getting all the publicity, going to the count. ... Again, not a man around. OK, Una didn't do terribly well with votes, but she got all the inches in the press and TV and radio – and abroad. And of course this was the first one since the suffragettes. I would say the bulk of women actually committed in the Movement, who didn't drop in when they finished their job, were lesbians and on the dole ... and we used state money to overthrow the status quo and fight for all these things.

Sappho had to come out every month. We had an office, monthly discos and weekly meetings, so that was completely full time. But so many people came forward to help it was just marvellous, and that's where I retained the collective concept, rather than being a separatist, although I reckon from 1974 on I was moving more and more into women's pragmatic action, rather than staying with the men.

I think contending with being a lesbian, an outsider – where to go, whether you are going to be attacked or whatever – is very absorbing. I thought a lot about it. . . . However, life changes and with all the politicking and getting to know some wonderful women, being a lesbian was not a problem any more, but being a *woman* was. And so it shifted. The *woman* came first. ... It was as though we had gone to the very *horizon* of lesbianism and we could take off or step out, but there was this much wider horizon of being a woman in society – work and care of kids, health, law. . . . That didn't deny any existence of lesbianism, it just meant it was all part of this wider thing.

In the 1980s those things were kept right up front. They have moved to one side now. There is not sufficient child care for women, and a lot of lesbians are having children. They're not having to have one-offs and marriage like the previous generations of lesbians had to, pre-Pill. And yet as lesbians we are job-based and we've got to earn money. Everyone says we are sex-crazed, but if there is a choice between sex and money, my God, one goes for the money and the job. Therefore, it is crucial that there should be nurseries. . . . It's not always that you can have a cosy mate to look after your child while you go out to work: *she's* got to work, too. That's all very basic stuff, but it should be always in focus.

Now you see, the guys don't have any of that problem at all. *They* don't care about having children, they don't mind offering semen in AID. *Now* there's the problem of AIDS. HIV and AIDS are appalling, but there are an enormous number of lesbians with breast cancer and other cancers, which never get a mention. There are women doing incredible contributions for HIV and AIDS, and yet cancer is never mentioned ...

Apparently in New York there's a purple ribbon sold from the AIDS support groups which is about cancer, so if you are wearing a purple ribbon your contribution goes towards cancer ... [But] people are so scared of cancer, it's such a *gloomy* kind of thing to have ... and to go rattling the bucket for breast cancer without it being really thought out – although I think it's absolutely crucial, it's got to be done in an incredibly imaginative way. And then, when you have the money, what are you going to do with it? Do you give it to a support group, or do you plunge it into this endless, bottomless research? . . . So one needs a lot of people getting together who have got it, have been cured of it, who care about people who have had it.

MORE ABOUT WORK

I toured the UK for Maurice Frost, a lecture agent. I was still churning out the same old stuff as on the American circuit, which worked very well. . . . Then I did get poor. I did a tally round. There was a shop called Edward Evans in Hammersmith, and I'd get in my little van and go and put my foot in the door and get people to buy a teapot and pay off 2/6 a week or something. I did that mostly in the evenings, which left me the afternoons to keep Sappho going. It was pretty shitty work, especially when we discovered that men doing the identical job were getting double the money. So we took it up with the TGWU and they said, 'We can't just come marching in.' About fifteen women were there and he called us 'Brothers'. Honestly! . . . (Funnily enough, we found out that four of us were lesbians, two became great friends, and one had a new lover who came to Sappho.) So we left. There was no way of it being unionized.

I'd got the basic salary and commission on what was sold. What I found more enjoyable was that it was like being a social worker. They'd say, 'Come and sit down, dear' and you had to – she was an old lady on her own, or the woman would come out with a shiner from terrible *scenes* the day before. That was fascinating, and just up the Harrow Road there was a tremendous black section and they invited me to a wedding. It was wonderful. I was the only white person. I loved the contact: it was a complete eye-opener, a whole new side of life . . . and that went on for about eighteen months.

Sappho was in our dining-room then. About 1975, Sappho moved out into Wardour Street, and at that time I was teaching [drama], because I thought, 'I must have some male balance.' I met this very interesting woman, Beryl, an educational officer at Ashford prison in Middlesex, and I also taught at Latchmere Remand Centre. I did that for about two years.

The Latchmere kids I couldn't stand – they were very bolshie, hardened criminals at something like ten years old. I didn't know how to handle them because they were children, but the guys at Ashford were different – much more interesting characters. At sixteen they would go to Ashford, and at twenty-one they would go to the Scrubs. The Ashford ones were more adult, we had very good classes then. I was on LBC with Denis Lemon (then editor of *Gay News*) talking about Gay Pride. It was a phone-in in the evening, and next day I went buzzing off to Ashford. And as I was walking from the gate past the 'box' where all the gate screws were, into the building, I passed them all and heard, 'Hallo, lessie'. I stopped in my tracks and thought, 'I'm not going to let this go. How dare they? I am *staff*.' I remember taking this deep breath and turning round, and just like little boys they all scattered, and I walked into the place and said, 'What was that you said?' 'I don't know what you are talking about, Miss.' I said, 'I distinctly heard the word lessie. I presume you heard the programme on LBC last night?' The most senior one said, 'No, we didn't, but all the lads who had radios in their cells did.' I thought, 'Oh my God, what am I facing when I go in today?'

However, I came into the class, and they didn't giggle or hoot at me. They were like little *angels* sitting there, these kids of eighteen or nineteen, in rows – packed class. I thought, 'When's it going to happen?', and then one of them said, 'Was that you on the radio last night, Miss?' I said, 'Yes – why?' 'Are you one of those lessies then?' I said, 'Yes.' 'Cor!' ... It was astonishing. I thought, 'They're not going for me,' – I, too, was *outside*, outside the law. Then they said, 'W*hy*?', and I said, 'Well, *having* a woman's body, a woman's body is very familiar, whereas a man's body is something different. ... By the way, can any of you draw women's genitalia?' 'Women's what, miss – er, Jackie?' '*You* know, like your winkie – draw the women's quim.' Anyway, one did, and I looked. ... Absolutely amazing how ignorant they were. No clitoris, of course, and no outer and inner labia. So I said, 'Now I'll show you how it's done,' and I called them and they said, 'C*or*! didn't know that,' and they were all grinning away. The screws were looking, and I don't know what they thought I was drawing. ... It was the most hysterically interesting class. At the end of it I was *shaking* ... and I thought, 'Well, if I can get through this there's nothing to fear.'

Then, when Beryl left – she was awfully nice – this Welsh guy came in, he was terrible. Beryl used to go and winkle all the boys out of their cells, whereas this guy wouldn't. So we had about two or three to a class – it was monstrous. In the end he said, 'I think we can dispense with your services', which was a pity because I was earning a lot of money.

That took me into 1977. After that I was totally Sappho until the early 1980s. Then I worked for a vascular surgeon, and from there I went to the British School At Rome in about 1984. We published amazing antique stuff from all these professors. ... We ran a competition every year for students who painted. If they won they had a whole year paid for in Rome. It was an incredible organization: this one woman ran it, who I got very fond of, there was *the* accountant and me – and we were the staff.

There were subscribers who had to be sent information. The language in all the documents was so sexist – everybody was *he*, so I soon had that changed. My boss was a pale feminist, but she thoroughly approved and we got it through. . . . There were these amazing people – women – who I don't think were safe. Incredible minds and thoughts, all living in the past or in canvases. Couldn't cross the street! . . . I'd never been to university – theatre was my university – and to meet these academics was fascinating. They closed the office down because of the lira *vis-à-vis* the pound and the ERM, and so on. . . . Everything was run from Rome and, I presume, still is.

They were good to me, because I should have left a year before, at sixty-five. They asked me to stay on another eight months until they closed the office down. I finished in 1991. It was a very nice salary and a beautiful setting in Regent's Park, all the students buzzing about. . . . I knew I had a very good reference, so I applied for other jobs . . . I really am up against it – the *age*. I doctored my age a bit, but I got terribly muddled working it out, doing it all in reverse.

That was a full, nice life. I was enjoying it thoroughly and that was what made it so hard to adjust to being redundant. I'd always promised, when I had free time, that I would help out at the Lesbian Archives – nothing had been done for years, and I used to get neurotic about the amount of work needing to be done. . . . Because there are no grants and no funding, and it is all voluntary, people are terribly enthusiastic for about three months. . . . But it's nice being among books and the sort of people who come in doing research – and the *treasures* in there. . . . The books, pictures, film, videos, postcards. . . . You think: 'God! Lesbians are *special*.'

I have never really *chosen* what to do, I have kind of dropped into it. The other thing I was 'midwife' to was the Lesbian and Gay Centre, which, again, the GLC [Greater London Council] got off the ground. I was in the working group that met at County Hall, and the women's group. Both combined to suggest the centre, found the property and the GLC said OK, which was very philanthropic. . . . And I was absolutely *purple* with the way those guys were running it, that appalling loss of money. . . . It was heartbreaking – and then to be told it was *closed*.

I was shocked to read in a Kenric newsletter and the gay press that *Sappho* was closing down. They had no mandatory right to do this. Nobody had been consulted. . . . Another woman rang me up and said: 'Who do they think they are? We'll have a meeting.' So I was sucked into all this, and then we decided to call it *Sappho Rising*. So it was like a new era, bringing it more into the 1990s.

People's eyebrows were going up and down because we had a display of sex toys, and there were non-sex toys, and people (in teams) had to tick whether they were sex toys or not, and if they won they got a prize. Then we had Kimberley Ann who pumps iron – tiny, five foot two, amazing body, delightful woman (straight). She gave a talk about how she got into pumping iron and winning all these championships. . . . Then she said, 'I will show you what I do'. She disappeared and came back in the flimsiest, briefest costume, and you saw this amazing muscle. I mean, this is Sappho?! . . . Then there were the serious speakers (e.g. Helena Kennedy and Alison Halford). . . .

I think now women just come in . . . and *use* Sappho and go away again; whereas before, it was their input that was so important, all those groups starting up – women came in with the ideas and suggestions and the collective carried them out or supported them. And so people would come to the meetings with some reason to be there, and I miss that. You can sit alongside two or three women all evening, with a speaker and questions, and you don't know anything more about them than at the beginning of the meeting. And they don't turn up again, because they got out of it what they wanted.

It is almost like migratory flocks coming in and moving on somewhere else. I was noticing that happening some years back and it depressed me . . . Of course, it was terribly lucky having the [Sappho] office and an address during the week – and the magazine. Women knew what they were coming to before they got there. They knew it was safe. The discos would attract a young crowd, who would then hear about the meetings. . . . More than once we had sixteen-year-olds and younger coming to the discos and meetings. I've always maintained it was far better they were in with us than wandering about the streets or moping at home, and I would rehearse them, I'd say, 'When were you born?' and 'How old are you?' 'Sixteen.' I said, 'That won't *do*, you can't be here in a pub . . . you've got to work out that you are eighteen and a half and *then* when you were born,' and they got very good at it. There was no threat to them and they were safe.

I remember one time – around 1977 – when we were at the Chepstow at Notting Hill Gate, a woman said to me, 'Psst! I want you to meet my friend.' And this was a policewoman off duty, but she was a lesbian and she said, 'I am just tipping you off that your discos [at the Sols Arms] are going to be raided. They are wondering if there are drugs, and what about the age limit?' So for a whole month the NCCL [Liberty] had an observer in there, and the solicitor said he'd help if we went to the law. So we inked his phone number on the inside of our wrists, and we were there ready, poised, every single Saturday ...

MONOGAMY

I watch with green and yellow envy all these babies skipping about, playing musical chairs. I missed all that for those thirty or so years of heterosexual phase. ... Personally, I am physically monogamous, I can't cope with more than one person at a time, but emotionally I am non-monogamous. I am very fond of some women, and I know they are of me, but there isn't the sexual push or desire for them – and they are the ones who last. ... I have never known multiple relations to work. I have seen people suffering, especially bisexual women. If you are bisexual or are in a 'multi' relationship, you are always *leaving* somebody, never going *to* anybody. What a state to be in – I couldn't possibly do that.

And this moving into SM – I am very leery about that. I was in New York around 1982 and went to Barnard University. Pat Califia, who wrote *Coming to Power*, was there. I had been to the women's centre and they were all up in the air about this and said, 'There has got to be a feminist response.' Barnard were so shocked at this they refused to circulate any papers or have any mention of this feminist conference. We were talking in the women's house, and they were all debating this new ideology and feminism, when in came this beautiful young blonde thing, all tanned, wheeling her bike into the room. She had come from San Francisco for this conference and she said, 'I just want you to know that Pat Califia and her group saved me from suicide, because I thought I was the only one in the world – I am a masochist.' Well, our mouths dropped open, we were looking for these terrible wounds. She had a flawless body and, of course, stopped us all in our tracks. So we said, 'Would you like to talk about it?', and she did. ...

She said it's mostly fantasy, it doesn't actually happen. I read *Coming to Power* and found it a big yawn. If these women are going to put on all these clothes-pegs and chains and masses of leather and be strapped to the bed, does the sexual desire survive all this? And how do you get out of it all?

The SM group here in Britain joined the lesbian Pride parade [the penultimate parade with the Sappho banner] and we met up in Holland Park and walked through High Street Kensington ... While we were ...

getting the banner out, a woman came and said, 'Jackie, can you come and settle an argument. . . . The feminists will not have the SM banner on the march.' I said, 'Well, what can I do?' 'Perhaps you can facilitate,' she said. I said, 'I'll do my best . . . '. And there were these enormously tall women, all in leather and tattooed – and this banner, which was so witty with women's signs like handcuffs all over it. . . . The only way I could reason was by saying, 'If we as a class of women are oppressed by the patriarchal heterosex society, how can we be judgemental about another minority? If we are saying, "Get off our backs", how can we say to a section of women, "No, you can't"? Are we not acting like heterosexuals?' [The SM group stayed at the back and the march moved off.]

I've never really resolved it but, again, the sense of injustice, of women dividing and being judgemental of other women – we can't afford to let that happen. . . . I remember being asked to dinner by this beautiful German woman in Toronto who used to buy from the furniture shop I was working in. It was a fabulous dinner and we had wine. . . . She's straight, and she disappeared, then I heard her voice from another room saying, 'Come on in, Jackie.' I went in there and she was stark naked on the bed lying face down and there was this ruddy great leather strap, and she said, 'Do it for me, hit me.' 'What with?' 'That strap.' I thought, 'Oh my God . . . .' She said, 'Harder, harder.' When these welts started coming up, I flew to the loo and threw up this exquisite dinner into the bog.

So I know I can't do it. There is some tremendous inner anger I have inherited at mutilation of a woman's body. So I know I can't compete in this or join it. At the same time, who am I to say, 'No, you can't?'

QUEER

I'm very anti-dildo. Why do we want to ape men? That puzzles me. Of the lovers I've had and couples I know, nobody has said they used dildos, so I don't know who these women are. . . . And this whole idea of queer politics – [the idea that] you can still define yourself as lesbian even if you sleep with gay guys and straight men – this, to me, is *crazy*. What I feel is happening is that lesbians are moving into male concepts as stereotypical dykes. Like the old days when a married woman in a lesbian group couldn't say that she was a mum and a *married* mum, I wonder whether we've been so repressed. . . . Nobody ever dared *talk* about wanting a dildo or using one, or being into SM. So who knows whether it is something that has been terribly suppressed, and that more women are getting to hear about it so that they are experimenting or going into it?

But it does seem to me that it is boxing us back into the 'box' of sex, and we spent a long time in the 1970s getting out of that. We did work, we had families and relatives and were committed to all sorts of things: politics, theatre, reading, books, gardening, housework, the whole thing. . . . Having broken out of that stereotypical sex-mad discussion, so-called politics is putting us back in that sex container again. I worry about it. . . . I still haven't got the courage, even when I go out and meet women I don't know, to say to them, 'Are you into SM?' I might get a real thump. Because there isn't the sort of group meeting where one can say, 'This will be the topic', and people will come and talk about it in 'consciousness-raising' style, can we ever find out?

Julia Tant

fifty-five, artist

I was in one of the very first Women's Liberation groups in this country – in Camberwell [South London]. It originally started in Peckham around 1969. I was having therapy at the time because of my sexuality. I'd come out and was then living with a woman. . . . I was a civil servant in Brixton and having a terrible time at work, being victimized. My therapist said I needed some support. I immediately said 'Women's Liberation', and he said: 'Why don't you join?' I said: 'I don't know where it is' – because you didn't see a list of them in the paper or anything. . . . Anyway, I discovered there was a group, phoned them, and that's how I started going.

I was living as a working-class person and didn't think of myself in any way as middle class . . . so I went to this group and I'd never been in such a big house in my life (it was in Camberwell). So the whole thing was quite disorientating for me.

Later they broke up into two groups and I joined the second group, and for the first time I was around a lot of middle-class educated women. I wasn't thinking in terms of *class*, but was aware that I couldn't just talk when I felt like it – I had to be careful, watch my manners. I felt really on my own. I didn't know anyone that was gay in the group either, they all seemed very hetero, so I wasn't going to open up with that too quickly.

Soon after that we met to talk about getting a women's centre together. It was about 1970 and we'd been meeting for about six months. They were busy discussing it all the time; whereas I wanted to just get on and *do* it, which is much more working class. I couldn't understand why they were having all these long deliberations over it, so I suggested a way we could do it – and I personally found them a house to have as a women's centre, in Vauxhall. Lots of things started to happen there – the first group for lesbians . . . I wasn't out then, but I helped to get this group going. We had a party, then I started going to the only feminist disco at that time, at the

Crown and Woolpack in Islington. By then everybody knew I was gay. I'd been with my girlfriend for three or four years and she didn't want to know about Women's Liberation at all.

I remember going to my first conference out of London, and feeling quite out of my depth again because there were such articulate women there. Women like Selma James of Wages For Housework were talking about world issues, and at the time all I wanted to talk about was something quite mundane, like being treated badly in my job, and I thought, 'I daren't bring that up here, they'll think I'm an idiot', so I kept very quiet. But as time went on and they had an action here, an action there, I'd go and join in, without realizing I was actually getting educated. I was changing how I spoke, learning to be confident. Finally, the time came when I stood up and said something, and before I knew it I was up on the platform speaking.

I got to know the women, I'd go to discos with them. And there would be the gay group versus the heteros, because at that time the Women's Movement didn't want to know about gay women because it might give the movement a bad name. So I was part of that whole *bandwagon*, and that made me strong because we were all united. I don't even know when the change came, I just know that it came and I became a different person. Even my family must have noticed it as well.

Though I didn't become conscious of it for ages, the class thing really started to take off – I can remember middle-class women standing on the platform saying, 'The Women's Movement can never grow until we bring in working-class women,' and I thought. 'What are they talking about? I'm a working-class woman and I'm already in here'. So I would put up my hand to speak, and say, 'Well, I'm working class', and they would just ignore me. This went on, and then I stopped saying it. I thought, 'They just don't want to hear.'

I joined the commune in South London when my relationship was coming to an end. It was the beginning of the end when I bought a 'Sisterhood Is Powerful' poster and put it on my wall at home. My partner told me to take it down – she said. 'We're not having things like that in the flat.' I wanted a room of my own, which meant we didn't sleep together any more. So I had my own room and put the poster over my bed, then I wrote to a newspaper and said, 'I've joined Women's Liberation', and somebody came around to interview me. I really got into it in a big way.

We didn't split up immediately – it was two or three years later, a slow process. Then I had to find somewhere to live quickly. I was now unemployed (I had given up the crappy job in the civil service), then I discovered some women were squatting, so I thought, 'Maybe I can join them', and that's exactly what I did. And that's how my whole life changed: from living in a very nice flat, with a car and a regular nine-to-five job, I end up in this squat where there's mice and no electricity. I got rid of my car and bought a little motorbike, and changed the way I dressed. I couldn't buy nice clothes any more, so overnight I became this completely different person, and cut my hair.

I was living in this gay community, in a squat, and feeling ever so depressed, having a sort of nervous breakdown, and I thought, 'I shouldn't be feeling like this. I've been in the Women's Movement for nearly ten years, I should be feeling really good.' They were having a party, it was a lovely hot summer's day (that hot summer of 1976) and although I felt spaced out and terrible, I decided I'd go along.

When I got there there were these big cheeses on the table, loads of records and loads of dope, and out in the garage were all these musical instruments: beautiful drum kits, trumpets, guitars ... and all of the women were sitting around smoking. They had a massive birthday cake and everyone was smoking joints and had their arms around each other, swaying to this feminist music – and I didn't feel like any of it. I didn't feel close to these women ... and I was thinking, 'We're all on the dole: how can they [afford] this and I can't? I must be really badly organized and un-together.' I couldn't have a party like this, I couldn't even afford to buy dope ... I thought I must just be antisocial, so I went back home.

I had a nice little squat, probably one of the nicest. There were two whole roads, all women. ... The middle-class women were trying to be downwardly mobile, dropping out; whereas I was trying to drop *up*. So I got my squat all nice and neat, little plants everywhere. ... As it happened, the squats were right on the council estate in Vauxhall where I'd grown up. Of course, the paving stones were still the same paving stones that I'd walked on as a child, but to all the middle-class feminists who were squatting, being downwardly mobile, it was like a foreign country because it was a very rough working-class neighbourhood, particularly at that time. It was all right for them, they could always go back to Mum and Dad. ...

I knew the reason why I was different, why I couldn't have big cheeses and all that, was this topic – *class* – which we never discussed. We were always supposed to be classless. ... [But] these women's parents were providing them with all this stuff. I didn't have parents who could do anything like that. In the beginning I only thought about class in a very *personal* way, like my feelings about being in this room with all these educated women. I was conscious of the fact that I was inferior to them. I thought they were exciting, and I wanted to learn to be like them.

I started my own feminist disco in Vauxhall after the Crown and Woolpack pub in North London closed. It went on for five years. Hundreds of women came twice a week, it was very famous in the 1970s, and so much to do with the feminist movement happened there. We played one of the first feminist records from the States there, by Chris Williamson, and a women's band, the Stepney Sisters Rock Band, played.

A woman called Joan came to stay in my squat. The two of us introduced [the title] 'Ms' to this country. About eight women stood outside the Passport Office with placards, we phoned the *Guardian*, made some leaflets. Within a week an airline announced they would start using 'Ms', and it snowballed. We managed to make it happen. People nowadays say, 'You can't do that, it will take for ever,' and I say, 'But you can – Joan and I did it.' You could then. Two women could go off and practically change the world.

I didn't have a smooth departure at all [from the Women's Movement], nor did Joan. ... She ended up having a breakdown. Fortunately, I held myself together. I've lived alone since my girlfriend went back to Australia in 1979. From then on I started doing things independently: I wrote letters to newspapers, did things for Stonewall. Then I got to art school, which was a big change in my life.

I went to St Martin's in 1985. It was a miracle that I got in because I'd done no art whatsoever. I saw this tiny ad in *City Limits*: 'Mature students wanted for a degree course. No qualifications necessary'. It was a five-year part-time course, in Fine Art and Critical Studies. It didn't address the class issue as I'd expected and I went through hell, but I did a good degree. No grant. I had to buy my own materials, which I couldn't afford on my dole money, but a charity helped me. I wrote to hundreds ... I lived on the dole, plus £150 from this charity. I eked it out over three years (with about £75 from another charity that helped older women). I finished art college in 1990. I left with a pound in my bank account but I managed to find a charity to give me £50 and eked that out to do a 9-month art project on Men in Drag. Then I had an exhibition (Voices of Women) at the Drill Hall and as a result of the (ensuing) publicity Greater London Arts came to see me and ended up giving me £1000, which, for me, was a lot of money.

So although it took me a long time and I had to go through a whole process of leaving my full-time job and changing into this alternative lifestyle, when I did decide to listen to those middle-class women it finally got me to where I'd wanted to be all my life: art school. I never could have gone there without having learned to live and survive in an 'alternative' way.

I did learn a lot. I changed to dress like them. They wore jeans and T-shirts: I started wearing jeans and T-shirts. Even how I talk is different. My family see me as being middle class now because of the way I talk. . . . Even my flat and the way I live in it is 'alternative' to the way my sister and my mum live. They think it's bizarre that I don't have a three-piece suite or central heating, a washing machine or fitted units. To them I'm this funny, 'alternative' person.

I see myself now as an educated, older, working-class feminist lesbian. I don't put them in a particular order, because your power shifts depending on the situation you are in. It's flexible.

It's harder to find lesbians to identify with. There are quite a lot of lesbians like myself who are not post-feminist lesbians or SM lesbians, and who are having the hardest, most isolating time. It's not at all acceptable to be a lesbian who doesn't want to fit into those categories. We have gone backwards. . . . It's very depressing. I just think we need to be more vocal. We've got to fight back.

*L*inda *B*ellos

forty-five, political activist, management consultant

I became a lesbian in 1980. It feels like it was only yesterday, and yet it also feels a lifetime. I have lived a new life since becoming a lesbian, it's been wonderful. In 1970 I got married. I was a heterosexual woman for ten years, for the whole of the 1970s, a period in which I felt like I was in prison. I had no idea what was going on in the rest of the world. I had two children.

I had absolutely no idea that I could be a lesbian. I knew the *word*, but I saw lesbians as white, and it hadn't occurred to me that I could be a lesbian. In 1980 I found this wasn't the case. I met somebody, C., and I realized that the feelings I had towards her were love. I spoke to her about it. She was the first lesbian I had met who had been out, a much younger woman than I, and she was very nice. She said that she was very flattered but that she couldn't have a relationship with me because I was married. I thought that was quite reasonable, but the more I thought about it the more I thought my feelings towards this woman were as natural as my so-called heterosexuality, and 'how come I never knew about this before?'

So, some of the things that I had learned about feminism – and from feminism – and had previously rejected, suddenly made sense, and I realized that there was a very *compulsory* element about heterosexuality, that we are not given a choice. I certainly wasn't, it wasn't on the agenda, and to some extent it still isn't, even though more and more of us are out. It is not something that every woman thinks about equally and then says: 'No, I prefer men'. Being a lesbian is such a *discouraged* activity, lifestyle, way of seeing the world, that I think it is true to say that heterosexuality is compulsory.

Meeting my first girlfriend, [N.], opened up that potential, but I was never persuaded by the logic that because it's difficult, therefore it couldn't be done. After all, it was difficult for me to be a black child in the 1950s. I didn't know this at the time, but apparently there were only 30,000 black people in Britain in 1950, the year I was born. It's very hard to be one of 30,000 in a population of what was then 50 million. But that's not a reason not to go out there and struggle and be yourself.

Love and lust were my motivators, and the politics was utterly essential to make sense of it. Without the politics of feminism, I don't think that I would have made sense of it. I might have continued to be a married woman who had affairs with women – I don't know. It was more than the object of *desire*: everything about feminism, and what feminism was saying, made sense about who I was.

I had always been a dutiful daughter. My way of getting away from my parents was to get married, and then after about four years I had children and did everything in a rather traditional way. [But] I discovered that there was more to me than just servicing other people. Being a lesbian is actually about being my own person.

When I realized that I fancied C. I defined myself as bisexual. I didn't think that I could *own* the title lesbian, because I didn't think I deserved it. I was living with a man, and it didn't seem to be appropriate. But once I'd met and gone to bed with N. I knew I was a lesbian, and I called myself a lesbian. Subsequently, it was necessary to define myself as a *black lesbian*, because it became immediately obvious to me that white lesbians saw me first and foremost as black. I'm talking about a period of tremendous euphoria and change.

I do find some men quite attractive – aesthetically attractive. I don't want to sleep with them. I wouldn't deny that some are beautiful. I just don't want to have that sort of relationship with them.

In the 1970s I was involved in community politics, a lot of stuff around my children – like the Queen's Park Community Association in Brighton. There is a sand pit in the park, and I was one of the leading lights behind it and made it happen. Organized a rota and dug. Got planning permission from East Sussex County Council. ...

I went to university in 1978. Prior to that I had been a finance worker. I worked in the Inland Revenue, then as a tax consultant for a while, and then I read politics at Sussex [University]. I went to a Students' Union lesbian and gay conference. There was a resolution and a presentation from PIE [Paedophile Information Exchange], and I spoke and organized against it, even though I was rather on my own on the issue. Most people didn't understand it. There is a very successful libertarian argument that anything goes, we are all oppressed minorities. It's still being used and I find it pretty distasteful.

And yet I am in fact opposed to censorship and would be described by a former colleague and lover, Sheila Jeffreys, as totally liberal. I am not. I am pragmatic, more than she is. I wish to counter some of the libertarian argument by being engaged with it as opposed to distancing myself and having 'safe space', as Sheila would put it. (We became lovers in 1981, for about nine months. It was terribly stormy – we're two quite strong personalities.) My current lover has a nice way of putting it: she says she's sick to death of being *against* things, she wants to be *for* them. I was initially quite interested in Feminists Against Censorship, but I really don't want to have an argument with one group of people versus another who wilfully misunderstand and misinterpret each other.

I got my degree and came back to London in 1981. I was on to my second [lesbian] relationship by then. ... I think it was absolutely right that I should have been a separatist, to help me get out of and away from the effects of heterosexuality, and having achieved that, I don't have to stay there. I think as a *process* it is essential for many of us. ... For my own part, I found that a period of complete separation was necessary to give me space away from men. I don't know whether I ever particularly deferred to them, but I certainly had to worry about their bloody egos ... and the constant reassurance that men always wanted, and still do. If I had been in a position of being close to them I wouldn't have had the space to think about what *I* felt about the world, as opposed to what I was worried about saying in front of them. Now, I feel sufficiently secure in my politics that I can be with them, because I am not interested in their egos, I am not there to reassure them and, if anything, I am accused of being a ball crusher – that's to say, I don't let them get their own way just because they're men.

Separatism was very necessary at that time, and many women continue to need it. I have slight problems about separatism as an end in itself. I think it gives men more power than they deserve. That's why I personally don't feel a tremendous desire to withdraw entirely from men, because I don't think it changes the world.

Working collectively, there were power struggles, but human relationships are about negotiating power. I found feminist practice and feminist process infinitely preferable to the 'left' stuff I had been familiar with previously. I was also involved in 'left' politics in Brighton, and the very doctrinaire way in which men operate. It was such a refreshing change to have a much more accommodating feminist process – and yes, we argued violently, but nobody said, 'You are not a feminist', unlike the 'You are not a socialist' argument or 'You are not really black'. So I experienced argument and dissent among women, and I found that positively healthy. People didn't break into their own separate groups, not speaking, and just condemn each other. . . .

When I joined the Women's Liberation Movement, my recollections are about working with, and respecting, women with very different points of view to me. I am still friends with them. I think of the co-operation there was among revvies and raddies – and, to some extent, socialist feminists. . . . There were two groups with slightly differing analyses, and we worked together. There was no political correctness of one view. I'd always experienced 'ideological soundness' as a joke. I used to do things like have sugar, and if I could get white sugar I'd use white sugar in my tea and coffee because it was ideologically unsound. I used to eat meat and drink alcohol and smoke cigarettes. And I do all those things now, because those aspects of political correctness used to drive me bananas, and so I used to do the opposite – except that I have now stopped smoking.

I define myself as a revolutionary feminist. I worked with radical feminists and socialist feminists on those issues to which we felt we had something useful to contribute. Someone would put an advert in the London Women's Liberation newsletter, calling a meeting on an issue. If I was interested I would go, and I might find some of my revvy friends there and I might find some of my raddy friends . . . I didn't have many socialist friends. Although I have always been a socialist and a feminist, I never defined myself as a socialist feminist, because my experience of socialist feminism is of middle-class do-gooding.

Whenever they talked about the working class it was 'those poor working-class women *over there*'. Working-class women are always white. Then there were black women. . . . I found the academic approach of socialist feminists as oppressive as anything that men ever did. It was not grounded in personal experience, and where they did try to talk about personal experience then they had to revert to Freud and psychoanalysis. . . . I felt that my revolutionary feminism and radicalism were about wholeness and a holistic approach to the world. I am not saying that they weren't also flawed, but there were elements of a kind of ideology of feminism which I continue to think are crucial.

Those women who still consider themselves revolutionary feminists would probably say that I am *not*, because of membership of the Labour Party and working with men, but scratch the surface of my feminism and you will find the same analysis as they have.

Early on I felt very marginalized as a feminist. What was articulated, demanded, had nothing to do with me. I remember one of the first things I did as a feminist – and to me, being a feminist and a lesbian feminist were the same – was to say at a NAC [National Abortion Campaign] conference: 'I can't support abortion on demand because it has a disproportionate effect on black working-class and white working-class women.' Free abortion on demand was essentially a demand from white middle-class women, but when you are black and working-class you can get an abortion, easily. I know of somebody who has been compulsorily sterilized against her will: a working-class woman, not a middle-class woman. And that analysis wasn't in the Women's Liberation Movement. That's why I couldn't relate to it. . . .

Joining the WAVAW [Women Against Violence Against Women] campaign, I felt – and still feel – that it is the one issue on which *all* women have a common experience. Whether you are working as a prostitute, whether you are walking down the street, whether you are the Queen, you could be threatened by men *as men* because you are a woman.

Sheila [Jeffreys] was one of the founder members of the Central London WAVAW, and has to be credited with the campaign *per se*. We spearheaded a whole series of Reclaim the Night marches in the early 1980s. . . . In 1983 I had dropped out of the Women's Liberation Movement – lots of us had. It had become so contentious, and there were so many fundamental arguments that could not be reconciled that I, like many other women, increasingly withdrew. I joined Black Sections of the Labour Party, and put all my energy into that. I was also at that time working at the GLC women's unit.

In 1981 I joined *Spare Rib*, the first black woman to join the collective and bring my revolutionary feminist politics there. I didn't like the majority politics, but there was a small group of us who were working class. I was the only black woman at the time. We had our differences, but we did have a common experience of the class assumptions of *Spare Rib*, which was middle class in a very oppressive way. . . . We had a common experience of a very negative time with some people who, in a sense, assumed they owned the world – and they did, and they do. I think they always took their class position for granted, and capitalized on it.

It was quite an exciting time, but not particularly happy. There were constant battles. . . . I left (after eleven months) because of a big argument about racism. I walked out, left the collective . . . I think I'd had some influence. It was necessary to put lesbian issues on the agenda as well.

That argument about 'we don't want to upset heterosexual women' was a view that I didn't share. It was not about upsetting: the magazine was also for lesbians, and if *lesbians* aren't a category of women, I don't know who is.

I think that whole period, not just in *Spare Rib* but in the Women's Liberation Movement, was a kind of collective naivety – to assume that sisterhood was sufficient to bind all women together, and that it was disruptive to recognize differences. That was the major argument then and, I think, still is. Politics is not enlarged to embrace and celebrate difference.

It is slightly better, and yet we have also become polarized around sex, and around SM in particular. It seems to me that there is a similar kind of intolerance around sex, which is an issue we talk about *least* as lesbians. Ironically, it is the issue that unites us and it is also the issue that currently divides us. From my point of view, there is tremendous ignorance, not just about sex but about the *history* of sex and sexuality. I wish people who call themselves supporters of SM would read more, I wish they would read the Marquis de Sade . . . It's not that I want them to change their minds, but it strikes me as bizarre that people should call themselves adherents to a politics and then be unfamiliar [with it]. It's a bit like Christians never having read the Bible, and then going out and proselytizing on behalf of Christianity when they don't actually know what they are talking about.

Equally, I think that those opposed to SM – vociferous opponents – really ought to be more familiar with the politics of libertarianism; not that they will agree with it, but their arguments will be better pitched. But I don't like 'either-or, anything goes', which is the libertarian argument, *or* the slippery slope – 'because we might be tainted by association with SM, therefore we must ban everything' . . . The trouble, it seems to me, with both points of view is that they are totally polarized and one is always invited to be in one camp or the other; and I think there is more overlap between them than they give credit for.

I think there are elements of sexual practice, which come within the ambit of sado-masochism, which are exciting, non-exploitative, generally worthy of further consideration. We have been very good at throwing labels at each other without looking at it in more detail. There is a great deal of hypocrisy about sex around lesbian feminists, people who say they are positively opposed to SM but feel slightly guilty that some of the things they do they fear might be SM. I think there is a more complex argument and debate beneath the surface that nobody articulates.

LIPSTICK LESBIANS AND DESIGNER DYKES

I think it is quite interesting and exciting. I wouldn't want to make a politics out of it, but I think that stereotypes are pretty harmful, and why do all lesbians have to look the same? Do they all have to be white, slim, to wear the same clothes – the *uniform*? Why is it OK to have one acceptable image of a lesbian? These are questions it's relevant to be asking now. It would be less so if there were fewer out lesbians. But now there are a lot – not enough, but quite a few – and we should be seen as diverse . . . I think it confronts stereotypes. When I come to work in a skirt and wear lipstick, I act exactly the same – the pretty stroppy individual I am, quite strong – and whatever the chaps might be thinking (or perhaps saying) about me looking different, because I am not quite fitting their stereotype, there is a sense in which I am doing something mildly revolutionary. It ain't going to change the world and it's not something I want to do every day, but I do want to do it occasionally.

I suppose I have a similar approach to butch and femme. Being stuck in butch – or femme – is problematic . . . We've fought for the right to be more wholly ourselves – we can't be entirely, we are products of this world, but we begin increasingly to define ourselves more as we wish to do so, and perhaps men can learn to do the same.

There isn't a substitute for talking, discussing, thrashing out ideas, listening to each other. We have to do it – and it's fun. It gets frustrating when we have unreasonable expectations and assume everybody has to say or think exactly as we do. I don't see it as conflict if there are different points of view. It can be extremely dynamic. I think most of the really strong politics that have come from women – feminist politics – have come from embracing difference.

Robin **G**orna

thirty, Head of Health Promotion, Terrence Higgins Trust

I first had sex with a woman when I was twenty-two. I was working full time as a volunteer at the Terrence Higgins Trust [THT] and had just graduated from Oxford with a degree in theology. I became a volunteer with THT after one of my closest friends at university, Jonathan, died in a car crash (he'd been driving home to see his lover Jason). Jonathan's death was very distressing . . . but it also politicized me around queer issues for the first time. I went to see Larry Kramer's play, *The Normal Heart*, soon after his death and THT were asking for volunteers as well as money, and during my last year at Oxford I trained as a volunteer for them and also worked on the local AIDS helpline.

So my final year was a very high-activity year, quite stressful. I was working incredibly hard for my finals exams. I was still doing some theatre (directing an anti-porn play), which I'd always done (also acting), and I started this voluntary work and got very enthusiastic about it. I was still grieving for Jonathan and got involved in a relationship with a boy called David, which was not the world's greatest relationship, but it tided me through that time. He was the first person I came out to about being bisexual, which is the identity I still have – that, and queer. Towards the end of that year-long relationship, I talked with him about my feelings for women, and one woman in particular. I had started working full time at THT as a volunteer organizing their buddy services. I guess my world was very different: from the alleged high-pressure life of an Oxford college and academia, to the high-pressure life of a major, very queer voluntary organization in London.

I loved working at THT, threw myself into it wholeheartedly, worked ridiculously long hours, thrived on the atmosphere. I got involved in large numbers of different projects and activities, I met a large number of people and I felt very comfortable and at home. Although I am sure I'd have denied it at the time, one reason I chose to volunteer at THT was to be in that queer environment and let myself explore my sexuality a bit more. It wasn't that I felt constrained or uncomfortable with my sexuality, but I lacked options or opportunities in the situation I was in at Oxford.

When the university term started again, I went back up to Oxford and had sex with Jane, the woman I'd been telling David I was lusting after. The next day I went round telling everyone I was bisexual. It wasn't that I didn't know I was bisexual, had sex with Jane and suddenly realized I *was*: quite the opposite – I'd known for a long time and never really felt I had a right to any kind of queer identity. But now it was like I had the proof.

I do wish I could use the identity 'queer', it would be so much easier and probably *truer* as to how I really feel about myself. P*roving* you are bisexual becomes very difficult ... and the minute I'm involved with anyone of either gender people make assumptions about my sexuality – that it's shifted or changed.

I was terribly naive and knew very little about queer politics. I assumed that all my new colleagues at THT would be delighted for this rather straight young graduate who'd just left her boyfriend. I thought I'd finally earned my queer credentials, but they didn't see it that way and I came under quite a lot of flak, particularly from older lesbians. And they still do it to me – ask me when I'm going to get off the fence, the obvious taunts. ... I'm still on the fence and I still like it here, but it was incredibly hurtful and difficult that people whom I expected would welcome me into the queer family seemed to be quite horrified and critical of my new-found sexual identity.

I get grief from lesbians, and most other people seem to accept me. ... I suppose the crunch came around AIDS as much as around my own sexuality. Anyone who stays friends with me has to put up with an awful lot of ranting about sex and queerness and AIDS and death ... and if they weren't going to be able to put up with that, they probably weren't going to be able to put up with my sexuality either. I did lose friends because of AIDS, because of the fear engendered by the subject of sexuality and death. I started working in it very early on, in 1986, before it was 'fashionable', and for a while I had an affair with an HIV-positive bisexual man, and that caused anxiety for some people – moving to the other side of dinner tables, that kind of thing. ... The friends with whom I stayed in touch are completely supportive. I wondered how they'd react when I was involved with a woman, and the majority of them have been fine.

I quite like having groups of friends that are 'traditional' and not queer. It makes it so much more of a challenge. It would have been easy for me at the time to have just let go of all of that past and immersed myself in the AIDS world and the queer world, and to deny I'd been at Oxford and all the privileges that come with that. But I think that would be a shame and I would lose opportunities to change their thinking a little bit.

My family is not very conventional: middle class, but immigrant. My grandfather is from Italy . . . very much the working-class boy made good, became a lawyer, made money, did the classic immigrant thing of being more British than the British, although still with that rather steamy Italian side. So we've never really fitted into the British class system or had any of those conventions that often make coming out difficult. . . . We're quite an eccentric bunch. The women in my family are very very strong and there's no sense of female subservience running through the Gorna clan. They're all very queer-positive. . . .

I'm an only child. We left my father when I was four, and I have no contact with him. I was born in Manchester. We moved to Leicester to live near my aunt, who was living there with her husband and two children. My aunt's a fairly wild figure. She's a barrister and does lots of media work and, under her influence and having made this extraordinary change in her life, my mum blossomed from being a timid mouse to being quite a wild and powerful woman in her own right. She went off to university when I was about seven, and when she'd graduated and got a job she and my aunt were still quite close. A lot of the important friends they made at that time were working in the theatre in Leicester, and among those were two gay men who were very camp, wonderful men. It was incredibly normal for me as a child to be around gay men, and pretty outrageous ones at that.

I don't remember coming out to my mum, which is weird. The only significant conversation that stays in my mind was when we went out to lunch and I asked her how she felt about me being bisexual. She said that she did have two problems with it: one was that she wanted grandchildren, and two that she'd never fancied a woman and so she didn't know how it felt, which I thought was quite a sweet reply. She actually outed me to my grandmother. My aunt had been telling my grandmother that I must be a lesbian because I didn't have a boyfriend and I was working in AIDS, and my mother put my grandmother straight, explaining that I was bi. My grandmother is Roman Catholic and goes to church every week, and is delighted that her granddaughter read theology. A couple of years ago she said to me, 'Robin, have you got a boyfriend?', and I said no, and she said, 'Have you got a girlfriend?' I said no, and she was quite disappointed. I was amazed that this eighty-year-old woman could take it on board so well.

When I was a child my mum had a number of black boyfriends. . . . Race politics have always been important within my home, as in my life with my mother, because that's principally the domain in which she's worked. She studied to be a community development worker, working with Afro-Caribbean communities. I remember the anti-apartheid movement from when I was pre-adolescent. I used to play in the steel band ... and so the sense of *difference*, which I suppose is part of the queer identity, was there from early on. Being the only white kid among a lot of black kids was part of my history, and so being different sexually didn't feel that terrifying. ...

Of all the labels I'd want to hang on to quite strongly, *feminist* is one [because] it seems to me that it's so derided, and that sense of identity around being a woman and fighting for other women, for women's rights, is such an outmoded idea but is crucial to the way I think about the world – and is very much why and how my AIDS work has shifted more and more to women's concerns. It often feels very strange for me to be working in an environment and having many friends whose sexual identity has been a major point of struggle in their lives, whereas mine hasn't. The only thing that causes me grief is having to prove I really am what I say I am. ... I was in a relationship with a woman and so many people seemed to leap with joy and decide they could confine me in the lesbian 'box', and I find that quite irritating. What good does it do? My identity needs to come from *within*. ... [Their] hammering away that I wasn't really bi certainly didn't inspire me to join the happy sisterhood of lesbians; it completely alienated me from the whole idea. ... How could they possibly *know*? It seems so ironic that the queer movement is founded upon the idea of being able to be honest about our sexualities and live them freely. ...

After my degree I was offered quite a number of jobs: civil service, diplomatic corps, THT ... I'd had no thought that [THT] might turn into a 'career'. It just felt like it was what I wanted – needed – to do. Within the AIDS field I've been through a shift from organizing the care work and also doing direct care myself, into more prevention-based activity. After that first year I was elected on to the board of directors of THT and started to do some freelance writing and research with the Community Development Foundation on community-based health education around AIDS. Then I moved to Oxford City Council on the health authority, where I was their AIDS liaison officer for a couple of years. After I left the board the then chief executive and a couple of board members went out to the European Commission, and were talking with them about the changes for 1992. The Commission offered them money to send someone from THT to link up the AIDS service organizations in Europe, and the Trust proposed me – principally, I think, because I spoke French. So off I went.

At the end of the first year of working with THT as a volunteer, I started to become more desperate for cash, and a fund-raiser was aware that the New York City Gay Men's Chorus was coming on a European tour and needed a courier who could speak languages, so she proposed me and I guided them round Europe for two weeks. This has become a significant event in my life. I mean, it was a crazy thing to be responsible for eighty queers on two buses, travelling from one end of Europe to the other, an absolute nightmare, but I have incredibly strong links with New York and have become very close friends with one of the people from the Chorus. I go out there a lot, and that really enriches my awareness of the queer movement and AIDS, not just the British side of it. It also makes life pretty shitty, because lots of them have died.

This ability to speak French came in very handy, and eventually I went out to Luxembourg in 1990. I left the flat I was renting, packed up all my possessions in a van and drove to Luxembourg, found a flat, moved in and a year later did the reverse journey. . . . In the long run I can see I've been very fortunate, in that I'm now able to help a number of AIDS organizations get European money – and I did get a lot of money out to small organizations when I was there, but it was a very frustrating business trying to enable people to network among the different European AIDS service organizations, to learn from each other and develop things on a pan-European scale. . . . During the year in Luxembourg I also took the Gay Men's Chorus from New York on their second European tour.

I was offered some work by Jonathan Mann, who was organizing the International AIDS Conference for that year [1992], and that led to me working out in Harvard for a couple of months, and then over in Amsterdam where the conference was held. I loved working in the States. . . . I worked for a woman, there were mostly women on my team. It gave me the opportunity to improve my knowledge about AIDS and to translate quite complicated social and medical research in simple terms. That's something I do more and more of these days, and is a skill I'm glad I learned. And it gave me more confidence in my writing skills – I had to edit the final report of the conference, which was quite a big piece of work and something I was proud of.

When that came to an end, I was a bit stuck: I was in the middle of Europe with a flat in Luxembourg, a country I loathed. . . . Miraculously, the health education manager of THT left and they employed me on a short-term contract to manage the health education team.

It was strange going back to the Trust. I'd always felt it was my home in many ways, and yet it was the first time I'd been a salaried member of staff. Clearly the place had changed a great deal between 1986, when I joined, and the end of 1992, when I worked for them again. That went on till the spring of 1993. It was nice to manage a team of very committed staff, and we produced a magnificent range of educational material for this short period of time. It felt very much like a maternal job, holding them all together in this interim phase when they were a bit lost between a much-loved manager leaving and the uncertainty of the future. . . .

I feel I've been very lucky to work for all these different institutions and understand how they work. . . . I've worked with THT in so many different capacities . . . I've done some work for one of the health authorities on sex education; I do training; I've done a lot of work with a group called the European AIDS Treatment Group, a group I funded when I was with the Commission. I'm very excited about that. I bring in a feminist slant and have been working on a lot of issues around treatment. I also do some writing for the National Aids Manual (I'm a trustee), and I do a lot of their women's stuff, not just around treatment but transmission and social issues too.

I write for a journal in the States, the *Journal of Physicians' Association of AIDS Care*: articles about conferences and various aspects of AIDS, like European activism. A lot of the work has been voluntary work, not paid. . . . I guess I'm very single-issue, in that it's principally AIDS work I do, but I don't really think that's a problem. I think there's something very important about those of us who've been doing this for a long time, continuing and finding ways of taking care of ourselves, because if we did all stop we'd lose a vast amount of expertise, and there are not that many of us who have been around that long.

I know that a lot of lesbians are very critical of women being involved with AIDS, because it's the Boys' issue not the Girls' issue. And I believe that's true, but [AIDS] is such a catastrophe that there's no way I could stop being involved with it. I think my commitment as a feminist to women's health is an important part of it, but, equally, I'm not at all separatist about that. A lot of the AIDS work I do is about gay and bisexual men, and that seems to me entirely right and proper.

I feel a bit weedy, like I ought to be involved in other lesbian and gay issues, but it seems to me that AIDS really is *the* queer issue of the 1980s and 1990s and, sadly, it's likely to be for many years to come. Frankly, when I'm not doing AIDS works I want to do things that are outside the realms of politics and campaigning.

Unless necessity forces me, I won't work in a situation where I need to be closeted. I can't imagine how that would be a realistic option for me. I'm not terribly good at keeping my mouth shut. I'd probably just blurt it out anyway. The whole fact of working around sexuality and sex means that I've reconsidered my sense of how I live my life. It's not just sexuality: it's also being confronted by so much death, so much loss. One of the things that many people with HIV and AIDS talk about is cherishing the moment and living fully for *now*, and quite a lot of that has rubbed off on me. My overall perspective on life has shifted profoundly. I don't think many people could be around the epidemic this long and not have their life changed by it.

I've had numerous short affairs but not many relationships since doing this work: not *long-term* relationships . . . and I'm sure that's been caused by the practical fact of mostly working and socializing with gay men for a long period of time, and also travelling so much. That's something I would hope to change . . . I've bought my own flat. I've decided I'm not going to just shoot off all over the world, like I used to. I have established some roots in London for the first time. I did spend quite a bit of time living out of a suitcase or in very nice, but impermanent, rented places. So, nesting, creating my own home and sticking tiles on the wall, making a garden, is very exciting and fun.

I guess this links into what I was trying to say about longevity and surviving working in the AIDS crisis. . . . There was a woman who cared for a friend of mine. He died in the summer of 1993 and she died of cancer a month later. She'd become like his 'wife', absolutely devoted to him for the last few months of his life, and I just think the toll this epidemic can take is extraordinary. It's not some trivial thing like burn-out and people needing to go away and have a rest for a week or two; it's *huge* and none of us know how to do it, because we've never had to face it before.

I think that AIDS work has been damaging for me in a number of ways. There was the practical sense of living all over the place, but also being around gay men and queer men's sexuality in-yer-face the whole time. It has felt overwhelming. It's like I've always been dealing with sexualities which aren't my own, which is partly why I tried to start some bisexuality and HIV work. It can be quite draining to be always thinking about what *men* are doing with each other. It leaves very little space for respecting one's own sexuality and the ways in which it may be very different. I don't go cruising, I'm lousy in bars, so where do I fit in with a lot of what my gay male friends and colleagues are talking about?

I'm part of a thing called the AIDS Mastery. It is a side of AIDS which is more spiritual, emotional, much more about living fully *now* ... and it's something I've become much more involved with since I moved back to London. I'm involved in a training programme, a workshop ... and that's given me opportunities to look more seriously at the different life choices I make.

In terms of identity, I often slip back to 'bisexual' because I feel so much resistance to the term 'queer'. My desire is to reclaim queer as an acceptable identity within the Movement. Being out as queer isn't a major problem. I remember one of my ex-tutors, who is now a bishop, talking to me about how he really believed and supported homosexual unions, but it was the bisexuals he felt sorry for. ... Coming out to him was pretty disastrous, and embarrassing. It was as if I'd metaphorically slapped him around the face. But I'm also conscious that for me it's been easy, because I'm from a privileged background in many ways.

There is so much more diversity now. ... I keep ranting on about queer, [but] the few images of 'lesbian' I had, before going to THT, were so dull, so stereotypical, that I didn't *identify*. ... Also, I do think there's quite a difference between being lesbian and being bisexual. ... I hope that at least the *concept* of diversity, of there being a *spectrum* of sexuality, will take root. ... I just hope we can build a respect for our differences and not get caught up in that nonsense about being the 'right' kind of dyke.

I see the Lesbian Avengers partly as a good thing, a fine thing, lesbians defining their own agenda and not getting caught up in queer men's agenda. Another side to me panics, because it can end up: 'That's what it means to be a good lesbian'. ... For me, it is a male and female thing. ... Lesbians and gay men are woven together. Our queer world has created itself economically *together*, because we haven't had the power as women to have our own separate world.

The future is hopeful if we can build a strong sense of the richness and diversity of lesbianism – within a politics that lets us work together because we are queer together. I don't want to do it just as the *Girls*, I want to do it as the *Boys* and the *Girls*. It's part of building a world that rejects the narrowing and constricting views of sexuality that the mainstream feeds us. ... We need to feed that back into the mainstream because it gives young women – and young men – much greater hope and possibilities for themselves, and for the options they can take in their lives.

Being in New York for Stonewall 25 made me incredibly hopeful because of the level of presence – and *difference* – that was so vibrant and exciting. We had whirling dervishes of naked ACT-UP protesters outside St

Patrick's Cathedral, and queer Christian groups singing their hymns – a fabulous *range*. ...

I was standing on the roof of a building on Christopher Street and it was the end of the day of the parade, and I started to think how twenty-five years ago a bunch of queers, drag queens and butch dykes were down at the [Stonewall] bar and they got angry and rioted ... and twenty-five years later, about a hundred of us were standing on the roofs, having had the most wonderful day and partied non-stop for a week, and we were watching fireworks which must have cost thousands and thousands of dollars, a magnificent display. ... The Empire State Building was lit up lavender, and I thought: 'Well, it's certainly not all rosy out there, but we've come a long way baby.' And, of course, we've got a long way to go, but it would be nice to step back for a minute and just celebrate a little bit.

III

Looking Forward

5 the future is lesbian

So as we approach the millennium, where next for lesbianism? Nearly all the women interviewed agreed that it was a lot easier to be out in the 1990s than at any time previously and that although pockets of prejudice clearly still existed, there was greater understanding and awareness and therefore less of the ignorance which breeds homophobia. One of the main reasons for this change in attitudes was the existence of prominent role models such as kd lang and Martina Navratilova, whose lifestyles may be remote from most 'ordinary' women, but whose decision to stand up and be counted has contributed to a climate of increased visibility. There was the additional foregrounding of lesbian characters and storylines in TV soaps and series such as *Brookside* and *Drop the Dead Donkey*.

Linda Semple: 'If you are coming out there is nothing to beat the sight of other people coming out – people with public personas becoming well known as lesbian or gay'.

Gillian Rodgerson: 'We need a lot more *different* kinds of role models. . . . I thought kd lang and Cindy Crawford on the cover of *Vanity Fair* was great fun, but not all lesbians are chic, nor do we want to be'.

Sophie Mills: 'I think there are many more possibilities and role models now, and that has to be a good thing'.

Jenny Wood: 'I would like to see more lesbians with a high profile coming out. It would make it so much easier for ordinary lesbians living in ordinary streets, in the North-East of England or wherever.'

Most women's optimism is, however, tempered with reservations about whether we are seeing lasting change, genuine social progress. As several pointed out, many of the issues which engaged lesbians in the Women's Movement of the 1970s remain contentious and unresolved in the 1990s: issues like custody, censorship, safety on the streets.

Linda Bellos: 'Being out is *better* than in the past, and it's better because we've made it better, but we haven't fully succeeded. It is not easy for every lesbian in any situation. There are lesbians in London feeling extreme isolation, and working – or living – in very hostile environments. It would be naive and foolish to pretend otherwise. I am not swept up in the euphoria of the media that makes it look like being lesbian is the most chic, radical thing to be, in and for itself. For the majority it ain't like that'.

Diane Langford: 'I don't think there's been any sudden "awakening" on the part of the general public, but on the other hand I do think the younger generation of lesbians are much more upfront and they are not going to be put down. I went on Hackney Pride [in 1994]. Frankie (my partner) was playing in the marching band, and these young women were there with their Lesbian Avengers T-shirts on and they were going up to car windows, shaking their collecting tins. There were these very dour-faced male drivers with their wallets out, putting money in the tins! The women were saying: "We need money for our action." I mean, I couldn't imagine myself ever having had the guts to do that'.

Mary Jennings: 'My mother sent me an Irish magazine where there was an interview with an Irish lesbian living in Cambridge. She's published a book and was invited to Dublin to appear on TV [in 1994]. . . . Things like that couldn't have happened years ago.'

Joyce Hunter: 'I still think that each person should be allowed to come out at their own pace. It's a process, and all of us must respect that process. I am not for outing, but I do believe that being out is healthy: it's good for your mental health and it's good for the younger people coming up to see role models. . . . I have been on Japanese TV and been interviewed on British TV. I am out to the whole world!'

Carol Uszkurat: 'I still get worried that the way things move forward is in the "identity" way, that heterosexual society – like the *Independent* or *Guardian* readers – would say, "Yes, they have a right to exist", not "This is something that I could do". It's not an "us-and-them" scenario. Lesbianism is an available activity for everyone . . . but I think there's a lot more leeway for hope . . . I myself feel more *informed*. I have moments of feeling fulfilled, but it's not a sustainable state to me because I always step back and question.'

Individual instances of homophobia, such as the media's vilification of Hackney head teacher, Jane Brown, produced powerful alarm bells among some interviewees, evoking feelings of 'There but for the grace of God go I'. Many young lesbians in the 1990s may have a marginally easier time than their predecessors in the 1970s and before, but listen to any radio phone-in about lesbian and gay issues and you will hear the real 'voice' of Britain in its most inglorious mode, sounding off about 'pervs', 'unnatural practices' and issuing dire biblical warnings. These kinds of programmes seem to attract the same type of antisocial, obsessional individuals who, if they were not listening to the sound of their own voices on air, would probably be hovering between soapboxes in Hyde Park, haranguing and heckling women like Sharley McLean. Peel away society's outer fabric of acceptance and you will uncover more than a modicum of naked hatred.

Mandy: '[Lesbianism] is perceived by a large part of the population as an unnatural way of life. The gutter press still pillory women, particularly lesbians . . . and I think that the experience of Jane Brown spells this out in very clear terms. I collected names for a petition for Jane Brown and that experience keeps very much at the top of the agenda – the knowledge that bigotry is there, rife.'

Geography has always been a crucial factor in any decision whether or not to come out, and in that sense little has changed. The younger, more gregarious woman based in a large town or city might not hesitate, but for the older, more introverted lesbian living in the sticks, the closet may represent the only safe option.

Linda Semple: 'If you are eighteen to twenty-five and living in London, Manchester, Edinburgh, Leeds, Birmingham, it's not so bad. If you are a 55-year-old woman whose children are grown up and who has just realized she's a lesbian because she fancies the woman next door, and she lives in 'Chipping Burpham' and the Ugly Duck pub in Little Small Hyde, twenty-two miles away, is gay once a year, then you're in deep shit!'

Jill Posener agrees: 'If you were born in the Shetlands you would have a really hard time coming out, and I think the same is true if you were born in the Midwest, somewhere in Wisconsin. When I was sixteen the article that made me call CHE was in *Honey* magazine and it was called: 'It's not all Gaiety'. I could buy it at the local train station in Richmond. Now you could probably go into, say, WH Smith's in Wolverhampton and pick up *Diva* because [lesbian and gay publications] are actually being handled by trade distributors. That has to have a terribly important impact on your identity.

Progress is always two steps forward, one back and three sideways, and it's a double-edged sword: with greater visibility comes increased attack. San Francisco has the biggest gay population in the world . . . and it's very probable that we'll elect a lesbian mayor within five years, and yet attacks on gay men – and on lesbians who look like myself – are rising dispropor-tionately to other crimes in San Francisco. Violent crimes, beatings, killings. .... That's the price of success, and we are hugely successful as a movement, but there are deep disappointments: lack of AIDS funding, the fiasco over gays in the military ... '

Money is another major determining factor. Lillian Faderman has said that 'if there's one thing that a woman needs to lead a lesbian lifestyle, it is economic self-sufficiency'.[1] Financial security frees up women to make choices, enabling them to live independently, without recourse to a man's income.

Wilmette Brown: 'People openly saying "I'm lesbian or gay" transforms everyone's possibilities on an individual level, but I don't think that struggle is over by any means. There are still many women, in both industrialized and Third World countries, who cannot afford to come out. They may be in marriages to men where they will lose custody of their children if it's known they are lesbian, or they do not have the money to leave a situation where they are living with a man. The dangers of being pushed back into invisibility and suicide are always there. As with any movement forward we know there is always a backlash against it. .... We are still in a very vulnerable position as lesbians. None of the gains we have made should be taken for granted – we had to fight for every single one.

Financial independence – a room of our own to live in, and an income – is the key to whether we can come out. .... One issue, which is very much an economic issue, is partnership legislation. The work that lesbian and gay people do making families is hidden by the fact that our partnerships are not legally and socially acknowledged ... and so we are financially ripped off in terms of benefits and other entitlements.'

She cites the 1994 Stonewall anniversary celebrations as evidence of the improved social climate for lesbians: 'By 1960s and 1970s standards, it's fantastic. It makes all the difference in the world that there is a massive lesbian and gay movement that's visible.'

Gillian Rodgerson: 'I think for younger women there is a more varied community to come out to ... and more support, but you have to be able to find it. Also, so much of the community is concentrating on the commercial scene. It's terrific having a wide choice of places to go, but for kids who are too young to drink, who don't like bars or can't afford to go to them, a collection of bars is not a substitute for a community. Sometimes we lose sight of that'.

Brenda Ellis agrees: 'I worry about the non-political side. At one time "lesbian" and "feminist" were synonymous. Now, it's lesbian feminists *or* lesbians who want to party. The thing is that lesbian feminists like partying as well as politics!'

Elaine Willis: 'I am worried about the politics within the lesbian and gay community ... I see a lot of incorporation going on into the gay men's agenda and I don't understand quite what's going on, but my gut feeling is that women are losing quite a lot of ground in terms of expressing what is distinctive about our needs as lesbian women ... I think a lot of the rhetoric disguises the fact that things haven't changed an awful lot for some women.'

A third issue, linked with money, is work. There will always be sensitive areas of employment, such as schoolteaching, the prison service and the police force, where coming out is deemed to be potentially damaging in terms of personal reputation or career prospects. Of my interviewees, police officer Beth Lambdon (Exeter) is out at work, but Becky, a younger recruit with the Metropolitan Police in London, is biding her time rather than risking the possible censure of colleagues.

Ann Wishart is a teacher and an area representative for Border Women: 'It really upsets me when I hear of women who have been living closeted lives for years and that this is their first contact with a lesbian. As a member of staff, I have encouraged the Students' Union to set up a lesbian and gay society. I am a manager and teacher and I work with disabled students, and when I hear of someone working in a shop or factory and feeling they can't be out, I feel that in some cases they are not nearly as vulnerable as I am. The answer is for people like me to be out. I have spoken to a few managers and made it my business to tell them I am out because I want them to address the issue. If managers at places of employment are out, it makes it a lot easier for those lower down the hierarchy to be out.'

Women who are self-employed, like Jenny Wood, Bridget and Savi Hensman, are probably the least likely to experience homophobia. Even the liberal, laid-back acting world may prove remarkably inhospitable to female actors who just happen to be lesbian. Former drama student, Harriett Gilbert, has women friends in the theatre who are either out 'selectively' or not at all: 'If you are an out lesbian the chances of you playing a mother thereafter are pretty low. .... I don't suppose it's ever that easy [to come out]. There is always that moment when somebody might react. Are they suddenly going to think that their children aren't safe with you? If it's a heterosexual woman friend, is she suddenly going to be a bit more careful about sitting close to you? ... I think all that still remains.'

Certainly, prospective students applying to do Harriett's journalism course are more upfront than would have been the case even a few years ago. In 1994 two women applicants made it plain that they were lesbian: 'They attached photographs to their application forms, and they've got earrings and crew cuts and all that.'

As evidenced in Chapter 2, lesbian mothers are generally treated more equitably in the 1990s, and most are given custody of their children. However, lesbians applying to be foster parents are often allocated children who are severely disabled, a deplorable situation which is denigrating to both parties. As someone who herself suffers from a disability, Brenda Ellis says the implication is that disabled children are considered somehow 'not worthy'.

Views on long-term prospects for lesbians ranged from deeply pessimistic to cautiously optimistic and positively euphoric. Many interviewees expressed concern at the emergence of an increasingly right-wing political climate in both the UK and the USA, fearing its repercussions for the lesbian and gay community.

Joyce Hunter: 'I see a backlash coming for all of us: people of colour, women, gay or lesbian. I am concerned about that and I think all the different communities within the wider lesbian and gay community need to stop beating each other up and start working together, or we are going to have a serious fight on our hands.'

Savi Hensman: 'To some extent in the lesbian community there's a complacency about what's been happening, a focus on very narrow issues, a lack of concern about the growth of racism and an assumption that the Far Right will stop their activities once they've dealt with black people, which I think is a dangerous thing for any lesbian to assume'.

Heather Cowan: 'I do believe that the more out we are the more accepted we become. How can you hate all gays when the nice woman working at the desk next to you is a lesbian? ... However, as the government becomes more conservative, antediluvian and rigid, to deviate from the white, male, able-bodied, heterosexual norm is unacceptable [sic], and lesbians miss out on at least two counts ... '

Mary Jennings takes a more positive view: 'I have seen dramatic changes in my own lifetime, like Mary Robinson becoming president [of Ireland]. She got elected almost the same week as Thatcher got thrown out [in November 1990]. So change (for the better) can happen. ... The thing I worry about is losing continuity with younger women. I think it is still underestimated how much lesbians contribute to the making of change for women in general. I do worry about that because – it's partly getting older, I suppose – I've known a time when there was no gay bars, discos, nothing. It's about keeping moving on, and we have to do that in different ways ... and so other people need to be doing other things. We can't spend all our time going out to discos and having a good time, because that will disappear. But – we can't go back'.

Beth Lambdon believes that young lesbian women in the 1990s owe an immeasurable debt to older lesbians for having such ready access to information about the lesbian and gay movement: 'They are not struggling by themselves. All those feminist women in the media struggled – and the kids in the discos took it for granted. They don't understand that a hell of a lot of women went through shit so these people can go out and be safe. If dykes hadn't walked through London in the 1970s, Martina couldn't have come out and said: "I'm gay".'

Del Dyer: 'You can *breathe* a bit better now. You can go to public places with a group of women and eight times out of ten you will be accepted. Because we are recognized in society as being not five, six, seven or eight but *thousands*, that in itself has changed the way people react, although of course there is still hostility . . . .

When I was *very* small, you had to be really brave to walk down the street with earrings and dyed hair. I do admire people like Quentin Crisp, because they are the early pioneers. We've got gay teenage groups, London Friend, established places to go to; whereas when I came out it was so limiting that if you didn't fit in there, well, tough, they bashed you up!'

Jackie Forster: 'All the opportunities are there – the support, the phone lines, bookshops – but I think it is still an extremely difficult personal decision to make, and once you are over that hump it is all out there; whereas before, where on earth did we go? There was only the Gateways and very little else that wasn't male-gay-run, or straight-run with trans-sexuals and transvestites – nothing that was lesbian-identified.'

Jill Posener: 'We've learned enormous lessons from the movements of the 1970s – how to work the media, how to work within the political structure; and outside of it. I think we've learned the process of assimila-tion, of developing our own businesses and financial centres for gays and lesbians. Of course, in the 1970s I was totally opposed to any of this, and now I can see the direct result in terms of the sheer power of our vote and of our money in the bank. . . . I think that England needs to catch up – there are a lot of things that we could learn from the American system . . . .

I honestly think that we're on a train that is unstoppable. One of the biggest problems in America, I think, is going to be this terrible conflict between the black community and the gay community. Open hostility, open warfare, without any real understanding that our aims and goals are the same.'

Diane Langford: 'I'm quite optimistic long-term because, despite all the setbacks that have happened in the world, things do eventually go forwards, not backwards ... but not in my lifetime.'

Hilde Morris: 'I'm very hopeful, merely because our society seems to be much more open now. Variations in behaviour are more easily accepted. It's evident in all sorts of things. Take fashion. Whereas previously you would have low hemlines or short skirts or particular rigid styles, now anything goes and, hopefully, it is the same with sexual preferences. ... Certainly, I would not feel anxious about either of my daughters if they told me they were lesbian. I would know that they would easily be able to find friends with similar preferences and that these preferences wouldn't affect their lives, whereas for me ... I lived a very isolated existence for very many years – for half my life, in fact.'

Mandy: 'One sure thing is that we shall always be there. Most of us will manage to continue the fight. I would hope that we do not have to back away from what we are and can be proud of what we are. And – I hate the word "acceptance"; I don't want to be accepted, it's so bloody patronizing – I hope that I can say quite clearly, if I have to or want to, that I am a lesbian and nobody is going to think any differently than if I'd said I was a carpenter or truck driver.'

Nettie Pollard: 'I'd like to see lesbians being part of a general movement for social change and sexual liberation. I'd like to see us change the sexism and power relations in society, because I don't believe that lesbians can be free while other groups are oppressed. I believe that none of us is free until we are all free.'

Perhaps the last word should go to American writer and professor Lillian Faderman. While researching material for her book, *Odd Girls and Twilight Lovers* (Penguin, 1992), she concluded that perceptions of lesbianism were continually changing, moving onwards:

> The only 'constant' about the lesbian was that she prefers women, that stereotypes are all stupid, that whatever politics we form are always subject to change and always will be changed by the next generation, that we can never rely on one concrete definition or one set of politics being there in the future. .... It seems that every generation thinks that this is the culmination of everything that went before. .... I can remember so well in the lesbian feminist 1970s feeling that: 'Now we've reached it, this is the climax'. Of course, the next generation comes along and laughs at that. It's fascinating.[2]

notes

INTRODUCTION

1. Veronica Groocock, 'Changes' (interview with Lillian Faderman), *Gay Times*, September 1992.
2. *Ibid.*
3. Survey findings quoted in Chrissy Iley, 'LA Lore', *Cosmopolitan*, January 1995.
4. 'One in five attracted to same sex', *Pink Paper*, 16 September 1994.
5. 'Public opinion: outlook improving', *Pink Paper*, 25 November 1994.
6. Valerie Mason-John, 'Women's launch for "sods" bill', *Capital Gay*.
7. Del Martin and Phyllis Lyon, *Lesbian/Woman*. Bantam, London, 1972, p. 179.

CHAPTER 1

1. *Ricki Lake*, 26 October 1994.
2. *Ibid.*
3. Pam St Clement, 'Making the argument by example', in Emma Healey and Angela Mason (eds), *Stonewall 25*. Virago, London, 1994, p. 51.
4. *Ibid.*, p. 53.
5. 'The case of the gay MP', *Daily Mirror*, 29 September 1977.
6. Deirdre Haslam, 'A long journey to the woman I really am', *Independent*, 2 February 1994.
7. 'The night I learned that my daughter's lover was a woman', *Daily Mail*, 29 October 1992.
8. 'The day when coming out is definitely in', *Evening Argus* (Brighton), 8 October 1992.
9. Quoted in Val Sampson, 'Sons and gay lovers', *Guardian*, November 1992.
10. *Ibid.*
11. 'Hopelessly devoted – living with a love that dare not speak its name', *Guardian*, 11 April 1990.
12. 'Women in love'/Open Space, *Guardian*, 19 April 1990.

13. Harriet Goldhor Lerner, *The Dance of Deception: Pretending and Truth-telling in Women's Lives*. Pandora, 1993, p. 30.
14. Judith Bradford and Caitlin Ryan, 'Who we are: health concerns of middle-aged lesbians', in Barbara Sang *et al.* (eds), *Lesbians at Midlife: The Creative Transition*. Spinsters Book Company, San Francisco, 1991, p. 149.
15. *Ibid.*, p. 155.

CHAPTER 2

1. Eleanor Stephens, 'Must a loving mother love men?' *Guardian*, 12 November 1976.
2. S. Golombok *et al.* 'Children in lesbian and single parent households: psycho-sexual and psychiatric appraisal', *Journal of Child Psychology and Psychiatry*, 1983. Quoted in Stephanie Norris and Emma Read (eds), *Out in the Open*. Pan, London, 1984, p. 177.
3. Stephens, 'Must a loving mother love men?'
4. *Ibid.*
5. Del Martin and Phyllis Lyon, *Lesbian/Woman*. Bantam, London, 1972, p. 141.
6. Victoria McKee, 'When two "mums" are better than one', *Independent*, 18 May 1994.
7. *Ibid.*
8. Beverly Kemp, 'When Mum's girlfriend comes to stay', *Independent*, 20 September 1994.
9. *Ibid.*
10. Angela Smyth and Julia Brosnan, 'Me and my mums', *Guardian*, 14 November 1994.
11. BBC TV, *Casualty*, 12 November 1994.
12. Chrissy Iley, 'Nothing to keep mum about', *Sunday Times*, 18 September 1994.
13. 'God didn't intend two women to be parents' (interview by Tony Gallagher and Paul Harris), *Daily Mail*, 21 September 1994.
14. Lynda Lee-Potter, 'Whose lives are they anyway?' *Daily Mail*, 28 September 1994.
15. 'Children's charity drops lesbian television star', *Pink Paper*, 7 October 1994.
16. *Ibid.*
17. Quoted in Vicky Powell, 'Baby power', *Pink Paper*, 1 July 1994.
18. *Ibid.*

CHAPTER 3

1. Sarah Schulman, *My American History: Lesbian and Gay Life During the Reagan/Bush Years*, Cassell, London, 1994, p. 236.
2. Emma Healey, 'Getting active: lesbians leave the Well of Loneliness', in Emma Healey and Angela Mason (eds), *Stonewall 25*. Virago, London, 1994, p. 96.

3. Kahlil Gibran, *The Prophet*. Heinemann, London, 1988.
4. ' "Follow God's word, not the church", says priest who marries gay couples', *Capital Gay*, 25 November 1994.
5. 'Spanish gays get set for same rights as hets', *Capital Gay*, 3 February 1995.
6. *Ibid*.
7. 'Airline hints at gay ban U-turn', *Pink Paper*, 20 January 1995.
8. 'British Airways opens cheap flight deal to gay partners', *Capital Gay*, 18 November 1994.
9. 'Germans elect gay Green', *Pink Paper*, 4 November 1994.
10. 'Name the day', *Pink Paper*, 13 January 1995.
11. 'Sharley McLean', in Suzanne Neild and Rosalind Pearson (eds), *Women Like Us*. The Women's Press, London, 1992, p. 79.
12. Chrissy Iley, 'LA lore', *Cosmopolitan*, January 1995.
13. 'Whither the pink pound?', *Capital Gay*, 12 August 1994.
14. Alison Gregory, 'Marking territory', *Pink Paper*, 4 November 1994.
15. Jo-Ann Goodwin, 'A marriage made in hell', *Guardian* (Weekend), 17 December 1994.
16. Sue George, 'Pounds, shillings and pink pence', *Guardian*, 29 June 1993.
17. Goodwin, 'A marriage made in hell'.

CHAPTER 4

1. Joann Loulan, ' "Now when I was your age": one perspective on how lesbian culture has influenced our sexuality', in *Lesbians at Midlife: The Creative Transition*. Spinsters Book Company, San Francisco, 1991, p. 11.
2. Adrienne Rich, *Blood, Bread, and Poetry: Selected Prose 1979–1985*. Virago, London, 1987, pp. 23–75.
3. Emma Healey, 'Getting active: lesbians leave the Well of Loneliness', in Emma Healey and Angela Mason (eds), *Stonewall 25*. Virago, London, 1994, p. 91.
4. Paulina Palmer, *Contemporary Lesbian Writing*. Open University Press, Buckingham, 1993, p. 53.
5. Sigrid Nielsen, 'Strange days', in Christian McEwen and Sue O'Sullivan (eds), *Out the Other Side*. Virago, London, 1988, p. 98.
6. *Ibid.*, p. 103.
7. *Ibid*.
8. John D'Emilio, 'Gay politics and community in San Francisco since World War II', in M. B. Duberman *et al.* (eds), *Hidden from History*. Penguin, Harmondsworth, 1991, p. 456.
9. Veronica Groocock, interview with Sheila Jeffreys, April 1994.
10. *Ibid*.
11. *Ibid*.
12. *Ibid*.

13. Sheila Jeffreys, *The Lesbian Heresy*. The Women's Press, London, 1994, jacket blurb.
14. Groocock, interview with Sheila Jeffreys, April 1994.
15. *Ibid.*
16. Nicci Gerrard, 'At the frontiers of feminism', *Guardian*, 22 April 1986.
17. Roddy Doyle, *Family*, June 1994.
18. Palmer, *Contemporary Lesbian Writing*, p. 53.
19. *Ibid.*, pp. 53–54.
20. Nielsen, 'Strange days', p. 106.
21. *Ibid.*, p. 105.

CHAPTER 5

1. Veronica Groocock, 'Changes' (interview with Lillian Faderman), *Gay Times*, September 1992.
2. *Ibid.*

bibliography

Sue Cartledge and Joanna Ryan, *Sex and Love — New Thoughts on Old Contradictions*. The Women's Press, London, 1983.

Martin Bauml Duberman, *et al.* (eds), *Hidden from History*. Penguin, Harmondsworth, 1991.

Lillian Faderman, *Odd Girls and Twilight Lovers: A History of Lesbian Life in Twentieth-Century America*. Penguin, Harmondsworth, 1992.

Feminist Review (eds), *Sexuality: A Reader*. Virago, London, 1987.

Sue George, *Women and Bisexuality*. Scarlet Press, London, 1993.

Kahill Gibran, *The Prophet*. Heinemann, London, 1988.

Harriet Goldhor Lerner, *The Dance of Deception*. Pandora, London, 1993.

Hall Carpenter Archives (Lesbian Oral History Group), *Inventing Ourselves: Lesbian Life Stories*. Routledge, London, 1989.

Emma Healey and Angela Mason, *Stonewall 25: The Making of the Lesbian and Gay Community in Britain*. Virago, London, 1994.

Sheila Jeffreys, *The Lesbian Heresy*. The Women's Press, London, 1994.

Del Martin and Phyllis Lyon, *Lesbian/Woman*. Bantam, London, 1972.

Christian McEwan and Sue O'Sullivan, *Out the Other Side*. Virago, London, 1988.

Suzanne Neild and Rosalind Pearson, *Women Like Us*. The Women's Press, London, 1992.

Stephanie Norris and Emma Read, *Out: People Talking about Being Gay or Bisexual*. Pan, London, 1985.

Paulina Palmer, *Contemporary Lesbian Writing: Dreams, Desire, Difference*. Open University Press, Buckingham, 1993.

Janice Raymond, A *Passion for Friends: Towards a Philosophy of Female Affection*. The Women's Press, London, 1986.

Barbara Sang, *et al., Lesbians at Midlife: The Creative Transition*. Spinsters Book Company, 1991.

Elaine Showalter, *Sexual Anarchy: Gender and Culture at the Fin de Siecle*. Virago, London, 1992.